Jack Coop[er]

WHO KNEW?!

Unusual Stories in Jewish History

gefen
publishing house
JERUSALEM ◆ NEW YORK   Est. 1981

Cover pictures taken from Wikepedia web site

Cover Design and Typesetting by S. Kim Glassman

ISBN: 978-965-229-476-0

1 3 5 7 9 8 6 4 2

Gefen Publishing House, Ltd.
6 Hatzvi Street
Jerusalem 94386, Israel
972-2-538-0247
orders@gefenpublishing.com

Gefen Books
600 Broadway
Lynbrook, NY 11563, USA
1-800-477-5257
orders@gefenpublishing.com

www.gefenpublishing.com

Printed in Israel   *Send for our free catalogue*

To my wife, Shayne,
my partner and friend for over fifty years and counting.

Contents

NEAR EAST: Early Times

WESTERN EUROPE: Trying to Fit In

CENTRAL EUROPE AND THE EAST: The Unwanted Diaspora

HOLOCAUST: Perpetrators, Bystanders, Rescuers

AMERICA: Finding a Home and Contributing

ISRAEL: Building and Defending a Nation

Foreword

This fascinating book by Jack Cooper points out to the reader the lesson that history is made by people, their heroism, foibles, vision and pettiness. There are also many "accidental" events, unplanned and unforeseen, which have almost cosmic consequences in the human story of events and personages. Thus history provides a fascinating patchwork of events and personalities that leaves all later generations to ponder and study.

This book deals mainly with the wondrous story of the Jewish people and of its events. It contains hundreds of facts and anecdotes, some tragic, some hilarious, some fateful and some seemingly unimportant if yet fascinating, that have helped make up the story of the Jews in world history. These facts are the pepper and spice that enliven the story of history which unfortunately when reduced to pure facts and dates can be very boring. Jewish history is always a revelation of the unseen role of the Creator in preserving the Jewish people against all natural odds. But even if the script is divinely inspired, the actors in the play of history are all human. They are the instruments through which the divine plan is somehow executed. The stories in this book prove this point in a very interesting and satisfactory manner.

Throughout history, Jews have had to live by their wits and perseverance, almost always being engulfed in a very hostile environment. These stories point out to the reader the many different mechanisms used by Jews to survive and even attempt to prosper. It was and is a slippery slope that Jews individually – and the Jewish people generally – have to traverse in this world. Even though many of the stories recorded in this book may at first glance appear to be minor in importance, the overall import and message of the book is very important and major. After reading this book the reader will have a different view and understanding of Jewish history and its twists and turns over the ages. The book combines entertaining reading, fascinating detail, and a sense of awe and inspiration regarding its subject matter. Enjoy reading this book; it will at the same time make you a better-informed person about the Jewish story.

Rabbi Berel Wein
Jerusalem
August 2008
Menachem Av 5768

Preface

In preparation for compiling these unusual stories, I have amassed a library of over a hundred books on Jewish history and read thousands of pages about a people that continually defies historical patterns of nations. Mark Twain summed up the indomitable spirit of the Jewish people when he wrote in *Harper's Magazine*, September 1899:

> If the statistics are right, the Jews constitute but *one per cent.* of the human race. It suggests a nebulous dim puff of star-dust lost in the blaze of the Milky Way. Properly the Jew ought hardly to be heard of; but he is heard of, has always been heard of. He is as prominent on the planet as any other people, and his commercial importance is extravagantly out of proportion to the smallness of his bulk. His contributions to the world's list of great names in literature, science, art, music, finance, medicine, and abstruse learning are also away out of proportion to the weakness of his numbers. He has made a marvelous fight in this world, in all the ages; and has done it with his hands tied behind him. He could be vain of himself, and be excused for it. The Egyptian, the Babylonian, and the Persian rose, filled the planet with sound and splendor, then faded to dream-stuff and passed away; the Greek and the Roman followed, and made a vast noise, and they are gone; other peoples have sprung up and held their torch high for a time, but it burned out, and they sit in twilight now, or have vanished. The Jew saw them all, beat them all, and is now what he always was, exhibiting no decadence, no infirmities of age, no weakening of his parts, no slowing of his energies, no dulling of his alert and aggressive mind. All things are mortal but the Jew; all other forces pass, but he remains. What is the secret of his immortality?[1]

---

1. Mark Twain, "Concerning the Jews," *Harper's Magazine* 99, no. 592 (September 1899).

The irony behind Twain's poignant words lies in the fact that Twain himself was no real friend of the Jews. But this is typical throughout my readings and evident in many of the stories that follow. The overriding theme that impressed itself on my mind in writing this book may be summed up in one word: *intolerance*. Many of the stories in this volume will deal with the efforts of Jewish men and women to overcome the obstacles put in their way and even just to stay alive. That they have been so successful in their endeavors can be attributed to the high level of intelligence and energy that they have applied to overcoming these man-made difficulties.

Other stories deal with Jewish responses to everyday situations in an atmosphere of relative freedom. The reader will be amazed at how, given freedom to function, Jews have scaled great heights in politics, business, and the professions.

As Jewish history now unfolds before our eyes in the twenty-first century, the reader can appreciate how this amazing people adjusts and prospers in all kinds of serious, and sometimes comical, circumstances. As the title suggests, these stories are *unusual* in their own right. Each has been included in the book because the story is something unexpected, even surprising. In other words, "Who knew?!"

I would like to thank Gefen Publishing House and my editor, Kezia Raffel Pride, for the opportunity they have given me to share these stories in the unbroken chain of Jewish history. I am grateful to my son Kenny for being the driving force behind the concept and direction of the publication; to my son Neil for suggesting the title for the book, his editing, and for guiding me to source material; and to my daughter Rhonda for her computer expertise.

This book could not have happened without the continuous inspiration of my grandchildren Jamie, Tara, Carly, Shelby, Josh, Mitch, and Zack. I am especially thankful to Shelby, Josh, Mitch, and Zack for letting me read these stories to them for their "stamp of approval" and for the many hours they spent on this book. Finally, I am grateful to all of the "people of the book" who lived the stories I was fortunate to write about.

Jack Cooper

Who Knew?!

NEAR EAST:
Early Times

When Moses came down from Mount Sinai with the tablets bearing the Ten Commandments, the Bible describes the scene: "And when Aaron and all the children of Israel saw Moses; behold the skin of his face sent forth beams: and they were afraid of him" (Exodus 34:30).[1] Although the English translation seems to be straightforward, the Vulgate, which is the Latin translation of the bible, confuses *karan* ("sent forth beams" or "was shining") with *keren* (horn) – both of which are spelled the same way in Hebrew – and translates *karan or panav* (the skin of his face was shining) to read *cornuta esset facies sua*, "his face was horned."[2] It is this reading which probably gave rise to medieval artists – including Michelangelo in his now-famous sculpture – portraying Moses with horns protruding from his forehead.

There may be another explanation for Moses' horns. Medieval Christians generally associated Jews with the devil.[3] Jews were obliged to appear in public with a distinguishing horn somewhere on their garb. In 1267 the Vienna Council decreed that Jews wear a horned hat, and Jews in medieval Germany were forced to bend the brim into a grotesque shape depicting horns.[4] Phillip III of France required the attachment of a horned figure to the regular Jew badge. In case there was any doubt, in at least one instance, the horned Jew was identified with the legend, in bold letters, "This is the Jew Devil."[5]

1. Rabbi Dr. Joseph H. Hertz, ed., *The Pentateuch and Haftorahs* (London: Soncino Press, 1952), 368.
2. Exodus 34:29. In verse 30 the Vulgate translates the same phrase as *cornutam Mosi faciem*, "the face of Moses [was] horned."
3. Israel Abrahams, *Jewish Life in the Middle Ages* (Philadelphia: Jewish Publication Society, 1896), 298.
4. Joshua Trachtenberg, *The Devil and the Jews: The Medieval Conception of the Jew and Its Relation to Modern Anti-Semitism* (New York: Harper and Row, 1943), 44.
5. Trachtenberg, *The Devil and the Jews*, 44, 46.

...Scriptural narratives added words to the English language

Each year during the Day of Atonement (Yom Kippur), services are held in synagogues all over the world and the description of the atonement is repeated. During the days when the Temple in Jerusalem was still standing, the high priest would engage in an elaborate ceremony to "cleanse" the congregation of their sins, so that they could start the New Year afresh.

As part of the ceremony prescribed in Leviticus, the high priest would lay his hands on a goat, symbolically transferring the sins of the people to the goat. The goat was then sent into the desert.[1] Today, in our everyday speech, we generally refer to somebody who takes the blame for somebody else as a "scapegoat."[2]

Another biblical narrative that has contributed to our vocabulary is the story of Abraham's nephew Lot who is visited by three men (really disguised angels) who have been sent by God to rescue him and his family from the destruction that is about to overtake the city of Sodom.

While the men are in Lot's house, an unruly mob gathers outside the house demanding that he surrender his guests "so that we may know them" (Genesis 18:5). The phrase "so that we may know them" is interpreted as the intention of the mob to commit homosexual rape on the three males in the house. Since the intention of God was to destroy the city of Sodom because of their licentious behavior, the city deservedly earned association with the word "sodomy."

---

1. "Azazel," *Illustrated Dictionary and Concordance to the Bible*, edited by Geoffrey Wigoder (Jerusalem: Jerusalem Publishing House, 1986), 140.
2. The Greek translation interpreted "scapegoat" to mean "goat that departs," i.e., (e)scape goat.

...a person's name is a mirror to his soul

A name is very important. People once believed that "a man's name is the essence of his being."[1] One Hebrew text says that "a man's name is his person"; still another saying is that "his name is his soul."[2] Acting on these beliefs, people had to carefully consider what was involved in choosing a name for their newborn infant.

According to biblical evidence, giving a child the name of a deceased relative or ancestor "would destroy and obliterate the soul and the remembrance of the departed and cause his soul to forsake its peaceful abode in heaven."[3] In those times, it was impossible for two family members to have the same name.

Another factor in limiting the naming of a child after a living person had to do with spirits or angels. When the spirits were engaged in their earthly interventions, they were just as likely as not to fail to distinguish one of the people bearing the name from the other. In order to eliminate the possibility of error, no two people in the family had the same name.[4]

However, by the time of the Talmud, the belief had shifted. By "giving a child the name of an ancestor, the memory would be preserved and kept alive."[5] Moreover, "the personality of the new-born infant would be protected from demonic assault by being 'screened' or 'covered' by the name of the older or distinguished ancestor."[6]

Another feature of naming babies was to make a careful study of the life of the person whose name the child was to bear. It would be imprudent to saddle the child with the name of a person who had been particularly unfortunate.[7]

Among more traditional Jews, whether the naming of a baby hearkens to the more ancient customs or to the more modern applications, the possibility of supernatural intervention is not to be discounted.

1. Joshua Trachtenberg, *Jewish Magic and Superstition: A Study in Folk Religion* (New York: Behrman's Jewish Book House, 1939), 78.
2. Ibid.
3. Benzion C. Kaganoff, *A Dictionary of Jewish Names and Their Origins* (New York: Schocken, 1977), 97.
4. Trachtenberg, *Jewish Magic and Superstition*, 79.
5. Kaganoff, *A Dictionary of Jewish Names*, 97.
6. Ibid.
7. Trachtenberg, *Jewish Magic and Superstition*, 78–79.

...Friday-night challah is reminiscent of a pagan custom

The Friday night Sabbath table in Jewish homes traditionally has two loaves of braided bread called "challah." The practice of setting out two loaves hearkens back to the biblical narrative of the Israelites being miraculously fed by God in their desert wanderings with the "manna" seemingly fallen from heaven. Each day they would gather their sustenance for one day. However, on the sixth day, the Israelites gathered twice as much so they would not violate the Sabbath by gleaning their food on the day set aside for rest (Exodus 16:5).

The question remaining is, why are the loaves braided? The answer is most likely to be derived from a pagan ritual. In ancient times the Teutonic goddess of fertility *Berchta* or *Perchta* was widely worshipped by women. As part of the ceremonies, the women would offer their hair to the goddess. After a period of time, the custom of offering the goddess their hair was discontinued. It was replaced by a symbolic offering of hair in the form of a loaf of bread fashioned from braided dough, the *Perchisbrod*.[1]

This cross-cultural sharing does not necessarily imply that the Jews were consciously practicing a pagan ritual. It merely represents adaptation through exposure. Some contemporary Jews will punctuate their conversation with the phrase "Knock on wood," derived from the Christian custom of touching a wooden cross for good fortune. It does not follow that the Jewish people employing the phrase are accepting Christianity.

---

1. Joshua Trachtenberg, *Jewish Magic and Superstition: A Study in Folk Religion* (New York: Behrman's Jewish Book House, 1939), 40.

For Jews who observe Yom Kippur (The Day of Atonement), the day is devoted to lengthy prayer sessions accompanied by a twenty-five-hour fast. This was not so in ancient days. The Talmud tells of an additional custom widely practiced on Yom Kippur.

Rabbi Shimon ben Gamliel said: "There were no festivals in Israel like the fifteenth of Av[1] and Yom Kippur. On those days the young women of Israel went out in borrowed white dresses [everyone borrowed a dress in order not to embarrass someone who did not have her own]...and danced in the vineyard" (Mishnah Taanit 4:8). As they danced, some of the young women advised their prospective husbands on the criteria for choosing a bride. Some stressed piety (Proverbs 31:30); others praised accomplishments (Proverbs 31:31); others stressed the suitability of a young woman to bear children (Taanit 31a); then there were those who posited beauty as a reason for choosing a mate. The Talmud goes on to say, "Young man, lift up your eyes and see what you choose for yourself" (Taanit 4:8).

The question arises as to why Yom Kippur was chosen for this practice. The Talmud offers an answer: "A bridegroom has his sins forgiven" (Bikurim 3:3).

Although the custom of courting on Yom Kippur has, except for very rare instances, been abandoned, Jewish customs still call for the bride and groom to fast on their wedding day, recite the Yom Kippur confession, and wear white garments.[2]

NEAR EAST: Early Times

---

1. After the sadness of the ninth of Av, which commemorates the destruction of the First and Second Temples in Jerusalem, the fifteenth of Av offers a hope of renewal in its focus on young romance.
2. A traditional Jewish wedding is described at http://www.aish.com/jl/l/48969841.html.

...there was a synagogue inside the Temple in Jerusalem

There is a widely held belief among many contemporary Jews that the establishment of synagogues was a direct result of the destruction of the Temple in Jerusalem by the Romans in the year 70 CE. While the destruction of the Temple put new and greater emphasis on the synagogue as a house of prayer and study, it does not follow that synagogues were unknown to the people before that time.[1]

During the rein of King Josiah (640–609 BCE) animal sacrifice was specifically prohibited (II Kings 22 and 23). However, the people continued to worship without sacrifices. Scriptural readings and sermons taking place within the Temple are described by Friedlander in his *History of the First Temple*.[2]

There is archeological evidence that a synagogue was dedicated in Alexandria during the reign of Ptolemy III, 246–221 BCE. Indeed, one of the many synagogues in Alexandria during this time was so huge that the voice of the precentor was inaudible to those in the rear of the synagogue, and signal flags had to be waved to indicate to the worshipers when they should make the appropriate responses.[3]

Rabinowitz gives the number of synagogues in Jerusalem at the time of the destruction of the Temple at 480.[4]

---

1. Gerson D. Cohen, "Talmudic Society," in Leo W. Schwarz, ed., *Great Ages and Ideas of the Jewish People* (New York: Random House, 1956), 162.
2. Louis Isaac Rabinowitz, "Synagogue," *Encyclopedia Judaica*, CD-ROM Edition (Jerusalem: Keter, 1997), 2–3.
3. Ibid., 2.
4. Ibid., 2–3.

The ritual murder accusation against the Jews is most commonly associated with medieval Christians accusing Jews of killing Christians for various religious rites. However, the earliest accusation that Jewish ceremonial practices require human sacrifices was first reported by the Greek philosopher Democritus (460–360 BCE).[1] Democritus alleged that the Jews captured a stranger every seven years and sacrificed him in the Temple.[2] About three centuries later, Ptolemy Apion (c. 116–196 CE), ruler of Cyrenica,[3] a Roman province of North Africa, reported the same story but reduced the time between sacrifices to one year and named Antiochus Epiphanes as one of the alleged victims.[4] Antiochus would be a logical "victim," since it was he who despoiled the Temple in Jerusalem and instituted pagan rituals.[5]

During the second century, ritual murder accusations were traded between Christians and pagans. Sometimes the allegations were directed at one sect of Christians by other Christians. As far as the Jews were concerned, the ritual murder charge came to be associated with the celebration of Purim,[6] when the villain of the story (Haman) was often burned in effigy.

It was in the Middle Ages that the ritual murder accusation against the Jews began to experience wide popularity.[7] By then the most common allegation was that Christian blood was required in the baking of the matzos for Passover. It is interesting to note that some rabbis enjoined their congregants not to use red wine for the Passover feast. This was so as to avoid any allegations that the wine included Christian blood.

The irony in the blood libel accusation is that the Bible specifically prohibits Jews from ingesting blood in any form whatsoever (Leviticus 12:10–14).

---

1. "Democritus," *Encyclopedia Britannica Micropedia*, vol. 4, 15th ed. (Chicago: Encyclopedia Britannica, 1990).
2. Joshua Trachtenberg, *The Devil and the Jews: The Medieval Conception of the Jew and Its Relation to Modern Anti-Semitism* (New York: Harper and Row, 1943), 126.
3. "Ptolemy Apion," *Encyclopedia Britannica Micropedia*, vol. 4, 15th ed. (Chicago: Encyclopedia Britannica, 1990).
4. Trachtenberg, *The Devil and the Jews*, 126.
5. Isaiah Gafni, "Antiochus," *Encyclopedia Judaica, CD-ROM Edition* (Jerusalem: Keter, 1997).
6. Purim is the holiday commemorating the saving of the Jews of Persia from a courtier who duped the king into giving him permission to kill all the Jews in the realm.
7. Trachtenberg, *The Devil and the Jews*, 127–28.

The holiday of Purim commemorates the deliverance of the Jews from extermination at the hands of the Persian King Artaxerxes (Achashverosh) in about 300 BCE. In the story, the grand vizier of the Persian Empire, Haman, wishes to do away with the king's Jewish subjects. The king foolishly gives Haman permission to do so before he learns that a certain Jew has recently saved his life. Unable to reverse his own decree, the king does the next-best thing by allowing the Jews to defend themselves. A battle ensues during the month of Adar, the Jews emerge victorious, Haman and his sons are hanged, and the remembrance of this event becomes an annual, joyous celebration among Jews all over the world.

Unknown to most of the Jewish community, there is a similar story which emanated from Cairo, Egypt, in the year 1524.[1]

Ahmed Shaitan (Jews see this as a play on words and read it *Satan*) usurps the throne of the kingdom of Egypt, which is bound to Suleiman's Turkish empire. Shaitan's intent is to plunder the Jews of their possessions and use the money to finance his rebellion against Suleiman.[2] The usurper approaches the master of the mint, Abraham deCastro (a Jew appointed by Suleiman himself), to have his name stamped on the coins. DeCastro requests the order in writing, secretly escapes from Cairo, and presents the order to Suleiman in Constantinople.[3]

Suleiman marches on Cairo, defeats Shaitan's army, and executes Shaitan. The Jews are saved. The twenty-seventh of the Hebrew month of Adar is set aside in Cairo as a Jewish fast day, and the twenty-eighth of Adar is given over to feasting and rejoicing.[4]

The style of writing in recording the story, the advent of a Jew who is close to the king, and the fast day preceding the celebration are strongly reminiscent of the Persian Jewish holiday of Purim.

---

1. Jacob R. Marcus, *The Jew in the Medieval World: A Source Book, 315–1791* (New York: Atheneum, 1938), 61–65.
2. Professor Heinrich Graetz, *History of the Jews*, vol. 4 (Philadelphia: Jewish Publication Society, 1894), 393.
3. Graetz, *History of the Jews*, 393, 396.
4. Marcus, *The Jew in the Medieval World*, 65.

During the early part of the second century BCE, a serious rift was develop-ing in the Jewish community of Palestine. On one side were the Hellenist Jews who wished to incorporate more of the Greek culture into their ev-eryday living. Ranged against them were the Hasidim,[1] those traditional Jews who resisted the encroachments of Greek living.

On a more superficial level, many of the Hellenist Jews were changing their names to be more Greek-sounding or were using two sets of names, one for the Greek society and one for the Jewish community and synagogue. Some wished to join the Gymnasium, which meant participating in the nude, something frowned upon by the Hasidim. The Hellenist Jews had come to the conclusion that Torah Law did not originate from the prophet Moses. They believed that the Torah as now written was "full of fables and impossible demands and prohibitions."[2]

In the contest of wills, the Hellenists had on their side most of the money of the Jewish community. They also had a close relationship with the Greeks, who had begun the practice of deposing the high priests and installing priests who were more in keeping with their taste.

For their part, the Hasidim had a fierce commitment to traditional Judaism. Their huge following was increased by the *amei ha-aretz,* the ordinary poor and unlearned people of the land. It was this group who were most disaffected by the tax-collecting Hellenists, since taxation fell most heavily on the poor.[3]

As the conflict continued, the Hellenists began to realize that they were on the losing end in their struggle. In order to bolster their position, they appealed to the Greek king Antiochus.[4] His response was a series of laws that virtually outlawed Judaism. Circumcision became a capital crime; the Temple was dedicated to Zeus; and the puppet priests abolished the traditional sacrifices and required the pious Jews "to make a symbolic sacrifice" on altars they regarded as pagan.[5]

When Jews refused to be subjected to these rituals, some were killed by the authorities. One such martyrdom took place in the town of Modiin. Protests grew into violence and a revolution commenced, culminating in the restoration of Jewish sovereignty, the cleansing of the Temple of its pagan sacrileges, rededication of the Temple, and the institution of the festival of Hanukah.[6]

NEAR EAST: Early Times

---

1. The anti-Hellenist second-century BCE group known as the Hasidim is not to be confused with today's Hasidic movement, which originated in eighteenth-century Europe.
2. Paul Johnson, *A History of the Jews* (New York: Harper and Row, 1987), 99, 101.
3. Ibid., 101–103.
4. Max Radin, *The Jews among the Greeks and Romans* (Philadelphia: Jewish Publication Society, 1916), 124, 137.
5. Johnson, *A History of the Jews*, 104..
6. Ibid.

...a Jewish author's work was set to music in many churches

Yeshua Ben Sira was a Jewish author who lived in Jerusalem circa 180–175 BCE. His work was written in Hebrew and translated into Greek by his grandson in Egypt, who added a preface. *The Wisdom of Ben Sira* (also called Sirach or the Book of Ecclesiasticus) is a text which was considered for inclusion in the Tanach (the Hebrew Bible, consisting of the Five Books of Moses, the Prophets, and the Writings), but it was instead relegated to the noncanonical writings called the Apocrypha.[1] Three major works of Ben Sira are *The Priestly Office*, *Now Praise the Lord*, and *Let Us Now Praise Men*.

Ben Sira's work *This Is the High Priest* has been set to music and has been used in Catholic churches for over four hundred years to honor popes and other high church officials.

Now Praise the Lord, a short hymnic passage, was adopted by the *Anglican Book of Common Prayer* more than four hundred fifty years ago and has been set to music by many composers in the English-speaking world. It has also appeared in German prayer books, and the composer Johann Sebastian Bach has used the chorale melody in his *Cantata Number 92*.[2]

It seems that this great Jewish purveyor of faith and wisdom is far more popular among Christian churchmen than among his own people.

---

1. Manfred R. Lehmann, "The Book of Ben Sira," http://www.manfredlehmann.com/news/news_detail.cgi/141/0.
2. Baathia Bayer, "The Wisdom of Ben Sira," *Encyclopedia Judaica*, CD-ROM Edition (Jerusalem: Keter, 1977).

...a devout pagan tried to rebuild the Temple in Jerusalem

Following the death of Roman emperor Flavius Julius Constantius II in 361 CE, his nephew Julian the Apostate succeeded to the throne. Julian was referred to as an apostate because he was critical of the Christian Church and had abandoned Christianity in favor of a sort of modified paganism.

Julian wished "to protect the oppressed of all nations and religions, to promote the well-being of all his subjects..."[1] This attitude would certainly put him in conflict with the Christians within the Roman Empire. Julian believed in the God of the Jews as being one of a number of gods, and he subscribed to the notion that this god had chosen the Jews as His very own people.

One of his first acts as emperor was to dispatch a letter to the Jewish congregations in which he reviled the practice of religious persecution and rescinded the special taxes levied against the Jews in favor of the Catholic Church. He further demonstrated his goodwill toward the Jews by allocating funds, materials, and workers to begin the reconstruction of the Temple in Jerusalem.

Work was actually begun on restoring the ruined Temple. However, when the workers began to clear away the rubble from the previous structure, a series of fires erupted, taking the lives of some of the workers. Historians generally attribute the fires to suppressed gases suddenly coming into contact with the air. Devout Christians attributed the fires to God showing his displeasure at the process of restoring the Temple of the hated Jews.

When Julian went off to war against the Persians, the work completely stopped. Julian was killed on the battlefield by an arrow, probably launched by one of the disaffected Christian soldiers in his own army. So ended the two-year reign (361–363) of Julian the Apostate. Christian emperors again ruled the empire and returned to their habitual persecution of Jews and other non-Christians.

---

1. Professor Heinrich Graetz, *History of the Jews*, vol. 2 (Philadelphia: Jewish Publication Society, 1893), 595–600.

...Jewish blacksmiths were blamed for insanity

Of all the reasons put forth for hating Jews, the most bizarre is being a blacksmith. In the early part of the sixth century, there was a sizable colony of Jewish blacksmiths in the country of Yemen. Because of their metalworking skills, they were considered sorcerers and were scorned by both their Christian and pagan neighbors.

Due to their close proximity, the Jewish smiths of Ethiopia and the Arabian Peninsula shared a similar pariah status. At that time of great susceptibility to superstition, metalworkers were associated with secrecy and sexual taboos.[1]

The Ethiopians had a word for the Beta Israel blacksmiths. They called them *buda*, possessors of the evil eye and Satanic powers. For centuries they had been accused of "being cannibalistic hyenas bred in hell."[2] Right up into the twentieth century, Jews in Ethiopia were blamed for spreading "*buda*-sickness," poisoning souls, possessing young women, and causing blindness, consumption, insanity, and death. This is all directly related to blacksmithing and Jews.[3]

In the rare case of an Ethiopian Jew attempting to better his lot by converting to Christianity, he usually found himself worse off than before. To the Amhara, the people of northern Ethiopia, he was just a baptized Falasha[4] and was therefore to be shunned. Rarely would he be able to find an Amharic girl who would consent to marry him. Worst of all, his fellow Jews would have nothing to do with him.[5]

By the late 1970s and early 1980s, most of the remaining Falashas in Ethiopia had immigrated to Israel, were free of the blacksmithing stigma, and were living as Jews in a free society.

---

1. Louis Rapoport, *The Lost Jews: Last of the Ethiopian Falashas* (New York: Stein and Day, 1983), 99.
2. Ibid., 100.
3. Ibid.
4. "Falasha" is the name given to the black Jews of Ethiopia.
5. Rapoport, *The Lost Jews*, 168.

...Jewish women's lib is two thousand years old

Because twelfth-century minors were not permitted to enter into contracts, it was commonplace for fathers of underage girls to enter into marriage contracts on their behalf. Very often, this practice led to great controversy in the family, especially if the girl had not been informed of the match.

While Muslim law was clearly on the side of the father in any dispute, it was not so among Jews. A marriage contract on behalf of a minor child was held in abeyance until the girl, now grown, would say, "I wish to marry this man." If such a declaration was not forthcoming from the young woman, the marriage would not take place.[1]

Moses Maimonides himself came down on both sides of the issue and said, "Although a father is permitted to contract a marriage for his minor daughter with whomever he likes, it is improper to do so, for our sages have disapproved of this."[2]

Lest we get the idea that the champions of the rights of women are a twelfth-century phenomenon, we need to go back to the first-century teachings of Rabbi Akiva. When called upon to rule on whether a working wife's earnings should belong to her husband, Rabbi Akiva put women's liberation a giant step down the road to emancipation. While conceding that the wife's earnings did indeed belong to her husband, he limited the husband's claim to the cost of her personal upkeep; any additional earnings belong to her.[3]

Could Akiva's ruling have been affected by the fact that his wife worked to put him through school?

---

1. S. D. Goiten, *A Mediterranean Society: An Abridgement in One Volume* (Berkeley: University of California Press, 1999), 370.
2. Ibid., 371.
3. Simon Noveck, ed., *Great Jewish Personalities in Ancient and Medieval Times* (Clinton, MA: Pioneer Press, 1959), 141.

Who Knew?!

WESTERN EUROPE:
Trying to Fit In

...Jews of Spain were expelled at least four times

The Iberian Peninsula was a place where Jews lived and thrived for hundreds of years. However, it was also a place from which Jews were often expelled. In fact, Jews were expelled from or outlawed in Spain at least four times!

In 613 the Visigoth Christians ordered that all Jews must either be baptized or leave the kingdom. In 638 the Sixth Council of Toledo ruled that only Christians might reside in Spain. Many Jews, however, went underground or secretly moved to other parts of Spain.[1] Between 672 and 680, Jews were expelled from many parts of Spain. In 681 the Twelfth Council of Toledo ruled that all Jews must accept baptism. Those who refused were to receive various punishments including confiscation of property and/or expulsion. They were also forced to sell their land holdings purchased from Christians at a price fixed by the government.[2]

In 1146, a fanatic Muslim group called the Almohads conquered much of Spain. Judaism was outlawed and synagogues and yeshivas were closed. Many Jews fled to Christian Spain or became secret Jews.[3]

As the Christians slowly expelled the Muslims from Spain, and as the various kingdoms of Spain became consolidated under a single ruler, conditions for Jews steadily worsened. The thirteenth and fourteenth centuries saw the long decline of the Jews of Spain. Riots, murders, forced conversions, confiscations, and disputations all led the way toward the final expulsion of Jews from Spain in 1492.[4] As always, those who became sincere Christians were allowed to stay.

---

1. "Spain," *Encyclopedia Judaica*, CD-ROM *Edition* (Jerusalem: Keter, 1997), 1.
2. Ibid., 2.
3. Ibid., 4.
4. Ibid., 7–13.

...Christian laws gave new meaning to a Jewish prayer

In ancient days some Jewish people would make a vow that if God would help them out of some difficult straits, they would perform some service to God in return. Since most of these promises were rashly given without adequate thought, the rabbis instituted a prayer entitled *Kol Nidre* (all the vows) to be said at the beginning of the Day of Atonement (Yom Kippur) service. This prayer is a renunciation of any vows a person may have made during the year. Many Jews, however, objected to the prayer. They complained that it would give Christians a positive proof that the word of a Jew was not to be trusted.

During the reign of Charlemagne, ruler of the Holy Roman Empire, a Jew involved in a court case requiring testimony was to be subjected to a humiliating ceremony involving the use of the Torah, the scroll containing the Five Books of Moses. Taking an oath on the Torah scroll is prohibited by Jewish law for all but the most sacred of occasions. But the Christian laws did not stop there. The Jew was required to hold the Torah in his hand, and wearing a girdle of thorns, descend into a pool of water. He was then required to spit on his penis three times and invoke the punishments mentioned in the Torah if his testimony were to be proven false. Moreover, a Jew was required to bring anywhere from four to nine witnesses, according to the importance of the case, while a Christian was only required to bring three witnesses.

These laws, modified somewhat from time to time and from country to country, remained in force until the nineteenth century. Prussia was the last country to abolish these practices in 1869.[1] However, the *Kol Nidre* prayer had now acquired a new significance. The humiliating and sacrilegious vows required under Christian laws were truly oaths to be renounced! *Kol Nidre* remains today as the most recognized of all the prayers of the Yom Kippur service.

---

1. Mark Waldman, *Goethe and the Jews: A Challenge to Hitlerism* (New York: Putnam, 1934), 26.

...Charlemagne changed the market day so Jews could trade

During the reign of Charlemagne, king of the Franks and emperor of the Holy Roman Empire (768–814), Jews prospered greatly. Because of their extensive contacts in the Muslim world, almost all of the French trade was in Jewish hands. During this time, Jews could freely migrate into the realm.[1] So great was Jewish influence in trade that the city of Lyon moved its market day from Saturday to another day to accommodate the Jews, who would not trade on the Sabbath.[2]

Charlemagne recognized the value of the Jews and protected them to the extent that the pope, who believed that Jews should not prosper, argued with Charlemagne to rein in the Jews. Charlemagne would not bend, although while Christian merchants were taxed one-eleventh of their income, Jewish merchants paid one-tenth.

Perhaps the best illustration of Charlemagne's relationship with the Jews is exemplified in the following event. The church had a strict law forbidding Jews from taking Church artifacts as a pledge for money borrowed. Penalties for infractions were severe. Charlemagne turned the law around. If a church official gave a Church artifact as a pledge for money borrowed, the offending official was penalized and the Jew involved was not charged.[3]

It is little wonder that Jewish immigration into the realm of Charlemagne greatly increased during his time on the throne, and the rise of Ashkenazic Jewry in Europe is traced to his reign.[4]

1. Eliot Rosenberg, *But Were They Good for the Jews? Over 150 Historical Figures Viewed from a Jewish Perspective* (Secaucus, NJ: Carol, 1997), 40.
2. Max L. Margolis and Alexander Marx, *A History of the Jewish People* (Philadelphia: Jewish Publication Society, 1927), 349.
3. Professor Heinrich Graetz, *History of the Jews*, vol. 3 (Philadelphia: Jewish Publication Society, 1894), 142.
4. Berel Wein, *Herald of Destiny: The Story of the Jews in the Medieval Era, 750–1650* (New York: Shaar Press, 1993), 50.

...a Jew commanded a Muslim army

Samuel Halevi (Samuel Hanagid)[1] was born in 993. He received an excellent Jewish education and learned the Arabic language and the Muslim holy book, the Koran. In 1013 he fled the Berber takeover in Cordoba, Spain, and settled in another Spanish city, Malaga, where he opened a spice shop near the palace.

After a time, the maidservant to the vizier, the highest-ranking member of the court of King Habbus of Granada, employed Samuel to write letters for her to the vizier while he was away. The vizier, Abu al-Kasim, was impressed by the wisdom of the letters and asked the maid who the letter writer was. She told him about Samuel and the vizier hired Samuel to work for him.

Samuel became the key advisor to the vizier, who served as the conduit for Samuel's advice from himself to the king. When the vizier became ill and was near death, the king bemoaned the fact that he was losing such a wise counselor. Al-Kasim assured the king that the Jew Samuel was the real source of the wise counsel the king had been receiving. Following the death of al-Kasim, King Habbus appointed Samuel vizier and chief councilor.[2] One of his major accomplishments in this position was the financing, creation, and distribution of books of holy writ, not only to the Jews of Spain, but to people all over North Africa and as far away as Palestine. Moreover, in addition to his duties of statecraft, and being the *nagid*, Samuel was one of the foremost poets of his day.[3]

The position of vizier eventually led to his appointment as commander of the king's army. He served in that position from 1038 to 1056. In one of the battles, Samuel gained a victory over a particularly vicious Slav ruler and his fanatic Arab vizier. This led to the institution of a Spanish Purim.[4] Sixteen of the eighteen years Samuel commanded the army were spent in warfare. Worn out by the constant combat, Samuel died in 1056.[5]

Samuel Hanagid had the distinction of being a Jew leading a Muslim army while also serving as *nagid* of the Jewish community.

---

1. *Nagid* is a Hebrew word for ruler or leader.
2. Jacob R. Marcus, *The Jew in the Medieval World: A Source Book, 315–1791* (New York: Atheneum, 1938), 297–98.
3. "Samuel ha-Nagid," and "Ismail Ibn Nagrel'a," *Encyclopedia Judaica*, CD-ROM *Edition* (Jerusalem: Keter, 1997).
4. Purim is a Jewish holiday celebrating the deliverance of the Jewish people from great danger. It commemorates an incident in ancient Persia, but there was also another such observation in Cairo, Egypt.
5. "Samuel ha-Nagid," *Encyclopedia Judaica*.

...Henry IV defied the pope to help the Jews

Henry IV (1040–1106), ruler of the Holy Roman Empire, was a great friend to the Jews. Under his rule, Jews were exempt from certain taxes and enjoyed liberal trading privileges. While Henry was on a trip to Italy, Jewish communities were victim to members of the First Crusade. Some were killed while others were forced to accept Christianity to save their lives.

When Henry returned home and received the news of what had occurred, he sent out edicts to shelter and protect the Jews. Those who had accepted Christianity to save their lives were excused to return to their faith. This last action on Henry's part enraged Pope Clement III, who said that it was a desecration of Church sacraments.

Not only did Henry ignore the pope, but he began to investigate the murders of Jews. There were convictions and even an archbishop was punished for enriching himself with valuables entrusted to him by terrified Jews.

It is paradoxical that Church leaders decried Henry's actions of "Christian charity" because the beneficiaries happened to be Jews.[1]

---

1. Eliot Rosenberg, *But Were They Good for the Jews? Over 150 Historical Figures Viewed from a Jewish Perspective* (Secaucus, NJ: Carol, 1997), 53–54.

The most famous and prolific commentator on all phases of Jewish Scriptures and writings was Solomon bar Isaac, better known as Rashi. Every page in the commentaries has a section devoted exclusively to Rashi, printed in a distinctive style of writing called "Rashi script."

While Rashi was preparing his commentaries, he frequently ran into situations wherein he was unable to explain himself in Hebrew (the language of the Scriptures) or Aramaic (the language of the Talmud). When this happened, Rashi would resort to using French words – transcribed in Hebrew characters – to cover given situations.

As a result of Rashi's efforts, we find some 3,500 of these French words in his commentaries on the Talmud and another 1,500 in his work on the Bible. Of course, much of the French language incorporated into Rashi's commentaries has changed over time, but the words he used are perpetuated in the holy books studied by Jews and others the world over.[1] Indeed, scholars of Old French find in Rashi's commentary a valuable source of information about that language.[2]

Use of Rashi's commentaries was not limited to Jews. Using Rashi's work, Christian biblical interpreter Nicholas de Lyre produced some outstanding interpretations of Scripture. One of the people who used de Lyre's translations was Martin Luther, who used them extensively in his own work. Luther went on to challenge the Catholic Church, and the Reformation was born.[3]

One would not expect such a famous scholar to involve himself in everyday, mundane matters of law, but Rashi agreed to take the case of a woman who claimed that her husband had divorced her and had denied her the amount of money stipulated in the marriage contract.

The husband claimed that his wife had an unsightly skin condition which she had not disclosed to him at their betrothal. The wife claimed that she had been healthy on her wedding day, and that the skin condition had developed after their marriage, to which effect she produced witnesses. Rashi delivered a verdict in favor of the wife and admonished her husband, using quotations from the Talmud to demonstrate that he was acting in a manner not befitting a Jewish husband.[4]

The range and depth of Rashi's work is even more amazing given that he earned his livelihood raising grapes and was a foremost vintner.

---

1. Esther Benbassa, *The Jews of France: A History from Antiquity to the Present* (Princeton, NJ: Princeton University Press, 1999), 34–35.
2. Maurice Liber, *Rashi* (1906; repr., Whitefish, MT: Kessinger Publishing, 2004), 56.
3. Abram Leon Sachar, *A History of the Jews* (New York: Knopf, 1964), 186.
4. Jacob R. Marcus, *The Jew in the Medieval World: A Source Book, 315–1791* (New York: Atheneum, 1938), 302–3.

...a Christian king sent Jews back to Judaism

William Rufus, king of England from 1087 to 1100, was noted for his scandalously impious behavior. He was constantly raiding the coffers of the church for his personal use and would do almost anything for money.

In one instance, a group of Jews offered Rufus a large sum of money if he would induce a number of their fellow Jews to return to Judaism after they had converted to Christianity. Rufus was successful in this endeavor and collected a handsome sum for his efforts.

Soon after, another Jew approached Rufus offering him sixty marks to get his apostate son to return to Judaism. The king attempted to do so, but the young man obstinately refused. When the father asked Rufus for his money back, Rufus refused, saying he had tried, but the young man was set on remaining a Christian. After a good deal of haggling, King Rufus decided to return half the money to the Jewish father.[1]

---

1. D'Blossiers Tovey, *Anglia Judaica, or, A History of the Jews in England*, edited by Elizabeth Pearl (London: Weidenfeld and Nicolson, 1990), 7–8.

...a French king expelled the Jews – and then wanted them back

Philip Augustus was king of France from 1180 to 1223. He was an implacable anti-Semite, and within one year of ascending the throne, he began his persecution of the Jews. In 1181 he had all the Jews in his kingdom arrested and imprisoned. They were released only upon the payment of a large ransom. He followed this with an edict that all Christians owing money to Jews did not have to repay their debt. He did, however, insist that 20 percent of the debt be remitted to the treasury. Having extorted all their money, Philip Augustus ordered the Jews out of the part of France ruled by him, which at that time was only the cities of Paris and Orleans.[1] The expulsion took place over the objections of counts, barons, and even bishops, because they felt their trade would suffer.

Following their expulsion, many Jews settled in areas controlled by other French nobles. Seeing his revenues drop precipitously with the departure of the Jews, Philip was forced to reconsider his edict of expulsion. This was not so easily done. He had to deal with many nobles, some with larger armies than his. Jews at that time were considered the property of the ruler of the area in which they lived. So valuable were they to the economy of their regions that the nobles, not wishing to lose them, imposed a kind of serfdom on the Jews in that they were not permitted freedom of movement.[2]

Once Philip decided he wanted his Jews back, he began to run into trouble. The nobles were loath to part with such a valuable segment of their population. Eventually, Philip struck a bargain with Thibaut, the ruler of the French district of Champagne, that each would send back any Jews who moved from one jurisdiction to another.[3] True to form, Philip violated his end of the bargain.

---

1. Professor Heinrich Graetz, *History of the Jews*, vol. 3 (Philadelphia: Jewish Publication Society, 1894), 402.
2. Ibid., 406.
3. Ibid.

...the illegal immigrant doctor brought his own minyan

In 1290 King Edward IV expelled all the Jews of England.[1] However, in 1410, King Henry IV was ailing and was seeking a new doctor. In violation of the edict of expulsion issued against Jews, he sent for Jewish doctor Elijah ben Sabbetai Beer. Dr. Beer had served Pope Martin V and his successor Eugenius IV. He also served as court physician to the duke of Ferrara and lectured in medicine at the University of Pavia. At the time of his summons, Dr. Beer was in Bologna.

In the previous year, the mayor of London, Richard Whittington, had summoned another Jewish physician, Samson of Mirabeau, from France to tend to his wife. What made Dr. Beer's trip different from others is the fact that he brought with him an entourage of ten men. While Jews may and do pray in private, public prayers require a quorum of ten adult males. Dr. Beer's stature was such that he was able to enter the country and to make his prayers more in keeping with that of a regular Jewish community.

The speed with which kings and popes would make exceptions to a national and/or Church policy when it suited their individual convenience is noteworthy.

---

1. Professor Heinrich Graetz, *History of the Jews*, vol.3 (Philadelphia: Jewish Publication Society, 1894), 645.

...Jews were only expelled if the balance sheet agreed

Whenever a country, in a fit of religious fervor, decided to expel its Jews, it would be faced with a choice between cleansing the realm of unbelievers and the attendant loss of revenues from the taxation of the Jews and the costs associated with the loss of trade conducted by the Jews.

In 1306, the king of France, with the unlikely name of Philip the Fair, issued an order of expulsion for all Jews in the kingdom and the confiscation of all their property. When the sale of the Jewish assets was totaled, it was found that the proceeds were insufficient to cover the loss of revenue occasioned by the departure of the Jews. Unwilling to suffer a negative balance, the king authorized the recall of a limited number of expelled Jews to recover the debts owed to them. The king would then be able to cut himself in on the proceeds and thereby to erase the negative balance.

In 1315, King Louis x (the Quarrelsome) issued a decree that the Jews could return to France for a period of twelve years. For a fee, he returned to them their confiscated synagogues and cemeteries. He also returned copies of the Torah (the Five Books of Moses), but he withheld the Talmud. The Jews were permitted to recover one-third of the debts due to them at the time of the 1306 expulsion with the remaining two-thirds accruing to the Crown. Although some Jews did return, it was noted that many of them left before the expiration of the twelve years.

In 1359, Charles of Normandy was acting as regent while Jean ii (the Good) was being held for ransom by his British captors. In desperate need of money, Charles decided to recall the Jews for a period of twenty years. This offer attracted few takers. The Jews were put off by the heavy reentry fee and the stiff annual residence charge. Another factor was the limited stay of twenty years. When Charles v ascended the throne in 1364, he extended the deadline by six years. In 1374, for the payment of a large sum of money, he added ten years to the length of residence for the Jews. With the death of the king in 1380, Louis d'Anjou, acting as regent, extended the stay of the Jews until 1401.

However the argument turned out to be moot. The burdensome taxes and fees so impoverished the Jewish community that they were no longer able to meet their financial obligations to the Crown, and they were expelled in 1394.[1]

---

1. Esther Benbassa, *The Jews of France: A History from Antiquity to the Present* (Princeton, NJ: Princeton University Press, 1999), 15–16, 20–21.

...Chaucer's *Canterbury Tales* could be outlawed today as hate speech

One of the great classics of English literature is *The Canterbury Tales* by Geoffrey Chaucer.[1] It is assigned reading in many high schools and colleges in the English-speaking world. The format of the book has a group of travelers deciding to help pass the time by having each of them regale the others with a tale. One of the stories is *The Prioress's Tale*.

The Prioress's Tale tells of a young Christian boy who becomes enamored of a liturgical song, "O Alma Redemptoris." Being gifted with a beautiful singing voice, the lad learns the piece by heart and sings it whenever he is moved to do so.

It happens that the boy's route to school takes him through a Jewish neighborhood. Satan tempts three Jews by giving them the idea that the song is offensive and should not be tolerated. The Jews hire an assassin who waylays the lad, slits his throat, and hides the body. The boy's widowed mother institutes a search for her son, and when the searchers pass nearby where the body is hidden, the boy miraculously breaks forth into song and is soon found. The Jews responsible are quickly rounded up, sentenced and quartered, and the boy is laid to rest.

If we juxtapose *The Prioress's Tale* into twenty-first-century Europe, we find the following paradox. The Council of Europe in 2002 passed a law criminalizing hate speech on the Internet as "any written material, any image or any other representation of ideas or theories which advocates, promotes, or incites hatred, discrimination or violence, against any individual or group of individuals, based on race, colour, descent or national or ethnic origin, as well as religion if used as a pretext for any of these factors."[2]

The Canterbury Tales, if it had been sent over the Internet today, would have been in violation of the law. Of course, the law was passed more than eleven hundred years after the writing, and the hate speech is in book form.

---

1. Geoffrey Chaucer, *The Canterbury Tales*, translated by Burton Raffel, with an introduction by John Miles Foley (New York: Modern Library, 2008).
2. Sean D. Murphy, *United States Practice in International Law*, vol. 2, 2002–2004 (Cambridge: Cambridge University Press, 2006), 245.

...Church ritual copies heavily from the Jews

Many of the most common Christian rituals are derived from ancient Jewish customs. Foremost in Christian ceremonies is baptism, which originated in the Jewish ritual bath. The Mass, which is the central part of the church service, stems from the Passover festive meal, the Seder, which means "order." The Last Supper is also reported to have been a Seder. Synagogues are usually constructed so that the worshipers face east toward Jerusalem. So, too, are many churches. The prayer book stems from the Psalter used in the days of the Jewish Second Temple.[1] The vestments of priests and bishops can be traced back to the ancient Israelite priests.

The rite of anointing was common Jewish practice long before it was adopted by Christians. Indeed, the term *Messiah* literally means "the anointed one." The church as a place of sanctuary derives from the cities of refuge as set forth in the Book of Leviticus. The poor boxes in the church are direct descendents of the Jewish practice of worshipers in the synagogue giving charity every day except the Sabbath and holy days.

The establishment of Jewish religious schools was common practice long before Christians opened Sunday schools. Rabbis are ordained by *semichah*, or laying on of the hands, and priests are ordained in a similar fashion.[2]

The observance of the Sabbath from the sunset on Friday to sunset on Saturday is a Jewish practice, which was changed to Sunday by the Christians.[3] It should be noted that some of the early Christians were more than eager to distance themselves from Judaism. In a rather bizarre incident, a conclave of Christian clerics called the Council of Laodicea passed a resolution in Asia Minor, *outlawing* resting during the Friday night–Saturday Jewish Sabbath.[4]

Nevertheless, all these similarities between Christian and Jewish rituals indicate that the daughter religion displays strong hereditary characteristics of the mother faith.

---

1. In the Roman Church, "Te Deum," "Magnificat," "Miserere," and "In Exitu Israel" are all from the Psalms. In the Greek Church, "The Trisagion" is based on the Kedushah of the Jewish service which is derived from Isaiah 6:3. The central service of the Catholic service (mass) or the Protestant service (communion) is derived from the wine and the unleavened bread used at the Passover Seder. The Canon Law of the Church originates from the table of forbidden relations from Leviticus 19. Augustine's *De Civitate* is merely Latin for the Jewish Kingdom of God or the widely used "Kingdom of Heaven." Even the concept of "original sin" takes as its starting point the Jewish concept of the sin of eating from the Tree of Knowledge (Genesis 3:1–7), although Christian theology develops the idea in ways that are contrary to the Jewish understanding. Joseph Jacobs, *Contributions of the Jews to Civilization: An Estimate* (Philadelphia: Jewish Publication Society, 1919), 90–95.
2. Ibid., 90–93.
3. Louis H. Feldman, *Jew and Gentile in the Ancient World: Attitudes and Interactions from Alexander to Justinian* (Princeton, NJ: Princeton University Press, 1993), 375–76.
4. Ibid.

...Jewish rituals limited Jewish deaths during the Black Plague

When the Black Plague struck Europe in 1348–1349, it is estimated that the death toll ran as high as one-third to one-half of the population.[1] But Historian Berel Wein puts the Jewish death toll at close to 20 percent of the Jewish population of Europe.[2] Why the wide discrepancy between people who lived in the same city and drank the same water? For the answer to that question, we must look to the ritual behavior of the Jews then and now.

Upon arising in the morning, an observant Jew must wash his hands on the following occasions: "On awakening from sleep, on leaving the lavatory or bath,…after taking off one's shoes with bare hands, after having sexual intercourse, after touching a vermin,…after touching parts of the body which are generally covered, after leaving a cemetery…or leaving a house where a corpse lay…" (Shulchan Aruch [Code of Jewish Law] 1:5).[3]

In addition, all Jews are mandated to wash their hands before eating, as well as before reciting the benedictions after the meal (1:137).

Meat that is prepared for Jews to eat must be thoroughly soaked, salted, and rinsed (1:116–17) so that there is not the slightest chance of ingesting any blood (an excellent medium for harboring bacteria).

A woman must cleanse herself thoroughly and then immerse herself in a ritual bath after the cessation of her monthly menstrual cycle (4:21).

Visiting the sick is an integral part of Jewish law. However, the primary objective of the visitation is to assist in caring for the sick person (4:87). If he is adequately cared for, then the visit may be in the more conventional sense of supplying company and good cheer.

When a Jew dies, Jewish law dictates that "His body shall not remain all night…but thou shalt bury him the same day" (4:101). Also, one should not eat in the same room where there is a dead body, even if it means one must go to another house (4:94).

The frequent washing and bathing, the soaking, salting and rinsing of meat and poultry for human consumption, the extra care given to the sick, and the prompt interment of the dead all tended to reduce the mortality among Jews exposed to the Black Death.

All of this did the Jews little good. They were accused of poisoning the wells and many were killed.

---

1. Barbara Tuchman, *A Distant Mirror: The Calamitous Fourteenth Century* (New York: Ballantine, 1978), 94.
2. Berel Wein, *Herald of Destiny: The Story of the Jews in the Medieval Era, 750–1650* (New York: Shaar Press, 1993), 120.
3. Rabbi Solomon Ganzfried, *Code of Jewish Law: A Compilation of Jewish Laws and Customs* (New York: Hebrew Publishing Company, 1961). This book is a compendium of Jewish laws distilled from literally thousands of scriptural and Talmudic sources. All ritualistic references cited will be shown in the body of the text with the volume number followed by the page number.

...during the Black Plague, killing Jews cancelled Christian debts

The Black Death, which decimated Europe during the fourteenth century, also provided Christian competitors and debtors of Jews with the opportunity to reap financial gain from the tragic events. A typical example of this type of behavior took place in the Alsatian town of Strasbourg.[1] Before the plague even reached the town, the butchers' and tanners' guilds, eager to eliminate the competition that Jews represented, attempted to begin their persecution. When the town council refused to go along with the plan, the guild members deposed them and instituted a council more to their liking. The Jews were then all put to death except those who accepted Christianity. The feudal lords went along with the extermination, since the deaths of the Jewish moneylenders meant cancellation of their debts.

In spite of a formal proclamation issued by the pope, exonerating the Jews from any complicity in spreading the plague, the extermination in Strasbourg was replicated in other places. When the process of extermination was completed, the money the Jews left behind was divided among the artisans of Strasbourg with a portion going to the Church and the cathedral.[2]

---

1. Barbara W. Tuchman, *A Distant Mirror: The Calamitous Fourteenth Century* (New York: Ballantine, 1978), 113.
2. Jacob R. Marcus, *The Jew in the Medieval World: A Source Book, 315–1791* (New York: Atheneum, 1938), 47.

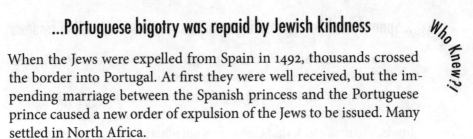

...Portuguese bigotry was repaid by Jewish kindness

When the Jews were expelled from Spain in 1492, thousands crossed the border into Portugal. At first they were well received, but the impending marriage between the Spanish princess and the Portuguese prince caused a new order of expulsion of the Jews to be issued. Many settled in North Africa.

About eighty years later, the Portuguese made an unsuccessful military foray into North Africa and were soundly defeated. Those who were not killed in the battle were offered as slaves to the descendents of the Jews previously expelled from Portugal. The humbled nobles, upon learning that their purchasers were Jews, were very much relieved. They knew that the treatment they would receive from the Jews would be much more humane than the "hospitality" their Portuguese ancestors had extended to their Jewish subjects so many years earlier.[1]

---

1. Rabbi Dr. Joseph H. Hertz, ed., *The Pentateuch and Haftorahs* (London: Soncino Press, 1952), 502.

In 1492, Columbus's proposed voyage of discovery was largely dead in the water. Four men of Jewish ancestry came to the rescue. First they convinced the Spanish royals of the merit of the project; then they found a converted Jew named Luis de Santangel to provide the funds.[1] To make sure that Columbus got where he was headed, a Jewish astronomer and mapmaker named Abraham Zacuto provided maps and charts to guide Columbus on his way. Another Jewish participant in setting up Columbus's voyage was Joseph Vecinho, who provided additional technical help to Columbus in a translation of Zacuto's work which Columbus carried everywhere.[2] Shortly after Columbus's departure, Zacuto was exiled from Spain with all the other Jews. He then settled in Portugal.[3]

When Columbus set sail on his epic voyage, he numbered at least half a dozen Jews in his crew. The ship's physician was a Jew named Maestre Bernal and the ship's surgeon was a Jew named Marco. The first sailor to sight land in the Caribbean Islands was probably one of the converted Jews. He was supposed to get a reward of ten thousand maravedis, but Columbus apparently kept the money for himself. When he found out he was not going to get the reward, he asked for his discharge, which was granted, settled in Africa, cast off the Christian religion, and returned to his "own faith."[4]

Another member of Columbus's crew was the newly converted Luis de Torres. De Torres was fluent in several languages and Columbus thought he would need an interpreter.[5] Columbus sent him into the interior to deal with the natives. It was here that de Torres found the natives smoking, and he is recognized as the first European to discover tobacco.[6]

Upon seeing a wild turkey, De Torres likened it to a peacock and called it by its Hebrew name, *tukki*, which eventually evolved to the present-day word *turkey*.[7] DeTorres asked for and was granted permission to settle. He received a grant of land and six slaves from the

1. Meyer Kayserling, *Christopher Columbus and the Participation of the Jews in the Spanish and Portuguese Discoveries* (Albuquerque, NM: Hubert Allen, 2002), 59, 74.
2. Ibid., 47–48.
3. "Abraham Ben Samuel Zacuto," *Encyclopedia Judaica*, CD-ROM Edition (Jerusalem: Keter, 1997).
4. Kayserling, *Christopher Columbus and the Participation of the Jews*, 90–92.
5. Ibid., 90.
6. Ibid., 94.
7. Harry Golden and Martin Rywell, *Jews in American History: Their Contribution to the United States of America* (Charlotte, NC: H.L. Martin Co., 1950), 9.

ruler of the island. He also received a yearly allowance from the king of Spain, a pension, and the title of Royal Agent for Spain. One version of his story has him living happily ever after in Cuba with many Indian wives, while others say that he and the thirty-nine other members of Columbus's expedition who stayed behind in Cuba were all murdered within the year.[1]

Meanwhile, having settled in Portugal, Abraham Zacuto was pressed into service by the Portuguese king. Portugal was preparing its own voyage of discovery to India by going around Africa. The expedition was to be led by Vasco da Gama. Zacuto provided da Gama with maps and charts for the voyage and trained the sailors in the use of the astrolabe (a navigation instrument used to determine latitude), which Zacuto had greatly improved by substituting copper for wood.[2]

By the time Columbus was ready for his second voyage, the Spanish treasury was filled with the wealth confiscated from the Jews exiled from Spain. Much of the money was specifically earmarked for Columbus's second voyage.[3]

When the Jews were expelled from Portugal, Zacuto, who had done so much for the Portuguese voyages of discovery, was among those expelled. The expulsions of the Jews from Spain and Portugal were not confined to the mother countries. The Inquisition was dedicated to the elimination of any Jews who might be found anywhere in the empires of Spain and Portugal, including the New World.

1. Rufus Learsi and Abraham J. Karp, *The Jews in America: A History* (Jerusalem: Ktav, 1972), 10; Ruth Behar and Humberto Mayol, *An Island Called Home: Returning to Jewish Cuba* (Piscataway, NJ: Rutgers University Press, 2007), 265.
2. "Abraham Ben Samuel Zacuto," *Encyclopedia Judaica.*
3. Kayserling, 105–6.

...a Jewish astronomer's charts saved Columbus and his crew

When Columbus set off on his voyages of discovery, he was equipped with astronomical tables and charts to help him in navigation. The charts had been prepared by Abraham Zacuto, a Jewish astronomer.[1]

During Columbus's fourth voyage, he ran into some serious trouble with one of his ships. The leaky vessel needed extensive repairs, and Columbus and his crew were marooned for over a year. Shelter and supplies were provided by the Indians, but after a period of time, the Indians complained of maltreatment by the Spaniards and began to withhold supplies.

Columbus asked for a meeting of the Indian chiefs on the evening of February 29, 1504. Using Zacuto's charts, he began by telling the Indians that their conduct was angering the gods, and as punishment, the gods were going to first remove the moon and then the sun. At first the natives were unimpressed, but as the full moon began to disappear, the Indians became alarmed and begged Columbus to return the moon. Columbus agreed to return the moon, and the Indians resumed provision of food for the Spaniards.

The Indians had probably seen eclipses before, but what impressed them was the ability of Columbus to communicate with the gods and enlist their aid in a specific problem at a specific time.[2] Of course, Columbus had a little help from Abraham Zacuto.

---

1. "Abraham Ben Samuel Zacuto," *Encyclopedia Judaica,* CD-ROM *Edition* (Jerusalem: Keter, 1997).
2. Ivars Peterson, "The Eclipse That Saved Columbus," *Science News,* http://www.science-news.org/view/generic/id/7809/title/The_Eclipse_That_Saved_Columbus.

For hundreds of years there has been speculation on whether or not Columbus had Jewish origins. While the following information does not purport to settle the question for all time, many reputable scholars have arrived at the conclusion that Columbus was a Jew.[1]

From Columbus's years before he came to Spain, there is ample evidence that he was more at home with the Spanish language than he was with Italian. His correspondence indicates that he was thinking in Spanish even as he wrote in Latin.[2]

Columbus was fond of making obscure references to the glories of his remote ancestors, and he frequently referred in his notes to certain facts of Jewish history.[3] In his will, he left "half a silver mark to a Jew who usually stands at the entrance to the Ghetto of Lisbon..."[4]

When Columbus was ready to depart on his voyage of discovery, he delayed his departure from August 2 (which fell on the Ninth of Av, a Jewish day of mourning) to August 3. Why the delay? Most Jews would be reluctant to begin a new enterprise on a day as tragic and unpropitious in Jewish history as the Ninth of Av.[5]

Then there is the matter of Columbus's name. He is variously referred to as *Columbus, Colombo, Colom,* or *Colon.* Columbus chose *Colon* and charged his children not to change it under any circumstances. Anybody acquainted with Jewish tradition would have chosen that particular rendering of his last name.[6]

Another linguistic clue is Columbus's reference to the destruction of the Second Temple in Jerusalem as "the Second House." Normal Christian usage of that time would have referred to the event as the destruction of Jerusalem. Columbus refers to the tragic event according to the Jewish reckoning as taking place in 68 CE rather than in the Christian rendering of the date as 70 CE.[7]

Finally, there is "...at the top left-hand corner of all but one of the letters addressed by Columbus to his son Diego"[8] the Hebrew letters *bet-hei*, meaning *b'ezrat Hashem* (with the help of God). No letters to outsiders bear this mark, and the letter in which Columbus omitted the appellation was one meant to be read by the king. Who but a practicing Jew would include that on his letters?

---

1. Cecil Roth, *Personalities and Events in Jewish History* (Philadelphia: Jewish Publication Society, 1953), 192–95.

2. Ibid., 197.
3. Ibid., 198.
4. Ibid., 199.
5. Ibid., 200.

6. Ibid., 205.
7. Ibid., 206–7.
8. Ibid., 208.

There has long been a tendency for Christians to harbor preconceived notions, mostly negative, about Jews. A widespread belief held by British people was that Jews were naturally fluent in foreign languages. This belief was fostered by the biblical narrative in Judges 12:2–6 in which a test was imposed by the Hebrews on suspected spies during a war. The suspects were asked to pronounce the word *shibboleth* correctly. Those who could not do so were immediately identified as unfriendly. Because Jews living in England could pronounce the word correctly, it was widely assumed that they could naturally master foreign tongues.[1] This reasoning was based on a misunderstanding, however; the original *shibboleth* test had to do with varying dialects; the Gileadites pronounced the word with an initial *sh* sound, while the Ephraimites had no such sound in their dialect.

Another belief about Jews concerned the centuries-old accusation that Jews used Christian blood to bake matzos for the Passover holiday (ironic given the Jewish prohibition on consuming blood, as stated in Leviticus 17:10–14). Thomas Calvert offered a different explanation. Because of their failure to accept Jesus Christ as the Savior, Jewish men were punished with a monthly emission of blood as are women during their menstrual cycle. The monthly loss of blood creates a need for Jewish men to replace the lost blood. Hence, the murder of Christian children takes place to provide blood donors![2]

The expulsion of the Jews from England in 1290 fostered the speculation that the Jews had emigrated to neighboring Scotland. James Howell, author of *The Wonderful and Deplorable History*, used this theory to explain why "the Scots were so tightfisted, and what else could explain their distaste for blood pudding?"[3]

In another bizarre statement, Henry Blount, author of *A Voyage to the Levant* (1636), wrote, "physical degeneration among Jews caused them to abandon the agricultural professions of their forefathers in favor of commerce."[4] Blount further states that "the Jewish complexion is so prodigiously timid, as cannot be capable of arms. For this reason, they are nowhere made soldiers or slaves."[5]

---

1. James Shapiro, *Shakespeare and the Jews* (New York: Columbia University Press, 1996), 30.
2. Ibid., 37–38.
3. Ibid., 40.
4. Ibid., 34. This thesis, of course, does not take into account that prohibitions on Jews owning land usually precluded participation in agriculture, and the guilds' exclusion of Jewish membership effectively shut Jews out of practicing the skilled crafts.
5. Ibid.

...Henry VIII sought Jewish scriptural opinions in his divorce

In 1527, England's King Henry VIII decided that he needed a new wife to provide the much-desired male heir that he lacked. Since Pope Clement VII was against the idea of Henry getting divorced so that he might remarry, Henry enlisted the aid of both Christian and Jewish scholars to prepare a brief to be submitted to the pope. Jews had been banished from England since 1290, so Henry had to send his ambassador Richard Croke to Italy to meet with Jewish scholars.[1] After protracted discussions, the weight of the Jewish opinion turned unfavorable to Henry. The rabbis actually sided with the position held by the pope.[2] Seeing that he could not win his case within the confines of the Church, Henry split with the Catholic Church and established the Church of England.[3]

Had the Jewish scholars sided with Henry, there may very well have been no establishment of the Church of England.

---

1. Michael Pollack, *Mandarins, Jews, and Missionaries: The Jewish Experience in the Chinese Empire* (Philadelphia: Jewish Publication Society, 1980).
2. Ibid., 377.
3. The Royal Household, "Henry VIII (r. 1509–1547)," The Official Website of the British Monarchy, http://www.royal.gov.uk/HistoryoftheMonarchy/KingsandQueensofEngland/TheTudors/HenryVIII.aspx.

...not all Jewish captives wanted to be freed

In 1530 Charles v of Spain gave the island of Malta to the Knights Hospitaller of the Order of Saint John.[1] Very soon the knights became full-fledged pirates preying on ships in the Mediterranean Sea. Among the booty derived from their piracy were captives, many of them Jewish.

Among the highest acts of Jewish charity is the obligation of Jews everywhere to ransom captives from wherever they may be. There soon grew up organizations called the confraternity for the redemption of captives,[2] devoted exclusively to the ransom of Jewish captives, mostly from the island of Malta where the majority of the hostages were being held. This organization raised funds and conducted negotiations with the pirates for the release of the captives. There were many such organizations.

To facilitate their work, the group maintained an office right on the island and was able to furnish the captives with a synagogue complete with Torah scrolls and a burial ground for those who might pass away during their captivity. They were even able to get the masters to permit the slaves to have Saturday and holidays off from work. All the while, the Jewish representatives would be working to effect the release of the captives.[3]

In 1666, a group of rabbis was captured. Among them was one Moses Azulai. Unlike other prisoners, Azulai did not demand rapid repatriation. Instead, he stayed to minister to the needs of his fellow captives. He was able to procure a perpetual calendar and an oven for baking unleavened bread. He even wrote bills of divorcement for some of the prisoners.[4]

After a time, the piracy tapered off, the number of prisoners dwindled, and Rabbi Azulai, lonely and advanced in years, requested repatriation. Unfortunately, before the process was completed, the rabbi passed away.[5]

1. Cecil Roth, *Personalities and Events in Jewish History* (Philadelphia: Jewish Publication Society, 1953), 113–15.
2. Ibid., 116.
3. Ibid., 115, 126.
4. Ibid., 131.
5. Ibid., 133.

...The Merchant of Venice mirrors Christian views

When Shakespeare wrote *The Merchant of Venice,* he was mirroring the widely held Christian view of the perceived differences between Judaism and Christianity.

Antonio, a Christian merchant, acts as guarantor for a loan contracted by a friend. Shylock, the Jewish moneylender, strikes a strange bargain with Antonio, his longtime tormentor. The loan will be interest free, but a pound of flesh must be forfeited if the loan deadline is not met. The time lapses and Antonio is unable to pay. Even though Antonio's friends raise more than the required amount, Shylock insists on the grisly fulfillment of the contract.

This episode displays two contrasts between perceived actions of Jews and Christians. On the one hand, Shylock slavishly adheres to the letter of the Venetian law in the fulfillment of contracts, just as Jews were perceived as following the letter of the Mosaic Law in their everyday dealings, regardless of the consequences. Also, by insisting on the exact performance of the contract, Shylock is displaying a distinct lack of mercy and compassion, another widely held perception of Jews in Shakespeare's time. By contrast, the Christians are depicted as willing to bend the law a little in the interest of mercy and forgiveness.[1]

A fake trial is held wherein Shylock is outwitted in the judge's injunction against shedding any blood during the excision of the pound of flesh. Shylock attempts to bail out of the contract, but he is held to the conditions, unless he will pay a major penalty. The ruling is that half of Shylock's estate is to be paid to the state and the other half to Antonio as a penalty for threatening the life of a Venetian citizen; Antonio magnanimously agrees to relinquish his half of Shylock's estate, if Shylock will become a convert to Christianity and will bequeath the remainder of his estate to his daughter Jessica at the time of his death.[2]

The legal injunction on Shylock hints to more themes of Jewish-Christian relations. From the late 1570s and early 1580s, Elizabethan England was deeply involved with the necessity of converting the Jews to Christianity; one writer even went so far as to say that only the conversion of the Jew stood in the way of the final judgment. Shakespeare is emulating a widely held belief.[3]

To add to Shylock's woes, his daughter Jessica converts and elopes with a Christian. This is another theme of Jewish-Christian relations: Jewish women are "young and desirable" while Jewish men are "invariably old and impotent," never accepted even after conversion to Christianity.[4]

1. Ross Douthat and David Hopson, *SparkNotes: The Merchant of Venice* (New York: Spark Publishing, 2002), 16.
2. Ibid., 42.
3. James Shapiro, *Shakespeare and the Jews* (New York: Columbia University Press, 1996), 134, 144.
4. Ibid., 132.

...Shakespeare plagiarized *The Merchant of Venice*

When the famous author Johann Wolfgang von Goethe was a child, his education included writing exercises in Latin. One of his selections relates the story of a court case involving a Jewish borrower and a Christian moneylender. In this case, a Jew named Welsch borrowed money from Johann George Junker. The Jew deposited a substantial security pledge and the package was sealed. When the pledge was redeemed, the package had been looted of most of its valuable contents, but the seal was unbroken. In the course of the trial, it was brought out that Junker had engaged the services of a seal maker to duplicate the original seal.[1]

Although these were the facts brought out at the trial, Goethe's story alters the portion where it would appear that the honest Jew was being victimized by a Christian knave.[2]

If this sounds similar to the story of Shylock and Antonio as told in Shakespeare's *Merchant of Venice*, that's because it is. The reversal of the roles is recorded by the Catholic biographer of Pope Sixtus v, Gregorio Leti. He relates that the victim who was to lose a pound of flesh was a Jew named Sampson Ceneda, and the villain was a Christian, Paul Secchi.

How much anti-Semitism was engendered by a plagiarized, fake story?

---

1. Mark Waldman, *Goethe and the Jews: A Challenge to Hitlerism* (New York: Putnam, 1934), 25.
2. Gerald Friedlander, *Shakespeare and the Jew* (New York: Dutton, 1921), 15.

As part of the Reformation, Protestants were encouraged to read the Scriptures. In doing so, many people had their first exposure to Jewish teachings as set forth in the Hebrew Bible. Some of the people were moved to emulate the practices of the people in the Pentateuch.

Among these was an Englishman named John Traske. Traske was an ordained minister preaching in London when he and some of his followers were arrested in 1618. Traske was accused of "having a fantastical opinion of himself with ambition to be the father of a Jewish faction."[1] Traske was convicted of "teaching that the laws of Moses concerning the differences of meats, forbidding the eating of hog's flesh, conies, etc., are to be observed and kept."[2]

Following his conviction, Traske was expelled from the ministry, fined, sent to prison, had one of his ears nailed to the pillory, and was burned with a "J" on his forehead. In prison, Traske was allowed to eat only the meats that Jewish law had forbidden.[3]

Traske subsequently won his freedom by recanting his Judaic views in a publication he issued entitled *A Treatise of Libertie from Judaisme*. Traske's wife refused to recant her views and was imprisoned for a long time. There were others who were similarly persecuted.[4]

Members of Traske's group later settled in Amsterdam and joined the synagogue there. A number of them are buried in the Spanish and Portuguese Jewish cemetery.

1. James Shapiro, *Shakespeare and the Jews* (New York: Columbia University Press, 1996), 23.
2. Ibid.
3. Ibid.
4. Ibid., 24.

...French anti-Semitism created great Jewish bankers

During the reigns of Louis XIV and XV of France (1638–1774), there was a protracted struggle between the Crown and the Parliament of Bordeaux. The kings wished to expel the Jews from the kingdom and enacted a series of restrictive measures including locking the ghetto at night. New Christians, those Jews who had recently become Christians, were being similarly squeezed into the position of being treated more and more like Jews, leading many to emigrate.

The government officials, on the other hand, wanted the Jews to stay. At issue was the French banking system. There was a woeful shortage of liquid capital, which was proving to be a major obstacle in improving the banking and credit system of France.

To this problem, the Jews could provide the answer. Because of the restriction on the Jews in purchasing real estate outside of their own residential districts, they possessed liquid capital and were willing to invest it. Moreover, they were able to successfully appeal to their Portuguese-Jewish brethren in England, Amsterdam, and the Iberian Peninsula to invest in the French endeavor. Thus it was that the Jews were launched into the French banking and credit system.[1]

---

1. Esther Benbassa, *The Jews of France: A History from Antiquity to the Present* (Princeton, NJ: Princeton University Press, 1999), 43–51.

...Spinoza was first offered a pension, then excommunicated

Baruch Spinoza began his career as a student in the Spanish-Portuguese school in Amsterdam. He was an outstanding student, and soon began to develop his own religious philosophy. It was rooted in the concept that "there is one God who demands justice and neighborly love and forgives those who repent."[1] Spinoza rejected the Mosaic authorship of the Pentateuch, and the possibility of genuine prophesy. He also insisted that miracles were impossible and that all tenets of religion should be subject to reason.

Soon Spinoza began to attract some negative attention in the Amsterdam Jewish community. There were many former *Marranos* (secret Jews) in the Jewish community who feared that if Spinoza converted to Christianity, it would have a devastating affect on Jews still within reach of the Inquisition.[2] (In fact Spinoza did not convert.)

The Jewish community of Amsterdam offered Spinoza the opportunity to recant his ideas and to accept a generous annual pension. Spinoza refused, and he was subsequently excommunicated from the Jewish religion.[3]

As his fame as a scholar and philosopher began to spread, Spinoza was offered in 1673 the chair of philosophy at the University of Heidelberg. He was to be given "freedom in philosophizing" provided that he would not "disturb the publicly established religion."[4] Spinoza declined the post saying that he "could not control the occurrence of religious dissension."[5]

Spinoza spent the rest of his life writing on philosophy, the Bible, and Hebrew grammar. He earned a modest living grinding lenses for eyeglasses and died in 1677 of a lung disease at the relatively young age of forty-five.

Some assert that Spinoza's ideas influenced John Locke,[6] who in turn influenced Thomas Jefferson in his writing of the Declaration of Independence. Spinoza is also credited with helping to undo the "Protestant (both Calvinist and Lutheran) denigration of mankind as infinitely unworthy of an all-powerful and distant God,"[7] and with paving the way for "an Enlightenment hope" that man could take responsibility for his own life.[8]

In spite of everything that happened to him and the content of his writings, Spinoza has frequently been referred to as "a God-intoxicated" person, and he is ranked as one of the major philosophers of all time.

---

1. Steven T. Katz, *Jewish Philosophers* (New York: Bloch Publishing Company, 1975), 141.
2. Professor Heinrich Graetz, *History of the Jews*, vol. 5 (Philadelphia: Jewish Publication Society, 1898), 93.
3. Ibid., 94.
4. Steven Nadler, *Spinoza: A Life* (Cambridge: Cambridge University Press, 1999), 311–14.
5. Katz, *Jewish Philosophers*, 139.
6. James Carroll, *Constantine's Sword: The Church and the Jews* (New York: Houghton Mifflin, 2001), 412.
7. Ibid.
8. Ibid.

In 1753 the British Parliament passed the Jewish Naturalization Act, more generally known as the "Jew Bill," granting citizenship to Jews. So great was the protest raised that the act was soon repealed. During the heated political debate that accompanied the passage and repeal of the bill, a central figure emerged: Shylock, the Jewish antagonist in Shakespeare's *Merchant of Venice*.

One of the fears expressed in the parliamentary debate was that one hundred years hence, in 1853, England would be ruled by Jews. A fraudulent publication called *The Hebrew Journal* made its appearance, showing that by 1853 a certain Jew named Shylock would be standing for election to the Sanhedrin[1] (no longer Parliament) in the land of Canaan[2] (no longer England). The ever-popular play *Merchant of Venice* would be banned from the British stage.[3]

Another contemporary writer cites Shylock's hatred of Antonio, Shylock's putative victim, when he says, "I hate him for he is a Christian." The writer continues with three more pages of continuous quotations from *The Merchant of Venice* and ends with the following admonition: "And now, Englishmen and countrymen, judge ye, what advantage it can be to you to have these Jews naturalized!"[4]

As the controversy heated up, the *London Evening Post* and shortly after the *Cambridge Journal* ran a parody entitled "The Thirty-Fourth Chapter of Gen[esis]," dealing with the rape of Dinah. The writer of the essay substitutes the names of some of the political figures, including Salvador and Pelham and, of course, Shylock. Those familiar with the biblical narrative will recognize the story relating to the rape of Dinah.

The essay reads in part as follows:

> And it came to pass, in the Year Seventeen hundred sixty-three, that the Daughters of the Britons, which their Wives bear unto them, went into the Synagogues of the Jews, to see the Daughters of the Israelites.
>
> And when the sons of Gid[eon], of Shylock...and Salv[ador] saw them, they took them, and defiled them...

---

1. The Sanhedrin was the ecclesiastical court/legislature that functioned during times of Jewish independence or autonomy under a larger empire.
2. *Canaan* was the biblical name given to the area that at the time encompassed Palestine.
3. James Shapiro, *Shakespeare and the Jews* (New York: Columbia University Press, 1966), 217.
4. Ibid.

And Gid[eon] and Shylock came to the Gate of the [Ex]change, and communed with the Men of their own nation...

And unto Gid[eon] and Shylock hearken'd all the Jews that went [in]to the [Ex]change. And they told the Pelh[ami]tes, who ordered every male to be circumcised...

And it came to pass on the Third Day, whilst their Private Parts were sore, that the Jews took their Swords, and slew every Male of the Britons.[1]

There were writings featuring Shylock too numerous to mention. Even in later years, after the controversy had died down, the fictional "Shylock" was still credited with writing books such as *The Jew Apologist* and *The Rabbi's Lamentation Upon the Repeal of the Jew Act.*[2]

All this from a character who never lived!

---

1. Quoted in Catherine M. S. Alexander and Stanley W. Wells, *Shakespeare and Race* (Cambridge: Cambridge University Press, 2000), 131.
2. Ibid., 221.

During the reign of Louis xv there was much talk about expelling the Jews from France. When the decision came *not* to expel the Jews, the dividends began to accrue rapidly. Among those who stayed in France was Jacob Rodrigues Pereire, an educator of the deaf. Pereire used his knowledge of physiology and anatomy to develop a system of sound articulation and lip reading. He earned great distinction for his achievement and was awarded a grant by Louis xv. A mathematical invention earned him another grant, and his work on increasing the speed of sailing vessels won him still greater recognition.[1] This Marrano returned to Judaism and became one of the leaders of the Sephardic Jewish community in France.

1. William Brickman, "Jacob Rodrigues Pereire," *Encyclopedia Judaica*, CD-ROM *Edition* (Jerusalem: Keter, 1997).

At the beginning of the French Revolution, a great deal of land had been confiscated from the Church and from the nobles and given to the peasants of the area known as Alsace. The peasants wanted to work the land, but lacking the money to do so, turned to Jewish moneylenders. The government had unfortunately imposed high taxes and devalued the money, making it very difficult for debtors to pay. They blamed the Jews for their problem, and a prominent French newspaper offered the opinion that emancipation of the Jews had been a great mistake. It further stated that the only way French Jews could become true Frenchmen was to convert to Christianity. Some wished to expel the Jews.

In answer to those who wanted to expel the Jews, Napoleon said, "It would be a weakness to chase away the Jews; it would be a sign of strength to correct them." Napoleon then declared a one-year moratorium on debts owed to Jews and convened an assembly of prominent Jews to "study ways of remedying the situation."[1]

The Jews gave generally satisfactory answers to all of Napoleon's questions, including one that asked if the Jews considered France their country and would defend it. When the Jews answered, "To the death!" Napoleon was very pleased and decided to convene a Jewish court of law called a Sanhedrin, to govern Jews according to Talmudic law.[2]

According to Napoleon's wishes, the Sanhedrin consisted of seventy-one members and included leadership patterned after that of Temple days. The Sanhedrin gave religious sanction to all the laws regarding Jews passed by the French Assembly except the laws relating to mixed marriages.

Once these decisions had been rendered, the Jews were perceived to have given up rabbinical jurisdiction, corporate status, and the hope for a return to the Land of Israel. They were now inseparably tied to France. As Abraham Furtado, one of the prominent French Jews, declared, "We are no longer a nation within a nation. France is our country. Jews, your obligations are outlined; your happiness is waiting."[3]

Although Napoleon was soon deposed and the position of the French Jews somewhat altered, the action of this short-lived Sanhedrin, in renouncing separate nationhood, had an effect on Jewish life in Western Europe for a long time to come.

---

1. Abba Eban, *My People: The Story of the Jews* (New York: Behrman House, 1968), 259.
2. Ibid.
3. Ibid., 261.

...an essay contest hastened the emancipation of French Jews

In 1785 the Société Royale des Arts et Sciences at Metz conducted an essay contest on the question "Are there possibilities of making the Jews more useful and happier in France?"[1] The contest was won by a French Catholic clergyman, Abbé Henri Baptiste Grégoire. In his essay, Grégoire suggested that the Jews should become westernized and integrated into French society. He further stated, as had been mentioned before in many times and places, that the social and moral shortcomings so often attributed to the Jews are the result of the discrimination practiced against them. He also suggested the abolition of social and political separatism, communal autonomy, Jewish quarters, Yiddish, and "the superstitious beliefs" to which the Jews adhered, because they had been misled by their rabbis.

Grégoire rejected the thesis that the Jews must forever suffer because of their guilt of deicide. He further pointed out that the prophets, at the destruction of Jerusalem, foresaw a time when the consequences of that disaster would come to an end. He suggested that it would be following the will of the Deity if the French nation would take the lead "in preparing by our humanity the revolution by which these people are to be reformed."

Using the topics raised in his essay, Grégoire was very active in raising the "Jewish question" to the French National Assembly. He also used his rhetorical skills to counter those who would deny emancipation to the Jews.

Largely through his efforts, emancipation of the Jews was granted in 1791.

Toward the end of his life, Grégoire became active in propagating the idea "of the fall of Rome and the renewed establishment of a Jewish Jerusalem as the capital of a reconstituted Christian world."[2]

---

1. Paul R. Mendes-Flohr and Jehuda Reinharz, *The Jew in the Modern World: A Documentary History* (New York: Oxford University Press, 1980), 53.
2. Professor Heinrich Graetz, *History of the Jews*, vol. 5 (Philadelphia: Jewish Publication Society, 1895), 440; Baruch Mevorah, "Henri Baptiste Grégoire," *Encyclopedia Judaica*, CD-ROM *Edition* (Jerusalem: Keter, 1997).

...French Jews gave aristocratic dowries

In eighteenth-century France, the Jews began to experience considerable economic success through ventures in buying and selling saddle horses and draft horses, silk, and silk goods.[1] During this period, the Jews also assumed a prominent role in the business of banking.[2] A measure of this rising prosperity was the size of the dowries that fathers of brides were able to bestow on their daughters.

During the last quarter of the seventeenth century, the average dowry of a Jewish bride was 590 pounds. By the years 1700–1709, the average dowry had risen to 730 pounds. By the years 1730–1739, the dowry size had risen to 1,650 pounds, and by 1760–1769, it was 6,787 pounds. By the eve of the revolution in 1789, the average dowry size had reached an astounding nine thousand pounds, comparable to that given by the most aristocratic families in France.[3]

There was an old Yiddish axiom that said, "*Alle far die kinder* (everything for the children)." The Jews of eighteenth-century France certainly lived up to that saying.

---

1. Esther Benbassa, *The Jews of France: A History from Antiquity to the Present* (Princeton, NJ: Princeton University Press, 1999), 44.
2. Ibid., 51.
3. Ibid., 44.

...French Jews urged repeal of their own voting rights

In 1808 the French government instituted a network of "consistories," semi-autonomous governing bodies, to handle the communal affairs of French Protestants and eventually French Jews as well. Members of the Jewish consistories consisted of one or two rabbis and three lay members nominated by the government and elected by the "notables," the rich and powerful.

Included in the general duties of the Jewish consistories were education, training for trades, and maintenance of the social order. More specifically, the consistories were charged with "charitable works, administration of religious affairs, and supervision of youth through the creation of primary schools for poor children and of vocational schools."[1] The consistories founded a new rabbinical school with the purpose of replacing the Talmud-oriented schools (yeshivot) which had been closed during the Reign of Terror. They eventually opened orphanages, children's homes, and a Jewish hospital.

By 1831, the government began to pay the salaries of rabbis as it had been doing for Protestant and Catholic clergy. In the light of past history, this was a remarkable achievement for the Jews of France.

However, all was not peaceful in the Jewish community. Because of the structure of the system for selecting members of the consistories, the power was held by the wealthier and more religiously liberal Jews. The Orthodox, generally the less affluent, were excluded from the governance of the community. When France extended the right to vote to Jews over twenty-five years of age, some of the Orthodox began to be admitted to the consistories. Seeing their power threatened, the ruling members of the Jewish consistories in 1851 amazingly called for the repeal of the decree of the December 1849 meeting that had given the Jews the right to vote.[2] In order to maintain their control, they were willing to bargain away what had taken the Jews of France more than a millennium to achieve.

---

1. Esther Benbassa, *The Jews of France: A History from Antiquity to the Present* (Princeton, NJ: Princeton University Press, 1999), 91.
2. Ibid., 92.

...Karl Marx's anti-Semitism hurt the communist cause

Although born a Jew,[1] Karl Marx came to associate Jews with everything detrimental to a socialist society. Jews represented, for Marx, a culture of merchants and hucksters whose God was money. Thus, it would appear that Jews, as a class, would not be welcome to the communist cause. In spite of this attitude by Marx, many Jews supported his ideology.

Marx's collaborator and lifelong friend was Friedrich Engels. After Marx's death, Engels was prompted to put some distance between himself and the anti-Semitism of Marx. Engels stated that "anti-Semitism falsifies the entire situation."[2] Engels went on to point out: "We here in England have had during the last twelve months three strikes of Jewish workers, and now we are to promote anti-Semitism to battle capitalism? ...Many of our best people are Jews."[3]

Marx, for most of his adult life, was financially supported by Engels, the son of a wealthy industrialist.[4] Thus we have Marx being maintained by the very class of people he was trying to bring down and permitting his self-hating anti-Semitism to blind him to the contributions that Jews were making and could make to the cause so dear to his heart.

---

1. Marx's father and later his mother converted to Christianity, and Marx was raised in a Protestant environment.
2. Elliot Rosenberg, *But Were They Good for the Jews? Over 150 Historical Figures Viewed from a Jewish Perspective* (Secaucus, NJ: Carol, 1997), 207.
3. Ibid.
4. Schneir Levenberg, "Karl Marx," *Encyclopedia Judaica, CD–ROM Edition* (Jerusalem: Keter, 1997).

...two Jews bought the Suez Canal for England

In 1875 Prime Minister Disraeli of England was dining with Baron Lionel Rothschild when a phone call informed them that the Khedive of Egypt had offered to sell his shares in the Suez Canal to the French. The negotiations had stalled and the British government had a chance to acquire the shares.[1]

Since Parliament was not in session at the time, the Prime Minister was unable to complete the transaction through the Bank of England. However, before the night was over, Disraeli and Rothschild had come to an agreement on the terms, and the deal was ready for the cabinet to meet and tender its approval.

This was a double victory for England. Not only had Great Britain stopped the French from adding to their commanding holding in Suez stock, but they also stood to gain an income that would indemnify them for the purchase price of the shares within three years.

It was with great pride that a jubilant Disraeli was able to write to the queen, "It is just settled; you have it, madam."[2]

---

1. In 1813 Benjamin Disraeli's father had a quarrel with the synagogue to which they belonged, and in 1817 he had his children baptized. Although nominally a Christian, Disraeli always expressed pride in his Jewish heritage and is included here as a Jew. It was his conversion which made him eligible to become Prime Minister of England, since Jews were barred from sitting in Parliament until 1858. "Benjamin Disraeli," *Encyclopedia Britannica Micropedia*, 15th ed. (Chicago: Encyclopedia Britannica, 1990).
2. Cecil Roth, *The Magnificent Rothschilds* (London: Robert Hale and Company, 1939), 73–77.

...Chaim Weizmann retained an anti-Semitic nurse for his children

In 1916, upon the birth of their second son, Chaim Weizmann engaged the services of a nurse, Jessica Usher. She remained with them for twenty-two years. With Chaim often away on Zionist business and Vera Weizmann busy with her own activities, the Weizmann boys were increasingly under the domination of this woman.

In her own way, Miss Usher saw her care of the Weizmann boys as her mission in life. She wrote, "I felt it my job as a Christian to come into that family and to give those boys, as far as possible, a normal life, because Jews are so cruel to their children. Jews have all these customs they impose upon them. Jews expect so much of their children, and I wanted to give those Jewish boys...a normal English life."[1]

A close friend of Vera Weizmann saw Miss Usher as a "malign influence" and tried in vain to have her dismissed.[2]

As a trained nurse, it fell to Miss Usher to minister to many of the medical needs of the family. Again she wrote, "Benji, Michael, Vera, and Chaim, because they were Jews, were always ill. Jews make a great thing about illness, and indeed, Jews actually enjoy illness.... Each member of the family used to have their own thermometer and [were] keen on having their temperatures taken."[3]

Benji, when he was grown, wrote of "Nurse's" "disgraceful behavior": "It is my firm conviction that we have had a Rasputin in our house for far too long."[4]

Finally, in 1938 Miss Usher suffered a nervous breakdown and retired from service.

---

1. Norman Rose, *Chaim Weizmann: A Biography* (London: Weidenfeld and Nicolson, 1986), 254.
2. Ibid.
3. Ibid.
4. Ibid., 255.

...Chaim Weizmann foresaw the Holocaust and the Jewish state

As early as the latter part of 1932, Chaim Weizmann was counseling German Jews to flee the country. Having read Hitler's *Mein Kampf,* Weizmann, on his last visit to Germany, advised the Jews of Munich, "Hitler means every word"; he told them it was time to flee. By March of 1933, Weizmann publicly denounced the German lapse "into barbarism."[1]

In 1933 Weizmann wrote to Felix Warburg, a member of a prominent German-American-Jewish banking family, "The world is gradually, relentlessly and effectively being closed to the Jews, and every day I feel more and more that a ring of steel is being forged around us.... It is all inescapable, and every ounce of my energy...is going toward the consummation of that end [Palestine]. Everything else is a palliative, a half measure, and merely postponing the evil day."[2]

In 1936, after appearing before the Peel Commission investigating Arab-Jewish conflict in Palestine, Weizmann told his private secretary Yeheskiel Saharoff, "I foresee the destruction of European Jewry..."[3]

Weizmann's pessimism deepened, and by 1938 he confided to a friend in an extremely prophetic utterance, "I am distressed that the Jews don't understand the apocalyptic nature of the times.... Part of us will be destroyed, and on their bones New Judaea may arise! It is all terrible but it is so – I feel it even here [in Rehovot, Palestine], and can think of nothing else...."[4]

---

1. Norman Rose, *Chaim Weizmann: A Biography* (London: Weidenfeld and Nicolson, 1986), 301.
2. Ibid., 301–2.
3. Ibid., 319.
4. Ibid., 310.

Who Knew?!

CENTRAL EUROPE AND THE EAST:
The Unwanted Diaspora

...Jewish traders kept Christians and Muslims in business

During the ninth and tenth centuries, diverse cultures and hostility divided Christians and Muslims. Trade between Europe and Asia virtually disappeared, as Christians and Muslims refused to use each other's ports.[1] Into this gap stepped a group of traveling Jewish merchants called *Radanites*. These people were masters of languages and spoke Arabic, Persian, and Greek, and the languages of the Romans, Franks, Andalusians, and Slavs.[2]

These intrepid traders, traveling by land and by sea, had several advantages: in addition to being conversant in all the languages encountered along the way, being neither Christians nor Muslims they were able to gain the trust of both sides. In addition, they were able to reduce or eliminate the risks of carrying cash over long distances. This was done by a system of checks or letters of credit, which would be honored by Jews all along the trading route. Moreover, they were able to eliminate language barriers among themselves by the universal use of Hebrew, known to all the Jews with whom they would be doing business.

For over a hundred years, almost every shipment of spices that came into Europe was a result of Radanite trade.[3] However, the virtual monopoly enjoyed by the Radanites was soon to end. Riots in China against foreign merchants hurt the Radanite trade. Another blow came with the fall of Khazaria – the Radanites had benefited from the goodwill of Khazaria's Jewish kings. Finally, the rise of Venice locked the Radanites out of the Mediterranean trade. Although the day of the Radanite traders had come to an end, the gold these traders had amassed helped them find a new line of work as bankers when Europe found itself in need.[4]

1. Matthew Goodman, "How the Radanite Traders Spiced Up Life in Dark-Ages Europe," *Forward* (May 30, 2003); http://www.forward.com/articles/8926/.
2. Joseph Jacobs, *Jewish Contributions to Civilization: An Estimate* (Philadelphia: Jewish Publication Society, 1919), 194.
3. Goodman, "How the Radanite Traders Spiced Up Life in Dark-Ages Europe."
4. Jacobs, *Jewish Contributions to Civilization*, 198–99.

...crusades spawned a "protection racket" against Jews

The crusades represented a turning point in the lives of European Jews. No longer were Jews being persecuted for their religion only. Now they had to contend with race aversion. In order to protect themselves, the Jews began to greet each new king or emperor with costly monetary gifts. They also gave generous gifts whenever some new danger approached. In return for the money paid, protection was extended to them. After a while, the tradition of Jewish giving evolved, and the Jews gradually became part of the feudal system. In the feudal system, each class owed allegiance to the class immediately above. Serfs belonged to the landowner and the land; knights were bound to their lord; lords owed allegiance to the king. Now the Jews belonged to the king.

The Jews assumed the status of *servi camerae regis*, servants of the royal chamber, and wards of the emperor. Kings and emperors were able to buy and sell them at their whim. If a king needed some money quickly, he was able to consign the revenue from "his" Jews to the person who was lending him the money. An ironic twist to this situation was provided by Emperor Albert, who sought to punish those who were killing Jews and destroying their businesses and possessions. He complained that they were maltreating his property and destroying his revenues! Incredibly, this system lasted for six hundred years.[1]

When Jews sought to emigrate from this "protective" environment, they were refused permission to do so, because they represented a steady and lucrative source of income. Here we have a prototype of the old gangster movies with their stories of protection rackets. The difference here is that the "gangsters" were the kings and the higher nobility.

1. Abram Leon Sachar, *A History of the Jews* (New York: Knopf, 1964), 192, 198.

A warrior setting forth to participate in a crusade often put himself into difficult financial straits. In an effort to alleviate the burden of those who were going off to war, Pope Innocent III issued decrees pertaining to crusaders who were in debt to Jewish moneylenders. The order stipulated that during the time the crusader was away, he was to pay no interest on his loans. Interest already paid to the Jewish financier was to be repaid to the crusader.

In the event the crusader could not pay his debt, there was to be a moratorium on payment until such time as the individual returned home to attend to his affairs. In cases where the Jewish moneylender was holding income property as collateral, the income was to be applied to reducing the principal, but no interest was to be paid.

As a result of these decrees, a crusader going off to war did not suffer financially due to his indebtedness. The Jewish moneylender, on the other hand, could do no better than to break even.[1] To add insult to injury, many of the crusaders participated in wholesale massacres of Jews while on their way to fight the Muslims.

---

1. Jacob R. Marcus, *The Jew in the Medieval World: A Source Book, 315–1791* (New York: Atheneum, 1938), 140–41.

CENTRAL EUROPE AND THE EAST: The Unwanted Diaspora

Who Knew?!

...Jews were instrumental in spreading the Renaissance

At the dawn of the renaissance, Europeans were becoming interested in the Greek philosophical writings that had been further developed by Arab scholars like Averroes and Avicenna. However, they were having trouble getting at the knowledge they were seeking. Barriers of religion and culture separating Christians and Muslims extended also to language. Few people in Christendom were fluent in Arabic. It was here that the Jews were able to bridge the gap. Having already translated the Arabic works into Hebrew, the Jews had no trouble rendering them into Latin, thereby making available an entire body of knowledge to Christian scholars. The major medical resource of the time was that of Avicenna, translated by the Jewish physician Master Bonacosa.[1]

The renaissance sparked a new interest in things Jewish. Christians began to study the Bible in its original Hebrew. The "works of Maimonides, Ibn Gabirol, and Yehuda haLevi became part of the new humanist curriculum," as did the Zohar and other works of Kabbalah.[2]

Some of the greatest Renaissance literature was heavily influenced by Jewish writings. The widely studied *Summa Totius Theologie* of St. Thomas Aquinas leaned heavily on the works of Maimonides, and the famous author Dante drew from Aquinas much of his theology and philosophy. Here we have a straight-line connection between Dante and Maimonides.[3]

Christians in the Renaissance began to desire to read Scriptures in the Hebrew. In order to accomplish this, some resorted to hiring Jewish teachers. However, the pope soon put a stop to this practice. Some of the clergy were disciplined for taking instruction from Jews. It was a lucky Christian who found a baptized Jew to teach him Hebrew.

Nevertheless, the thirst for Hebrew language continued. Some classes in Hebrew were available for purposes of fostering conversions to Christianity, but in Italy Hebrew was a subject in its own right.[4]

The Jewish Kimhi family of rabbis did their major work in Hebrew grammar and critical interpretation of the Bible during the period from 1105 to 1235. The great German intellectual Johannes Reuchlin may have

---

1. Cecil Roth, *The Jews in the Renaissance* (Philadelphia: Jewish Publication Society, 1959), 65–66, 71.
2. Berel Wein, *Herald of Destiny: The Story of the Jews in the Medieval Era, 750–1650* (New York: Shaar Press, 1996), 246, 258.
3. Roth, *The Jews in the Renaissance*, 87.
4. Ibid., 137–39.

based his groundbreaking 1506 *De Rudimentis Hebraicis* on the work of the Kimhis; it became a valuable tool of Renaissance scholars.[1]

When the Authorized Version of the King James Bible was compiled in about 1611, the Jews were officially absent from England following their expulsion in 1290. However, it was generally accepted that the influence of David Kimhi was present on every page.[2]

Another renaissance figure mentioned elsewhere in this volume is Abraham Zacuto. He is credited with supplying Christopher Columbus and Vasco da Gama with the astronomical charts used in their epic voyages of discovery. However, like other Renaissance figures, Zacuto stood on the sturdy shoulders of some earlier Jewish scholars.

In the thirteenth century Alfonso X of Castile commissioned Abraham ibn Sid, the cantor of the Jewish community, to compile a revision of the Ptolemaic planetary tables. This compilation was translated into Hebrew by Moses ben Nimes in 1460. These tables were further revised by Zacuto before he presented them to Columbus.[3]

Conversely, France was quite tardy in reaping the benefits of the Renaissance because the country was largely devoid of Jewish influences.[4] Thus it was that amidst expulsions and ghettoization, the Jews were able to make substantial contributions to the Renaissance.

1. Gordon Laird, "The Kimhi Family: Their Writings in the Reformation," http://www.glaird.com/kim-hom.htm.
2. Israel Abrahams, *Jewish Life in the Middle Ages* (Philadelphia: Jewish Publication Society, 1896), xix, 372.
3. Raphael Patai, *The Jewish Mind* (New York: Scribner, 1977), 125.
4. Ibid., 222.

...Renaissance Jews were renowned dancing masters

During the Italian Renaissance, Hebrew teachers in cultured households instructed the pupils, not only in Bible and Talmud, but also in music, singing, and dancing.[1] Relationships between dancing instructors and their pupils were extremely close, so much so that the clergy in 1443 ordered the closing of schools of music and dancing kept by Jews.[2]

Because of their popularity, some Jewish dancing masters continued to teach Christians. However, it was very difficult to do so when the pupils were royal personages and their presence was conspicuous.

One of the great Jewish dancing masters, Guglielmo de Pesare, converted to Christianity,[3] presumably so that he could continue in his profession.

---

1. Cecil Roth, *The Jews in the Renaissance* (Philadelphia: Jewish Publication Society, 1959), 275.
2. Ibid., 275–76.
3. Ibid., 278.

...Jews *deliberately* invited the Inquisition to censor their books

Moses Maimonides (Rambam) was possibly the greatest commentator on Jewish religious topics. He was, however, not without some severe critics. So controversial were his writings that some of his opponents, in 1232, put Maimonides' writings under a ban.[1] Moreover, in order to strengthen their proscription of Maimonides, they foolishly invited the Dominicans and the Franciscan Friars to assist them in rooting out the writings that they opposed.

While the Inquisition was limited to converted Christians returning to Judaism, this invitation by the Jews themselves was too good to pass up. Before long, the Inquisitors were looking into a wide array of Jewish writings. Tens of thousands of volumes of the Talmud and other Hebrew writings were burned by the Inquisition in widespread locations.[2]

Pope Gregory IX instituted debates concerning Jewish writings with the inevitable result that the books were consigned to the flames. When Louis XV permitted the Jews to return to France after their expulsion, he stipulated that nobody would be allowed to own a copy of the Talmud.[3]

So it was that what should have been a scholarly discourse among Jews on the validity of Maimonides' writings turned into an unmitigated disaster lasting right up into modern times.

---

1. Joshua Trachtenberg, *The Devil and the Jews: The Medieval Conception of the Jews and Its Relation to Modern Anti-Semitism* (New York: Harper and Row, 1943), 178.
2. Ibid.
3. Ibid., 179.

...a woman with marital problems needs a cantor

During the eleventh, twelfth, and thirteenth centuries in the Middle East, cantors did much more than lead their congregations in song. As a minimum requirement, a cantor had to be literate and musical and had to be familiar with a number of variations of the tunes he was to perform. Cantors were also linguists whose abilities were often put to use.

Aside from the musical requirements of the job, cantors of those days were required to appear as beyond reproach in their religiosity and moral conduct. Once the cantors had attained these personal credentials as pillars of the community, they were well positioned to begin performing all the community functions required of them.

Officiating at weddings, funerals, and other family affairs, cantors lent dignity and honor to the proceedings as well as providing additional income for themselves. Another source of income for the cantor was "the tour." From the eleventh through thirteenth centuries, cantors would visit nearby towns to demonstrate their skills, and grateful patrons would reward their efforts by monetary contributions.

Since cantors spent a great deal of time on the road, they were often entrusted with bearing public announcements to other towns and were also engaged to carry goods from place to place.

Cantors also functioned within the legal system of Jewish communities. The cantor might be retained to visit the homes of women experiencing problems in their married life. The depositions taken down by the cantor might very well be used in a subsequent legal proceeding. Indeed, cantors frequently were vested with power of attorney by virtue of their reputed honesty. Because they traveled to other places, such powers of attorney might eliminate the necessity of somebody else making additional trips outside their immediate vicinity.

The time-honored practice of ransoming captives was another area where cantors were pressed into service. Cantors also were charged with seeing to it that needy Jews were provided for by public funds.

Finally, cantors frequently acted as matchmakers. If the match eventuated in marriage, the cantor might logically be engaged to perform the nuptials.[1]

---

1. S.D. Goitein, *A Mediterranean Society: An Abridgement in One Volume*, revised and edited by Jacob Lassner (Berkeley: University of California Press, 1999), 278–81.

...Maimonides practiced medicine lying down

Moses Maimonides (Rambam) was one of the greatest Jewish philosophers and commentators on the Talmud who ever lived. In addition to his accomplishments in the Jewish religion, Maimonides was much sought after as a physician. When Maimonides was sixty-four years old, his friend Samuel ibn Tibbon, who lived far away, wrote that he would like to come for a visit with the great man.

Maimonides wrote back that he would love to have the visitor, but he had to forewarn him of his grueling schedule and lack of time for visitors. In his letter, Maimonides describes his daily routine. Each morning, he rides about two miles on horseback from his home in Fustat to Cairo, where he serves as the physician to the Sultan, his family, and members of his court. He is obliged to stay there at least until the noon hour, but is often required to stay later into the afternoon, if there are many patients to see.

After leaving the palace, Maimonides rides home, where he is greeted by a throng of patients awaiting his return. He hurriedly eats his only meal of the day and begins to see the patients who have come for treatment. This lasts until the evening and sometimes until about eight o'clock at night. So exhausted is he, that he describes himself as follows: "I converse with and prescribe for them [the patients] while lying down on my back from sheer fatigue; and when night falls, I am so exhausted, I can hardly speak."[1]

He goes on to say that on the Sabbath after services he instructs the people until noon, and some of them come back in the afternoon. This is the only time he has for conversation.

At the age of seventy, Maimonides died. "The cause of death was listed as weakness."[2]

1. "Maimonides," *Encyclopedia Judaica,* CD-ROM *Edition* (Jerusalem: Keter, 1997).
2. Ibid.

...there was a Golden Age for Jews in Lithuania

In 1388, King Vytautas of Lithuania (1392–1430) granted the Jews of his country a charter exempting synagogues and Jewish cemeteries from taxation. Jews were allowed freedom of transit and trade and were allowed to mint coins. While most Catholic countries outlawed Jewish land ownership, Jews of Lithuania were able to obtain property rights through licenses purchased from the government. Jews were allowed to trade in liquor and had rights to peddle or sell in stores equal to the rights enjoyed by Christian merchants.

Christians owing money to Jews were expected to pay on time. A late interest payment by a Christian obligated him to pay twice the sum due. Jews did not have to make payments on time if the due date fell on the Sabbath or Jewish holidays. Jews were also exempt from jurisdiction of Church or municipal courts, because those courts were traditionally biased against Jews.

By papal order, the blood libel was proscribed. Christians testifying against Jews had to have their evidence corroborated by a Jewish witness, and Christians bearing false witness against Jews faced confiscation of all their property and possessions. Jewish property, including synagogues and cemeteries, was protected by statutes.

A Christian who was guilty of killing a Jew was subject to having all his property seized. Injuring a Jew made the Christian liable for medical care and a fine. In other situations, one who killed a townsman had to remit twelve *shoks* to the exchequer. Killing a Jew or a nobleman required the payment of one hundred *shoks*.[1]

King Vytautas was succeeded by the thirteen-year-old boy king Casimir the Great (1444–1492). Under pressure from the Catholic Church, Casimir was forced to sign the Statute of Niezawa limiting the freedoms enjoyed by the Jews. Having signed the statute, Casimir disregarded its provisions, continued Jewish freedoms, and also continued to appoint Jews to responsible and lucrative positions.[2]

These statutes were truly remarkable for that period of time. It should also be noted that pagans were rulers in Lithuania during most of the "golden age" for Jews.[3]

---

1. Masha Greenbaum, *The Jews of Lithuania: A History of a Remarkable Community, 1316–1945* (Jerusalem: Gefen Publishing House, 1995), 8–9, 16.
2. Ibid., 10–11.
3. Yaffa Eliach, *There Once Was a World: A 900-Year Chronicle of the Shtetl of Eishyshok* (Boston: Little, Brown, 1998), 22–24.

...kosher slaughter was a capital offense

In the thirteenth or fourteenth century, a group of Jewish merchants presented gifts to the Mongol Khan, a powerful Asian ruler. The Khan, in turn, held a banquet for his guests. Noticing that the Jews were not eating the food set before them, the Khan inquired as to the reason and was told that the food was "not clean," which meant more specifically, not kosher, because the animal had not been slaughtered according to the Jewish dietary laws.

The Khan was furious and issued the following decree:

> From now on, the people with green-blue eyes, and The People of the Book are forbidden to slaughter sheep by slitting their throats [the kosher method of slaughter]. Sheep must be disemboweled in the Mongol fashion. Whoever slaughters a sheep by cutting its throat shall be executed in the same manner. His wife and children shall be confiscated and given to the man who has exposed them.[1]

An indication as to how serious were the Jews in their observance of the rules of ritual slaughtering is the fact that they were known as the Sinew-plucking Religion.[2] This process of removing a certain vein from the hind quarter is so labor intensive that this part of the animal is rarely prepared for Jewish consumption and is routinely sold to non-Jews.

It is not known how widespread was the injunction of the Mongol Khan, nor how long it was in effect, but its enforcement would have had serious consequences for Jews coming under the Khan's edict.

---

1. Sidney Shapiro, *Jews in Old China: Studies by Chinese Scholars* (New York: Hippocene, 2001), 195–96.
2. Ibid., 41.

...Torah reading was interrupted for adjudicating a grievance

For many years, organized Jewish communities have had well-defined procedures for adjudicating grievances, disagreements, and violations of community standards. However, in some particularly serious or emergency conditions, one or more congregants would resort to the interruption of the reading of the Torah[1] in order to get an immediate hearing and possible resolution of their case.

One such case occurred in the shtetl (small town) of Eishyshok, involving a group of Jewish soldiers who had been drafted into the Polish army. These soldiers were being subjected to an array of discriminatory practices among which was the frequent delay or nonpayment of their salaries. This practice posed a particular hardship to men of modest means.

On the day the men resorted to the interruption of the Torah reading, the congregation voted to supply the soldiers with a monthly stipend out of their own coffers to make up for the shortfalls occasioned by the discriminatory practices of the Polish army.[2] Only then was the worship service resumed.

---

1. The Torah reading is the recitation of a portion of the Scriptures at a given point in the synagogue service. Such readings take place on Mondays, Thursdays, Sabbaths, and holidays.
2. Yaffa Eliach, *There Once Was a World: A 900-Year Chronicle of the Shtetl of Eishyshok* (Boston: Little, Brown, 1998), 84–86.

...the story of *Faust* has virulently anti-Semitic origins

One of the most popular and enduring literary works of all time is the story of Faust. Faust is a scholar on a quest for the true essence of life. In order to attain it, he is willing to barter his soul to the devil. The story has been retold in literally hundreds of dramas, operas, classical music, popular music, and movies, and has been presented in every conceivable medium all the way to comic books and advertising.[1] However, this seemingly benign tale has more sinister overtones in its origins.

From very early times, Christians have attempted to associate Jews with the devil. Depictions of Satan give him decidedly Semitic features. The mandatory Jew badges often display horns or other features associated with the Devil. Because of his failure to accept Christianity, goes the reasoning, the Jew is much more vulnerable to the temptations set out by Satan. If a Christian were to be tempted by Satan, he would most likely have a Jew serve as the intermediary. In some instances, the Jew *is* the Devil.[2] Michelangelo's horned *Moses* is probably more than a mere mistranslation of the Hebrew text.[3]

In countless passion plays and Christmastime presentations, the Jews and the Devil are shown working together. Moreover, very few people doubted the use of Christian blood in Jewish ceremonials on Passover, circumcisions, and at weddings.[4] Perhaps Shakespeare summed it up best in some lines from *The Merchant of Venice*: "Let me say amen betimes, lest the devil cross my prayer, for here he comes in the likeness of a Jew" (act 3, scene 1, lines 19–21).[5] In act 2, scene 2, line 27, Shakespeare puts it as plainly as could be: "Certainly the Jew is the very devil incarnation."[6]

1. Theodore Ziolkowski, *The Sin of Knowledge: Ancient Themes and Modern Variations* (Princeton, NJ: Princeton University Press, 2000), 5.
2. Joshua Trachtenberg, *The Devil and the Jews: The Medieval Conception of the Jew and Its Relationship to Modern Anti-Semitism* (New York: Harper and Row, 1943), chapter 1.
3. The verse in Exodus 34:29 describes Moses coming down from the mountain after receiving the Torah (Five Books of Moses), and *karan or* (his skin was shining); the Latin Vulgate translation of the Pentateuch mistranslated *karan* (was shining) as "was horned," a cognate meaning.
4. Trachtenberg, *The Devil and the Jews*, chapter 1.
5. William Shakespeare, "The Merchant of Venice," in *The Riverside Shakespeare*, edited by G. Blakemore Evans (Boston: Houghton Mifflin, 1974), 267.
6. Ibid., 261.

...a Christian scholar saved the Talmud from a book-burning Jew

In 1509, an apostate Jew named Johannes Pfeffercorn conspired with the priests of the Dominican Order to have all Jewish writings, except for the Bible, burned because they allegedly contained material defaming Christianity and the Church. Their special target was the Talmud, and permission for the confiscation of the books was given by the German Emperor Maximilian. Pfeffercorn and the Dominicans recruited Johannes Reuchlin for assistance in this endeavor. Reuchlin was one of the most respected Christian scholars in all of Germany. He was learned in Hebrew and a master of the Kabbalah (Jewish mysticism). Although he knew little of the Talmud, he realized that the Dominicans and Pfeffercorn knew even less. He told them that the Talmud had been around for centuries, and if it was blasphemous toward the Church, it would have been destroyed long ago. Moreover, Reuchlin told them that the entire Christian faith rested on Jewish writings.

Realizing that Reuchlin would not participate in their scheme, Pfeffercorn wrote a scurrilous pamphlet called "*Handspeigel*" (Mirror) impugning Reuchlin's integrity and scholarship. Reuchlin countered with a writing of his own, the "*Augenspeigel*" (Eyeglasses). As the controversy continued, the emperor commissioned Reuchlin to examine the writings in question and report to him whether or not they should be consigned to the flames.

Reuchlin's report was that the books were not as the Dominicans and Pfeffercorn had claimed and, therefore, should not be burned. This did not end the matter. Among the conspirators was a heretic hunter named Hoogstraten, who had the authority to bring Reuchlin and the "*Augenspeigel*" to trial on charges of heresy, insulting the Church, and favoring the Jews. Reuchlin was about to be condemned and burned, when Archbishop Uriel of Cologne put a stop to the proceedings allowing one month to sort out the problems.

Reuchlin, knowing that he was still in grave danger, wrote a Hebrew letter to the Jewish personal physician of Pope Leo x to intercede on his behalf in obtaining a change of venue. The pope granted it, the trial was held before the bishop of Speyer, and Reuchlin was acquitted.

All of this was going on at the time that the Protestant Reformation was on the rise in Germany. Because of Reuchlin's prominence, the case had become a national issue. The scandalous behavior of the Dominicans caused great damage to the Catholic Church, and many historians feel that Reuchlin's intervention on behalf of the Talmud hastened the spread of the Reformation.[1]

---

1. Jacob R. Marcus, *The Jew in the Medieval World: A Source Book, 315–1791* (New York: Atheneum, 1938), 157–64.

...burghers of Cracow posted a bond against violence toward Jews

King Sigismund of Poland was a rare kind of ruler. To allay the fears of the Jews in Cracow against the possibility of riots, Sigismund in 1530 ordered the burghers (townspeople) of Cracow to post a bond of "ten thousand gulden...as security for the maintenance of peace and safety in the city." The king proclaimed that anyone who had a quarrel with the Jews "should proceed in a legal manner, and not by violence..."[1]

While this measure was successful in its own right, the Polish officials managed to pass anti-Jewish statutes in 1538 in a "constitution" with an entire section devoted to limiting the activities of Jews. Nevertheless, this was classed as a period of prosperity for the Jews of Poland and Lithuania. The king even forbade the merchants from holding a market day on the Sabbath so that Jews could trade.[2]

---

1. Simon M. Dubnow, *History of the Jews in Russia and Poland*, vol. 1 (Philadelphia: Jewish Publication Society, 1916), 76.
2. Ibid., 84–85.

...a "bobe mayse" is not an old wives' tale

Generations of people have become familiar with the term *bobe mayse*, meaning a tall tale, a white lie, a likely story – anything but a truthful utterance to be taken seriously. This was not always so.

In the fifteenth and sixteenth centuries there was a book circulating in Western Europe about a fictional action hero named Buovo, the Italian form of the Anglo-Norman Bevys. He was a type of hero patterned after Robin Hood and Sir Lancelot.

The book was quite popular and was translated into a number of languages. Finally, in 1507–1508, it was translated into Yiddish by Isaac Levita and published in 1541.[1] It was the first non-religious book printed in Yiddish.[2] The story in its Yiddish form deals with Bove's adventures in avenging his father's murder, seeking his stolen patrimony, and resisting the efforts of would-be proselytizers to induce him to leave his faith.

The *Bove Buch*, as it was called, was a great success and remained in print for almost five-hundred years. In the late 1700s, modernized versions began to appear under the title *Bove Mayse*. The last popular edition appeared in 1900–1910, still titled *Bove Mayse*.[3]

Interest in the type of hero exemplified by Bove eventually began to wane, and people even forgot who he was. However, the unbelievable tales of Bove were transformed, over a period of more than one hundred years, into tall tales told by your grandmother...[4] hence *bobe mayses*.

---

1. Currently available in a version by Jerry C. Smith, *Elia Levita Bachur's Bovo-Buch: A Translation of the Old Yiddish Edition of 1541* (Tucson, AZ: Fenestra Books, 2003).
2. Michael Wex, *Born to Kvetch: Yiddish Language and Culture in All Its Moods* (New York: St. Martin's, 2005), 32.
3. Ibid., 34.
4. Ibid., 35–36.

...A Jewish graduate has to pay for uninvited guests

In fifteenth-century Italy, Jews seeking higher education frequently ran into laws meant to exclude them from university training.[1] If, however, a Jewish scholar reached the point where he was to be awarded a degree, he found himself with an added problem. In Padua, for example, the Jewish graduate had to provide "an open table with food and drink for all who cared to come."[2] After a while, every Jew, on his graduation, had to provide to an official of the university a quantity of "sweetmeats for the academic attendants, and for each of the many 'nations' into which the student body was divided."[3] It was estimated that it cost twice as much for a Jew to graduate as for a non-Jew.[4]

---

1. Cecil Roth, *The Jews in the Renaissance* (Philadelphia: Jewish Publication Society, 1959), 37.
2. Ibid.
3. Ibid.
4. Ibid., 37–38.

In 1600 three Jewish editors in Venice put out a new edition of *Sefer Bedek Habayit*, a commentary on rabbinic law, by Joseph Caro. In order to protect themselves against copyright infringement, the men secured a writ ordering excommunication, ban, and anathema for any who would dare to make unauthorized copies of the book. The order was then published in every synagogue in Venice.

As an added deterrent to would-be pirates, the following curse and blessing were appended to the writ:

> Upon any one who may transgress against this our decree of excommunication, ban, and anathema – may there come against him "serpents for whose bite there is no charm," and may he be infected "with the bitter venom of asps"; may God not grant peace to him, etc.
>
> But he that obeys – may he dwell in safety and peace like the green olive tree and rest at night under the shadow of the Almighty; may all that he attempts prosper; may the early rain shower with blessings his people and the sheep of his pasture.[1]

1. Jacob R. Marcus, *The Jew in the Medieval World: A Source Book, 315–1791* (New York: Atheneum, 1938), 404–5.

...Jews voted themselves out of a job

The job of tax farmer (collector) was a lucrative position often assigned to Jews by their respective governments. In 1580 Polish law explicitly forbade Jews from holding this position. Instead of complaining about the discriminatory nature of the law, the representatives of the self-governing body of the Jews met to ratify this law affecting them. So fearful were they of arousing the ire of the Christian population that the Jews worded their statement in part saying that "certain people, thirsting for gain and wealth to be obtained from extensive leases, might thereby expose the community to great danger."[1] In this way the Jewish community officially distanced itself from the task of tax farming, should the opportunity present itself in the future.

---

1. Simon M. Dubnow, *History of the Jews in Russia and Poland*, vol. 1 (Philadelphia: Jewish Publication Society, 1916), 109–10.

...missionaries were one book short of converting all the Jews

It was a long-held belief in some Christian circles that the Jews had expunged from their sacred Scriptures all the references that would prove conclusively to the world that Jesus was indeed the long-awaited Messiah whose second coming would usher in the Messianic Era. All that was needed was a pure and unedited text.[1]

In 1642, Jesuit missionary Alvarez Semmedo brought to the attention of his contemporaries the existence of a Jewish sect in Kaifeng, China, who had absolutely no knowledge of Christianity. This would mean that any Torah in possession of these Jews would not have been altered. The rabbis would be exposed for having perpetrated a massive fraud, and the Christians would have all the proofs of the truth of Christianity. The Jews would no longer have any reason to continue to reject Christianity, and the entire Jewish community would convert.[2]

However, problems with this thesis soon became evident. The scrolls in possession of the Chinese Jews proved, upon inspection, to be substantially the same as the scrolls extant in Europe.[3] Furthermore, Jewish defenders of the charge of falsifying the Torah scrolls pointed out that it would require widespread alteration of books belonging to thousands of people. Why were there no records of strong protests against the wholesale tampering with sacred Scriptures? How could so many people, in such widely dispersed areas, many of them not Jewish, simultaneously participate in wanton desecration of holy writ? What about the scrolls in possession of the earliest Christians? Would they have acquiesced in having such a blow dealt to their newfound faith?[4]

Interest in the Kaifeng Jewish community continued for centuries more, but the isolation of the congregation eventually caused it to be assimilated into the larger Chinese population.

---

1. Michael Pollack, *Mandarins, Jews, and Missionaries: The Jewish Experience in the Chinese Empire* (Philadelphia: Jewish Publication Society, 1980), 29.
2. Ibid., 29.
3. Ibid., 104, 105, 155.
4. Ibid., 29–30.

In 1643, the Warsaw Diet (parliament) embarked on a scheme to impair the livelihoods of Jewish merchants by a discriminatory system of regulating prices. It was designed to put Jewish merchants at a distinct disadvantage in a competitive market. A Polish Christian was limited to a 7-percent profit margin. A Christian foreigner was limited to a 5-percent profit margin. A Jew had to limit himself to a 3-percent profit margin. While this sometimes resulted in a lowering of the quality of the merchandise Jews had to offer for sale, it also meant that higher-quality merchandise sold by Jews could undersell the same products sold by Christians.[1]

When shoppers came to the market, they found that they could consistently buy the same product from the Jews for a lower price. At this point, Christian merchants could let all the business go to the Jews, or they could lower their prices. In either case, this system would invariably incur the displeasure of the Christian businessmen, but it was the law of the government that made it so.

1. Simon M. Dubnow, *History of the Jews in Russia and Poland*, vol. 1 (Philadelphia: Jewish Publication Society, 1916), 99.

...Christian prophecy promoted a Jewish false Messiah

Some Christian mystics predicted that 1666 was to be "a year of wonders, of strange revolutions in the world, and particularly, of blessing to the Jews."[1] So desperate was their need for salvation that many Jews were guided by these Christian prophecies. When false Messiah Sabbatai Zevi proclaimed himself to be the Messiah in 1648, many Jews truly believed that they were at the dawn of the Messianic Era.

Not knowing exactly how to conduct themselves in such an apocalyptic time, some Jews made radical changes in their behavior. Some began to engage in prolonged fasting in order to hasten the coming of the Messianic Era. Others buried themselves in the earth with only their heads exposed, had melted wax dropped on their shoulders, rolled in the snow, bathed in icy waters, or had their bodies pricked with thorns followed by having themselves afflicted with thirty-nine lashes.[2]

Believing that their sustenance would be miraculously provided for in the Messianic Era, some Jews ceased all business activities and sold their personal and business assets, often at a fraction of their value.

Word of the supposed Messiah reached Nehemiah Cohen, a Polish Jew who had predicted the imminent coming of the Messiah, but it was not to be through Sabbatai Zevi. Nevertheless, Zevi hastened to send for Cohen that they might meet. The meeting took place, and Cohen came away unconvinced that Zevi was the Messiah.

Cohen's skepticism almost cost him his life from irate supporters of Zevi, but he escaped to Adrianople. There he posed as a Muslim and reported Sabbatai Zevi's plan to take the sultan's throne. Sabbatai was arrested, offered the choice of conversion or death, chose conversion, and his movement ceased to be a threat to Jews or Muslims. Nehemiah Cohen took off his turban, returned to Poland, and lived quietly without publicizing what he had done.[3]

Even after Sabbatai Zevi converted to Islam, many of his followers believed this was part of a grand plan and followed him into apostasy.[4]

---

1. Jacob R. Marcus, *The Jew in the Medieval World: A Source Book, 315–1791* (New York; Atheneum, 1938), 261–62.
2. Ibid., 263–64.
3. Professor Heinrich Graetz, *History of the Jews*, vol. 5 (Philadelphia: Jewish Publication Society, 1895), 152–53.
4. Marcus, *The Jew in the Medieval World*, 268.

...a Jewish woman claimed the ability to deflect bullets

During the Cossack and Tatar rebellion in Poland in 1648–1649, the rebels singled out Jews for annihilation, partly out of bigotry and partly because some Jews had acted as representatives of the ruling landowners in collecting taxes and crops. Whole villages of Jews were faced with the choice of baptism or death. Most chose death.

It sometimes happened that a Cossack would select a particularly attractive Jewess to be his bride. In one such case, while the procession was on the way to the church, the young Jewish woman engaged her prospective bridegroom in a strange conversation. She told the Cossak that she had the uncanny ability to cast a spell over bullets in order to divert them from their target. She convinced the gullible Cossack to permit her to display this ability by having him shoot at her. The Cossack did so and the young woman fell down mortally wounded.[1] In this way, she chose death over apostasy as did so many of her coreligionists.

1. Simon M. Dubnow, *History of the Jews in Russia and Poland*, vol. 1 (Philadelphia: Jewish Publication Society, 1916), 147.

For almost two millennia, Jewish communities dealt with the rescue of captives held for ransom. The Lithuanian National Jewish Council had a set of procedures for dealing with this problem. One of the considerations was not to pay excessively to redeem captives lest this encourage more capturing for strictly monetary purposes.

The following measures were adopted by the Lithuanian council.

Communities were enabled to spend up to ten gold pieces without any application or authorization to rescue a captive. For sums from ten to sixty gold pieces, the community had to apply to the nearest jurisdiction with sufficient rabbinical authority to approve the amount. For amounts exceeding sixty gold pieces, permission had to be granted by one of three higher-level designated jurisdictions.

When funds were being raised to redeem captives, each community was supposed to meet its assessed obligation and to do so within certain time constraints. In the event they failed to do so, the offending community was subject to sanctions imposed by the council.[1]

While most people were ready and willing to do their share, the involuntary characteristic of this fundraising showed the importance stressed by the Jewish community of looking after the welfare of each Jew, even it that person was a captive in a far-off land.

---

1. Jacob R. Marcus, *The Jew in the Medieval World: A Source Book, 315–1791* (New York: Atheneum, 1938), 454–58.

...when Jews are expelled the economy suffers

In 1741 Czarina Elizabeth Petrovna, hoping for a mass conversion of Jews to Christianity, issued an edict expelling all the Jews from the cities of Great Russia and Little Russia. Her intentions were twofold. One possible consequence she expected was mass conversions of Jews to Christianity. Secondly, she thought she was giving a commercial advantage to the Russian businessmen.[1]

Aside from the fact that not even one Jew accepted Christianity, severe damage to Russian commerce occurred. Complaints from Russian merchants and Greek contractors began to arrive in the Senate. The merchants were suffering because their affairs were so closely intertwined with the Jews. Revenues to the exchequer were also down. The Senate endorsed the petitions and sent them along to the czarina.[2] The empress turned down the petitions, saying, "From the enemies of Christ I desire neither gain nor profit."[3]

In 1764 Catherine II, the new czarina, received a petition from the nobles and elders requesting that the Jews be permitted to enter the kingdom for purposes of trade. Catherine, however, was afraid to make a beneficial gesture toward the Jews as her first major decision. She declined to intervene, the Jews remained expelled, and Russian commerce continued to suffer.[4]

CENTRAL EUROPE AND THE EAST: The Unwanted Diaspora

---

1. Simon M. Dubnow, *History of the Jews in Russia and Poland*, vol. 1 (Philadelphia: Jewish Publication Society, 1916), 255.
2. Ibid., 256–57.
3. Ibid., 257.
4. Ibid.

...coins and pogroms helped propel the Rothschild fortune

Meyer Amschel Rothschild was born to an Orthodox Jewish family in 1743. At a young age he entered the banking business. Through his interest in collecting old coins, Rothschild became friends with William the Landgrave.[1] During their friendship, Rothschild became drawn into William's brokerage business. After a while, William became the elector[2] to the region of Hesse-Cassel, a district in Germany.

When Napoleon invaded Germany, William was forced to flee, leaving Rothschild in charge as his financial agent. It so happened that William possessed a large amount of bullion, which the French soldiers searched for diligently. Their efforts were in vain, because Rothschild had hidden it in secret catacombs built by the Jews as a hiding place during the murderous pogroms that periodically devastated the Jewish community. Despite threats and bullying by the soldiers, Rothschild was not intimidated into revealing the hiding place of the fortune in bullion.

Through shrewd investing, Rothschild was able to quadruple William's capital while earning healthy commissions in the process. By the time William returned from exile, Meyer had enough capital from the commissions to go into business for himself, and the Rothschilds' empire was born.[3]

---

1. A German count having jurisdiction over a large territory of land.
2. One of the German princes entitled to vote for the emperor of the Holy Roman Empire.
3. Howard M. Sachar, *The Course of Modern Jewish History* (New York: Vintage Books, 1990), 130.

...if you talk during services, you will pay a fine

In 1756, Frederick II of Prussia (also known as Frederick the Great) issued the *Règlement*, a constitution governing Prussian Jewry. Two barons in the Franconian village of Sugenheim immediately followed suit with their own constitution regulating Jewish life in their village. While Frederick's constitution covered thousands of Jews, the Sugenheim document covered only twelve households.

The Sugenheim document levied fines for various infractions of the constitution. Minor fines were paid in wax to be used for candles for the synagogue or in cash. Major fines were paid in cash, and the proceeds were divided evenly between the local Jewish community and the village. Some of the constitutional provisions are as follows:

> **Article I.** There will be a fine levied for anybody failing to come to the synagogue on Mondays and Thursdays (when the Torah is read).
>
> **Article II.** There will be a fine levied for anybody failing to come to the synagogue for prayers on the day before the celebration of the New Moon.
>
> **Article III.** The cantor will call the people to services and will be subject to fine if he fails to do so.
>
> **Article IV.** There will be a fine levied for idle talk in the synagogue.
>
> **Article VI.** Fines are levied for wrangling in the synagogue.
>
> **Article VII.** Fines are levied for quarreling, fighting, and striking one another in the synagogue.
>
> **Article XIV.** A fine will be levied for wrangling about book-stands.
>
> **Article XV.** A fine will be levied against anybody who moves a bookstand so as to interfere with the worshiper taking his three steps backward.
>
> **Article XXIII.** limits excessive celebrating on the festive holidays of Purim and Simchat Torah. Fines will be levied against revelers who overstep the bounds of decorum.[1]

It seems strange that two Christians would write such a treatise on synagogue behavior. It probably was the last resort for Jewish factions who couldn't police themselves.

---

1. Jacob R. Marcus, *The Jew in the Medieval World: A Source Book, 315–1791* (New York: Atheneum, 1938), 212–19.

...Goethe had to hire a Christian to teach him Yiddish

Before his twelfth birthday, the encyclopedically learned Johann Wolfgang Goethe of Germany took up the study of Judeo-German, more commonly referred to as Yiddish, a language spoken almost exclusively by European Jews. The Yiddish lexicon at that time consisted of about 70 percent German, 20 percent Hebrew, and 10 percent "Slavic and other elements."[1] Goethe's interest in Jews and Jewish topics was not limited to the study of Yiddish. His exercises in translating material into Latin included stories about David and Goliath, Joseph in Egypt, and Moses freeing the Jews from slavery. He was a sometime visitor in the ghetto, frequently went to services in the synagogue, and attended a circumcision and a Jewish wedding. He also became familiar with the Feast of Tabernacles (Sukkot), an eight-day Jewish holiday commemorating the wandering of the Israelites in the desert.

In order to practice the array of languages Goethe had acquired, he wrote a play in the form of letters sent among family members. One family member wrote in German, another in a German vernacular, another in Latin, one in English, one in French, one in Italian, and the youngest member of the family contributed his part in Yiddish. Unfortunately, this work of Goethe's has not survived.

However, one of Goethe's Yiddish productions has outlived the author. It is *Die Judenpredigt* (the Jewish sermon). It deals with a Jewish Messiah legend in which the Jews are saved, but the Christians come to an unfortunate end.[2]

It is ironic that Goethe's instructors in Yiddish and later on in Hebrew were Christians, since Jews were by law not permitted to serve as tutors of non-Jews.

---

1. Mark Waldman, *Goethe and the Jews: A Challenge to Hitlerism* (New York: Putnam, 1934), 36.
2. Ibid., 58–60.

...Felix Mendelssohn was Jewish until he sang a Christian song

Felix Mendelssohn, the grandson of the famous Jewish intellectual Moses Mendelssohn, was an accomplished pianist by the age of nine. At the age of ten, he was enrolled in the Berlin Singakademie, where he was exposed to the finest of choral music. At the age of twelve, he had already composed several symphonies, fugues for string quartets, operas, and other works.

One day, while the chorus was singing Bach's *Passion According to St. Matthew*, another boy in the group taunted young Felix, saying, "The Jew boy raises his voice to Christ!"[1] Felix went home in tears. His father, feeling that being Jewish would hamper Felix's prospects for succeeding in the world of music, took his son and his sister Fanny to be baptized in the Protestant religion. The parents, Abraham and Leah Mendelssohn, soon followed their children into Christianity.

Abraham Mendelssohn added the name Bartholdy to their last name, saying that "a Christian Mendelssohn is an impossibility."[2] His father wanted Felix to perform under the name of Felix Bartholdy, but Felix refused and achieved fame as Felix Mendelssohn. His sister Rebecca often signed her letters Rebecca Mendelssohn Meden Bartholdy.[3] The Greek translation of *meden* is "never."[4]

Fanny Caecille (Zipporah) Mendelssohn was a musician in her own right, and Felix relied on her advice and taste in music. He incorporated six of her songs with his, but he did not identify her as the composer. So similar in style were her works that they were indistinguishable from those of her famous brother. Under her own name, Fanny published four books of piano pieces, two books of solo songs, and one book of part-songs. She died suddenly at age forty-two. More of her work was published posthumously.[5]

The combination of Fanny's untimely death and Felix's busy schedule of composing, directing, and playing wore him out, and he died at the age of thirty-eight.

---

1. Milton Cross and David Ewen, eds., *Milton Cross' Encyclopedia of the Great Composers and Their Music*, vol. 1 (New York: Doubleday, 1953), 473.
2. Dika Newlin, "Felix Mendelssohn," *Encyclopedia Judaica*, CD-ROM Edition (Jerusalem: Keter, 1997).
3. Ibid.
4. Ibid.
5. Ibid.

...if you are a prostitute, you can stay

For many years, the objective of the czarist Russian government was to exclude Jews from their empire. In 1823, there were no fewer than 1,230 clauses in the *Code of Disabilities* heaped upon Jews.[1] The last survey of Russian regulations concerning the Jews was *Gimpelson's Statutes Concerning the Jews*, which ran for an astounding thousand pages.[2] A giant step forward in this direction was the establishment of the Pale of Settlement, an area to which all Jews were supposed to be confined.

However, there were exceptions to the rule of confinement of Jews to the Pale. People belonging to certain professions were permitted to travel or live outside the Pale. Among these were discharged soldiers, some mechanics, distillers, brewers, and artisans. Jews privileged to reside outside the Pale were permitted to have two assistants or servants.

The police would run periodic checks to see if these aides were indeed employed in the work designated on their permits.[3]

A rather bizarre case involved a young Jewish woman wishing to continue her university training. Unable to gain entry to St. Petersburg or Moscow as a student, she gained her "yellow ticket" by registering as a prostitute. When the police discovered that she was studying instead of practicing prostitution, she was summarily expelled from the city.[4]

---

1. Simon M. Dubnow, *History of the Jews in Russia and Poland*, vol. 2 (Philadelphia: Jewish Publication Society, 1918), 34.
2. Paul Johnson, *A History of the Jews* (New York: Harper and Row, 1987), 359.
3. Ibid., 360.
4. Dubnow, *History of the Jews*, 345.

...Jewish soldiers might have to serve for thirty-one years

The Russian government had long seen Jews as an unassimilated body within their midst. This they felt needed correction.[1] The answer lay in a scheme to neutralize the Jews by taking them into the army for a period of twenty-five years. Their purpose was to render them as "un-Jewish" as possible. In 1827 an order was sent out to begin drafting Jewish boys.

In order to ensure that the conscripts would be rendered as assimilated as possible, the army would take children as young as twelve years of age. Since they could not be considered useful soldiers until the age of eighteen, the draftees would undergo a period of indoctrination prior to their actual military service. Only upon reaching the age of eighteen would a conscript's term of service begin. This system ensured that a Jewish cantonist would be obliged to serve from a minimum of twenty-five years to a maximum of thirty-one years, if he was enrolled at the age of twelve.[2]

Once the boys were in the military setting, the process of removing their Jewishness began in earnest. They were subjected to lectures designed to convert them to Christianity. Those who resisted baptism were beaten, and food was often withheld from them. Refusal to eat non-kosher foods also resulted in severe punishments. The mortality rate for the conscripts was alarmingly high. The younger the recruit, the more likely he was to be dead within a very short time.[3]

Responsibility for supplying recruits was forced upon the Kahal, the Jewish organization responsible for governing the Jewish community and collecting and remitting taxes due to the government and providing Jewish recruits for the army.

Many of the young men eligible for the draft fled. Others resorted to chopping off the index finger (trigger finger) of the right hand.[4] However, since the Kahals were responsible for supplying the required number of recruits, they had to be meticulous about hunting down Jews for service in the Russian army.[5] The "hunters," as they were called, resorted to violating the law by kidnapping boys under the age of twelve. Sometimes they took boys as young as eight by falsifying their ages. They often snatched their recruits by nighttime home invasions.

In this way, as in many other eras before and since, the Jewish community was forced to terrorize its own members.

---

1. Simon M. Dubnow, *History of the Jews in Russia and Poland*, vol. 2 (Philadelphia: Jewish Publication Society, 1918), 14.
2. Ibid., 19.
3. Ibid., 26–27.
4. Stephen Birmingham, *The Rest of Us: The Rise of America's Eastern European Jews* (Boston: Little, Brown, 1984), 36.
5. Dubnow, *History of the Jews*, 23.

...the House of Rothschild made a bad investment

In 1851 Pope Pius IX reimposed restrictions on Jews living in the Papal States. He also brought pressure against other rulers to revoke Jewish rights granted in 1848. In several cases he was successful in getting revocation of rights granted to Jews.[1]

In 1858, a Jewish child named Edgar Mortara was forcibly removed from his parents' home. The Christian babysitter claimed that she had had the child secretly baptized when he was seriously ill. Under the laws, a baptized child could not be raised in a Jewish home. The case went to Pope Pius IX, who ruled against the Jewish family, and the child was taken to be raised as a Catholic.[2]

In 1867 this same pope supported a charge of ritual murder against the Jews, and lent support to the charge that Jewish law *required* the murder of Christian children. The pope even declared a holiday commemorating a Christian child who allegedly was the victim of a ritual murder by the Jews.[3]

All of these actions against the Jews were taken after the House of Rothschild made a fifty-million-franc loan to the pope on condition that the ghetto walls would come down. Pope Pius IX took the money, but the ghetto remained.[4]

---

1. David I. Kertzer, *The Popes against the Jews: The Vatican's Role in the Rise of Modern Anti-Semitism* (New York: Knopf, 2001), 114–15.
2. Ibid., 119.
3. Ibid., 127–28.
4. Ibid., 115.

...converts *from* Judaism still made contributions to their people

When rabbis predicted dire consequences from the *Haskalah* (enlightenment), they were often very accurate. Many Jews converted to Christianity, but a large number of the converts continued to write in Hebrew on Jewish topics and to participate in Jewish activities.

One such person was Daniel Chwolson (1819–1911). Son of Orthodox parents, he received a traditional Jewish education in a yeshiva, a school of rabbinical studies. In 1841 he left for Germany to pursue studies in Oriental languages. By 1855, he was back in St. Petersburg, accepted an appointment to the university as professor of Hebrew and Semitic languages, and converted to Russian Orthodox Christianity.

His writings made important contributions to Hebrew paleography, the study and interpretation of ancient writings. He also tried to maintain his membership in the Society for the Promotion of Culture among the Jews, but his apostasy led to his being expelled from the group. However, he still maintained contact with Jewish scholars and leaders and was sensitive to the dangers surrounding his people.

When the Russian government threatened closure of yeshivas, Chwolson was quick to intervene on their behalf. He also intervened when the Russian government sought to prevent the publication of new printings of the Talmud.

Perhaps the most noteworthy of Chwolson's contributions to the Jewish people was his successful defense against the Russian government's attempts to outlaw Jewish ritual slaughter.[1]

It is interesting to note that Chwolson's scholarly pursuits were a direct outgrowth of his earlier Jewish education.

---

1. Masha Greenbaum, *The Jews of Lithuania: A History of a Remarkable Community, 1316–1945* (Jerusalem: Gefen Publishing House, 1995), 122–23.

...Freud was a staunch Jew but had strange ideas about Judaism

Sigmund Freud, the father of psychoanalysis, was born to a Hasidic Jewish family in Moravia. He studied medicine but soon gravitated toward treating problems of the mind. Freud theorized that religion was a form of collective delusion.[1] For example, he said that Moses was an Egyptian who taught an Egyptian monotheism to the children of Israel. He further postulated that the Israelites rebelled against Moses and had killed him, thereby creating self-perpetuating unconscious guilt feelings felt by Jews.[2]

When we look at Freud's writings, we might see him as estranged from Jews and Judaism. This was not the case. None of his children converted or married outside the faith. One of his sons became a Zionist. Freud himself went out of his way to declare that he was neither a German nor an Austrian, but a Jew.

When he was savagely criticized, he turned to his B'nai B'rith lodge brothers for solace. Freud would never accept royalties when his writings were translated into Hebrew or Yiddish.[3] Moreover, Freud ascribed great powers to the Jewish spirit. At one point he counseled his friend Max Graf, "If you do not let your son grow up to be a Jew, you will deprive him of those sources of energy which cannot be replaced by anything else."[4]

Freud further wrote regarding the Jews, "We preserved our unity through ideas, and because of them, we have survived to this day." He also believed that the founding of the religious school at Yavneh after the destruction of the Jewish state by the Romans was "for me one of the most significant manifestations in our history."[5]

One might wonder how Freud would have analyzed a person who cultivated his Jewish identity and lauded Jewish values while proclaiming that "religion is a form of collective delusion."

---

1. Paul Johnson, *A History of the Jews* (New York: Harper Row, 1987), 413.
2. Louis Miller, "Sigmund Freud," *Encyclopedia Judaica,* CD-ROM *Edition* (Jerusalem: Keter, 1997).
3. Johnson, *A History of the Jews,* 414.
4. Quoted in Moshe Gresser, *Dual Allegiance: Freud as a Modern Jew* (Albany: SUNY Press, 1994), 110.
5. Johnson, *A History of the Jews,* 414.

...the Madonna hung out with Lithuanian Jews

Lev Samuilovich Rosenberg, later Léon Bakst, was born in Russia in 1864. After graduating from the high school, he was a non-credit student at the St. Petersburg Academy of Arts and supported himself as a book illustrator.[1]

Bakst created quite a controversy when he chose as his subject in a contest *The Madonna Weeping over Christ*. In an effort to emphasize the Jewishness of Christ, he painted the Madonna surrounded by a group of Lithuanian Jews. The enraged judges defaced the painting and Bakst was expelled from the academy.[2]

However, Bakst was not finished with the world of art. He associated himself with the Russian Ballet, commonly known as the Ballets Russes. Between 1909 and 1914, Bakst was the designer of sets and costumes for eleven ballets and outfitted such greats as Pavlova and Nijinsky.[3]

At its inception, the Ballets Russes was funded by a Jew, Gabriel Astruc, and was helped by another Jew, Baron Gunzberg. The Ballets Russes, founded and brought to prominence by Jews, was not strong enough to confer special privileges on Bakst. Although his father was a privileged Jew and Leon was already world famous, he still could not regain admission to St. Petersburg as late as 1912 because he was Jewish.[4]

The son of a peddler, and himself a former military tailor in the Crimean War, Bakst was – for a time – the teacher of the famous Jewish artist Marc Chagall. Bakst's work is still shown in exhibits of Russian art.[5]

---

1. Charles Spencer, *Leon Bakst and the Ballets Russes* (London: Academy Editions, 1995), 225.
2. Paul Johnson, *A History of the Jews* (New York: Harper and Row, 1987), 411.
3. Ibid.
4. Ibid., 412.
5. Alfred Warner, "Leon Bakst," *Encyclopedia Judaica*, CD-ROM *Edition* (Jerusalem: Keter, 1997).

...one anti-Semitic writer could have so many editors

In 1864, the French writer Maurice Joly wrote a political pamphlet called "Dialogues in Hell between Machiavelli and Montesquieu" that attributed ambitions of world domination to Napoleon III.[1] Joly seems to have borrowed the idea from a tawdry novel by Eugène Sue, *The Mysteries of the People*, which describes a similar imagined Jesuit plot.

In 1868, German anti-Semite Hermann Goedsche, using the pseudonym Sir John Retcliffe, wrote a novel called *Biarritz* in which representatives of the Twelve Tribes of Israel meet with the devil. The plot is based on a scene in a work by Dumas, *Joseph Balsamo*, which describes a secret meeting held by the "Unknown Superiors," but Goedsche brought in elements from Joly and Sue, and made the Jews the plotters.[2] Goedsche's story was again copied and modified by members of the Russian secret police, who, in an 1873 pamphlet entitled "The Jews, Masters of the World," reported the secret meeting as if it were fact.[3]

In an effort to strengthen Czar Nicholas II, they rewrote Goedsche's work showing Jews as enemies of the czar and plotting to take over the world. The czar was not taken in.[4] However, the story refused to die. A right-wing Russian political group called the Black Hundreds came out with its own version, the first to use the title *Protocols of Zion*.[5] During the Russian Revolution, anti-revolutionary propagandists used the *Protocols* to incite the masses against the "Jewish Revolution." In 1921, a British journalist exposed the fraudulent nature of the *Protocols*, but met with limited acceptance.[6]

The Germans, seeking to explain their defeat in World War I, seized upon the *Protocols* as the "stab in the back" inflicted on them by the Jews. In 1934, the Swiss government prosecuted and convicted the disseminators of the *Protocols*. This did not dissuade the Nazis from extensive propaganda use of the *Protocols*. Indeed, Hitler had mentioned the *Protocols* in his book *Mein Kampf*.[7]

To this day the *Protocols* are still being used by the Arabs in their struggles with Israel. Additional research by a British university professor has traced in detail the fraudulent nature of the *Protocols*, but the beat goes on.[8]

1. Leon Poliakov, "Protocols of the Learned Elders of Zion," *Encyclopedia Judaica*, CD–ROM Edition (Jerusalem: Keter, 1997).
2. Umberto Eco, *Six Walks in the Fictional Woods* (Cambridge, MA: Harvard University Press, 1994), 136.
3. Ibid.
4. Poliakov, "Protocols of the Learned Elders of Zion."
5. Stephen Eric Bronner, *A Rumor about the Jews: Antisemitism, Conspiracy, and the Protocols of Zion* (London: Oxford University Press, 2000), 76.
6. Poliakov, "Protocols of the Learned Elders of Zion."
7. Ibid.
8. Ibid.

...a Jewish banker helped establish the German Empire

In 1866, Otto von Bismarck, the head of the German state, was about to embark on a war which was to establish the German Empire. Finding it difficult to obtain financing for this expensive undertaking, Bismarck turned to his Jewish personal advisor and banker Gerson Bleichroeder. The money was advanced and Bismarck went to war. In 1869, under Bismarck's leadership, the subject of Jewish emancipation was raised. The final statement read in part: "All still existing limitations of the... civil rights which are rooted in differences of religious faith are hereby annulled."[1]

At a later date, when Bismarck's opponents in the Reichstag attempted to embarrass the chancellor for his Jewish connection, Bismarck replied: "It is true that Bleichroeder brought me in the year 1866 the means for waging war which nobody else wanted to advance to us. This was a deed for which I was obligated to feel gratitude. As an honest person, I don't like to be spoken ill of, nor have a Jew say that I have used him and then held him in contempt in spite of services rendered which I, as a statesman, had to value highly."[2]

This was a remarkable statement from a man whose past was documented with sporadic incidents of anti-Semitism. However, Bismarck had enough character to look beyond religion to the worth of a man. Bleichroeder was eventually raised to the nobility.

Alas, times did change. In 1881, Bismarck said that "while he was opposed to anti-Semitic agitation, he had done nothing against it because of its courageous stand against the Progressives." With this utterance, anti-Semitism gained the respectability it was lacking.[3]

---

1. Joachim O. Ronall, *Encyclopedia Judaica*, CD-ROM Edition (Jerusalem: Keter, 1997).
2. Elliot Rosenberg, *But Were They Good for the Jews? Over 150 Historical Figures from a Jewish Perspective* (Secaucus, NJ: Carol, 1997), 177.
3. Howard M. Sachar, *The Course of Modern Jewish History* (New York: Vintage, 1998), 260–61.

...Rasputin had a Jewish business manager

The Romanov dynasty in Russia was perhaps the most anti-Semitic court in the history of Russia. The very superstitious Czarina Alexandra came under the influence of an illiterate preacher named Grigory Yefimovich Novykh, better known as Rasputin. The Czarina "believed that Rasputin had been sent by God to represent the mystical union between the peasants and autocracy."[1] Once Rasputin became ensconced in a position of influence, he began to exploit his station for personal gain.

Typical of Rasputin's dealings was his experience with a wealthy Jew expelled from St. Petersburg for illegally residing there. Rasputin used his influence to get the Jew residence privileges. For his efforts, Rasputin received an expensive fur coat. So extensive were Rasputin's bribery cases that he hired a Jewish business manager to handle his booming financial affairs.[2]

Thus it was that under the very watchful eyes of the violently anti-Semitic Romanovs, Jews and other sufferers under czarist persecution could benefit.

1. Elliot Rosenberg, *But Were They Good for the Jews? Over 150 Historical Figures from a Jewish Perspective* (Secaucus, NJ: Carol, 1997), 200.
2. Ibid.

...an anti-Semitic Jew coined the word *anti-Semitism*

In 1879 Wilhelm Marr, the son of a Jewish actor, published a German-language pamphlet entitled "The Way to Victory of Germanicism over Judaism." He accused the Jews of developing "industry and commerce in order to achieve world domination" and cultivating "liberalism as a façade for their activities."[1] As the founder of the Anti-Semitic League, Marr was able to attract quite a sizeable following, including members of the German intelligentsia. He also preached racial purity. According to Marr, the struggle between Jews and Germans would only by decided by victory of one and death of the other. In 1912, eight years after Marr's death, the league that he founded adopted racism as its policy. Marr is seen as a major link in German racism leading up to the Holocaust.[2]

---

1. Howard M. Sachar, *The Course of Modern Jewish History* (New York: Random House, 1990), 234.
2. Ibid.

...Wagner hated Jews but he needed one named Hermann Levi

In 1881 Hermann Levi was probably the foremost conductor in all of Europe. He was also very close with the well-known anti-Semitic composer Richard Wagner. As the time came close for Levi to conduct Wagner's *Parsifal* at the notoriously anti-Semitic Beyreuth Festival, pressure began to intensify on Wagner to replace Levi on the podium and "to keep his work pure and not allow a Jew to conduct it."[1] Wagner was not willing to entrust his masterwork to anybody but Hermann Levi. He was heard to say, "No Levi, no *Parsifal*."[2]

In 1888, when illness prevented Levi from conducting the *Parsifal* at the Beyreuth Festival, word went out from the festival that "*Parsifal* had at last been delivered from 'Jewish hands' and given back to Christianity."[3] A critic of the festival that had been "given back to Christianity" ranked it "scandalously inferior."[4]

---

1. Peter Gay, *Freud, Jews, and Other Germans: Masters and Victims in Modernist Culture* (New York: Oxford University Press, 1978), 220.
2. Ibid., 222.
3. Ibid., 224.
4. Ibid.

...a Chinese shopkeeper priced his goods in Hebrew

The ancient Jewish congregation of Kaifeng, China, began to attract much attention in the late 1800s and on into the twentieth century. Many people and organizations had good intentions, but there was little they could do to rescue the nearly extinct congregation from sinking into oblivion due to emigration.

One of the visitors on a potential rescue mission was Noach Mishkowsky. In conversation with a shopkeeper, Mishkowsky tried to ascertain how much of his Jewish heritage the man had retained. The shopkeeper knew that his forbears were monotheists, rested one day a week, and avoided polygamy. He did know there was a language called Hebrew, and he was familiar with the characters. His wife was a Buddhist, but he considered his children to be Jewish.[1]

Mishkowsky was interested in purchasing a basin in the shop and inquired as to the price. The man looked at the bottom of the basin and told him it cost twenty-five units of Chinese money. Mishkowsky looked at the markings on the basin and was astonished to see the Hebrew letters *chaf-hay*, the numerical equivalent of twenty and five.[2]

In Jewish circles, it is quite common to use Hebrew letters in listing dates and in the pagination of books written in Hebrew. How did this shopkeeper have this particular knowledge? In answer to Mashkowsky's question, the shopkeeper indicated that it was the numbering system used by his father and his grandfather. He did not know the names of the letters or the phonemes they represented.[3]

---

1. Michael Pollack, *Mandarins, Jews, and Missionaries: The Jewish Experience in the Chinese Empire* (Philadelphia: Jewish Publication Society, 1980), 229.
2. Ibid., 229.
3. Ibid.

...Jews were too intelligent to be tolerated

For many years, the Russian government was always dealing with what it called "the Jewish problem." Government action regarding "the Jewish problem" usually took the form of expulsions and/or limitation of occupational pursuits permitted to Jews. There seemed to always be some perceived injustice perpetrated by the Jews against the Russian populace.

In 1881, following widespread and horrendous pogroms against Jewish communities, the governor general of Kiev, a man named Drenteln, offered to the czar an astounding rationale for the suppression of Jewish mercantile activity. Among other things, Drenteln said that legal measures were necessary "in order to counteract 'the intellectual superiority of the Jews.'"[1]

Drenteln also advocated the adoption of measures "to shield the Christian population against so arrogant a tribe as the Jews, who refuse on religious grounds to have close contact with the Christians."[2] At the same time, the official Church position was that Christians ought to maintain their distance from Jews, following the Christian injunction to "hate the murderers of the Savior."[3]

In an era when machines and brain power were rapidly replacing muscle power, the Russian government was striving to neutralize the intellectual gifts of an entire segment of its population. Others would make that same mistake.

---

1. Simon M. Dubnow, *History of the Jews in Russia and Poland*, vol. 2 (Philadelphia: Jewish Publication Society, 1918), 276.
2. Ibid., 276.
3. Ibid., 379.

...In czarist Russia, Jewish families had only one son

During the latter part of the nineteenth century and the early twentieth century, the czarist army had a policy of not drafting "only sons" into the military. They would also exempt sons who were the sole support of elderly parents.

It was in this area that there arose a practice of families having "only sons." The first male child would receive the family's surname and be recorded as the son of the family. Each subsequent birth of a male child would be recorded with a different surname as the child of an entirely new set of parents.

Other males might be recorded as having died in infancy and still others were recorded as starting life as four-year-olds to make them eligible at an earlier age to be the sole support of aging parents. It was rare indeed for a son to have a "brother."[1] Such were the lengths to which Jewish families had to go to ensure the safety of their children.

---

1. Yaffa Eliach, *Once There Was a World: A 900-Year Chronicle of the Shtetl of Eishyshok* (Boston: Little, Brown, 1998), 12.

...Jews kept British and German guns firing in World War I

In 1916, the British war effort in World War I began to experience a dire shortage of acetone, a vital ingredient of cordite, which in turn was necessary for the manufacture of munitions. Chaim Weizmann, the famous Zionist, was also a renowned chemist. He devised a system of extracting acetone from corn, thereby keeping the British from running out of ammunition.[1]

On the German side, the army was suffering from a shortage of ammonia, also an essential ingredient for the manufacture of munitions. Fritz Haber, a German-Jewish chemist, was able to synthesize ammonia from nitrogen and hydrogen. For this he won the Nobel Prize in chemistry, and the German guns did not fall silent. Haber, as director of the Kaiser Wilhelm Research Institute, was also instrumental in developing the German chemical weapons chlorine gas and mustard gas, which were so deadly during World War I.

After the war, Haber continued to be the leading chemist of Germany, but when Hitler came to power, he instructed Haber to fire all the Jewish employees. Haber, who by this time had left Judaism, refused to do so and resigned from his position.[2]

In an ironic twist of fate, after leaving the Kaiser Wilhelm Research Institute, Haber was offered a position at the Seiff Institute in Palestine by none other than Chaim Weizmann, the man who was his scientific opponent during the war.[3]

Haber set out for Palestine to assume his new position, but his health began to fail him and he died in Switzerland, still wondering why his country, for which he had done so much, would not protect him from what was to come.

Weizmann, on the other hand, went on to become a vital force in the founding of the State of Israel and was its first president.

---

1. Julian L. Meltzer, "Chaim Weizmann," *Encyclopedia Britannica* (Chicago: Encyclopedia Britannica, 1990).
2. Samuel Aaron Miller, "Fritz Haber," *Encyclopedia Judaica,* CD-ROM Edition (Jerusalem: Keter, 1997).
3. Ronald W. Clark, *Einstein: The Life and Times* (New York: Avon Books, 1984), 225.

...Jews had German army helmets engraved on their tombstones

The most prestigious member of the Jewish community is the *Kohen* (priest), a descendent of Aaron. One of his functions in the services held in the synagogue was to offer a benediction with his hands shaped in a triangle with the thumbs touching and the forefingers outstretched and touching. This image was often placed on the tombstone of a Kohen.

Next in the hierarchy of Jews is the *Levite*, a descendent of the tribe of Levi. The Levite assisted the Kohen during Temple times. One of his functions was to pour water onto the hands of the Kohen. Thus, we often see a water pitcher engraved on the tombstone of a Levite.

On the High Holy Days, or other momentous occasions, a ram's horn, or *shofar,* is blown in the synagogue. The *shofar* blower often had the *shofar* engraved on his tombstone.

The *mohel,* or circumciser, might have the inscription of a knife to denote his occupation in life.

In an extreme bit of irony, Jewish veterans of the German army, proud of their service to Germany, especially in World War I, often had the distinctive German army helmet engraved on their tombstones.[1]

---

1. Peter M. Daly, "Funeral Symbolism on Jewish Tombstones and Monuments," Constructions of Death, Mourning and Memory Conference, Woodcliff Lake, New Jersey (Oct 27–29, 2006); Nolan Menachemson, *A Practical Guide to Jewish Cemeteries* (Bergenfield, NJ: Avotaynu, 2007).

...you can pay for it, but you can't use it

The end of World War I and the convening of the peace conference at Versailles brought high hopes for the Jews. Written into the treaty were guarantees of equal treatment for the Jews.[1] A mood of exhilaration accompanying the treaty and its assurances of civil rights for the Jews prompted a Jewish businessman from Rumania to demonstrate his goodwill for all the citizens of the university town of Cernauti. He had a fine new social center constructed and furnished for the benefit of the university's students. "The first step taken by the authorities was to exclude any Jewish student from the use of the new center."[2]

Failure to provide for enforcement of the treaty led to similar denial of the rights of Jews in other countries supposedly covered by the treaty.[3] It seems that, when it suited their purposes, countries were willing to make promises they had no intention of keeping.

1. Abba Eban, *My People: The Story of the Jews* (New York: Behrman House, 1968), 344–48.
2. Ibid., 353.
3. Ibid., 352–53.

...selling a birthright could be a *good* thing

Aby and Max Warburg were the sons of a German-Jewish family of bankers. Aby, the eldest, was, at an early age, a "passionate bookworm."[1] When he was thirteen years old, Aby "sold" his birthright to his younger brother Max in return for the promise that Max would pay for all the books he might wish to own.[2]

When the time came, Max entered the family business, while Aby continued to pursue the interest that would make him a renowned art historian. By 1911, Fritz Saxl was engaged to organize the fifteen thousand volumes in Warburg's collection.[3] In 1921, Warburg's library became "a research institute in cultural history."[4]

Warburg died in 1929, but the institute continued to function in Germany until Hitler came to power. It was then that the institute was transferred to the University of London. It is now a "member-Institute of the University's School of Advanced Study."[5]

While Esau of the Bible came to rue the day he sold his birthright, it was probably the best decision of Aby Warburg's life. Today his institute is a respected library, serving many scholars.

---

1. Peter Gay, *Freud, Jews, and Other Germans: Masters and Victims in Modernist Culture* (New York: Oxford University Press, 1978), 127.
2. Ibid., 127.
3. Ibid., 130.
4. As described on the website of the Warburg Institute, http://warburg.sas.ac.uk/institute/institute_introduction.htm.
5. Ibid.

...Albert Einstein was a poor student

Albert Einstein's early years did not show the promise he was to realize later in life. He was late to begin speaking, and his parents thought he might be learning impaired. His Greek teacher was so unimpressed with Einstein's performance that he declared Einstein would never amount to anything.[1]

Einstein chafed under the rigidity of the rote learning system at the Gymnasium (high school). Irritated by Einstein's attitude and by his precocious questions, his frustrated science teacher exclaimed, "your mere presence in class destroys [the other students'] respect for me."[2] Einstein promptly remedied this by dropping out of school.

When he was sixteen, his father told him to "forget his 'philosophical nonsense' and apply himself to the 'sensible trade' of electrical engineering."[3]

His lack of a Gymnasium diploma precluded Einstein's matriculation at most universities. He was, however, eligible to enter the Swiss Federal Institute of Technology without a diploma providing, of course, he would be able to pass the entrance examination.

Einstein failed the entrance test despite the fact that, at the age of sixteen, he had written a paper on "the relationship between electricity, magnetism, and the ether, the hypothetical nonmaterial entity which was presumed to fill all space and to transmit electromagnetic waves."[4] Perhaps he should have submitted the paper to someone other than his uncle.

In any event, Einstein spent another year getting ready for the test. This time he passed and was admitted to the institute. He ignored his father's advice and continued his studies in physics.

---

1. Maja Winteler-Einstein, "Albert Einstein: A Biographical Sketch," in *The Collected Papers of Albert Einstein: The Early Years, 1879–1902* by Albert Einstein, translated by Anna Beck and Peter Havas (Princeton, NJ: Princeton University Press, 1987), xx.
2. Mark A. Runco and Steven R. Pritzker, *Encyclopedia of Creativity*, vol. 1 (San Diego, CA: Academic Press, 1999), 644.
3. Ronald W. Clark, *Einstein: The Life and Times* (New York: Avon Books, 1965), 41.
4. Ibid., 41.

...Albert Einstein used his fame to benefit the Berlin poor

While Albert Einstein jealously guarded his privacy, he frequently gave his name and his time to a worthy cause. In 1930, while en route to Pasadena, California, for a lecture series, he agreed to two radio broadcasts from aboard the ship. For each speech, he earned one thousand dollars, which he promptly remitted to a charitable fund for the poor people of Berlin. From those who sought his autograph, he charged one dollar. For autographs of memorabilia, he charged five dollars. All of the proceeds went to this charity.[1]

None of this could transcend the fact that Einstein was Jewish. Within a few short years, Einstein's scientific work was relegated to the bonfire,[2] and he himself had to escape Germany with a price on his head.[3]

---

1. Ronald W. Clark, *Einstein: The Life and Times* (New York: Avon, 1984), 520–22.
2. Ibid., 571.
3. Ibid., 600.

...Albert Einstein was helped by other brilliant Jewish minds

Albert Einstein's place in the world of science is certainly secure. However, like almost all scientists, Einstein did not work in isolation. His epic discoveries were aided by the work of other brilliant minds.

Tulio Levi-Civita (1873–1942) was an Italian mathematician whose work in absolute differential calculus provided the basis for Einstein's relativity theory.[1]

Leopold Infield, a professor of mathematics at Toronto University, was a collaborator of Einstein's and he contributed to his work on mathematical physics.[2]

Albert Abraham Michelson is credited with providing Einstein with direction to his famous relativity theory. This German-born Jew, residing in America, constructed a giant interferometer which proved extremely useful in the famous Michelson-Morley experiment.[3]

Hermann Minkowski (1864–1909) was a teacher of Einstein. Minkowski postulated the Minkowski world, a four-dimensional space in which the fourth dimension is time and a single event is represented as a point.[4] This fusion of time and space was, of course, crucial to Einstein's work.

The mere promulgation of any theory, especially one as revolutionary as Einstein's theory of relativity, does not always bring instant acceptance. It still remained for other scientists to investigate and verify its truth.

Karl Schwartzschild (1873–1916) was one of the foremost mathematicians and astronomers in Germany in his time. His research in space and gravitation helped prove Einstein to be correct.[5]

Another major proponent of Einstein's work was L. Silberstein (1872–1948). He delivered a series of lectures at several universities and eventually published his course in a book entitled *Theory of Relativity.*[6]

Max Born of the University of Göttingen also issued a publication entitled *Einstein's Theory of Relativity*, first in German and then in English.[7] Each of these works by fellow Jews helped solidify the veracity of Einstein's work.

---

1. Dagobert D. Runes, ed., *The Hebrew Impact on Western Civilization* (New York: Philosophical Library, 1951), 93.
2. Ibid., 97.
3. Ibid., 120.
4. "Hermann Minkowski," *Webster's Encyclopedic Unabridged Dictionary of the English Language*, 1983.
5. Runes, *The Hebrew Impact on Western Civilization*, 110.
6. Ibid., 124.
7. Ibid.

Who Knew?!

HOLOCAUST:
Perpetrators,
Bystanders,
Rescuers

...Jews became anti-Semites to prove they were Germans first

In the latter part of the nineteenth century and on into the twentieth century, there was a great passion among German Jews to be Germans first and Jews second. One of the easiest ways to make common cause with their German counterparts was to express their disdain for the *Ostjuden*, the Jews from Eastern and Southern Europe who were entering Germany as refugees from persecution.[1]

Another way for German Jews to bond with the German population was to help publicize the slanders about Jews including their alleged "corrosiveness," "materialism," and "hatred of tradition."[2] The newspapers running the anti-Semitic slanders were often Jewish owned or Jewish managed. Sometimes the writers themselves were Jewish.[3] Nor were the expressions of anti-Semitism limited to the mass media. Even in personal relationships, the hatred surfaced. The famous music conductor Hermann Levi was not immune to the viciousness. His correspondence "often bore anti-Jewish barbs."[4]

In spite of all this pandering to German society in an effort to be accepted as Germans, it was becoming evident to the Berlin Jews that the other Germans did not see them in the same way. "The Jew was the only citizen of Germany, it seemed, for whom religious conversion was not the road to acceptance but a cause for suspicion."[5] It was the tardy realization of the disconnect between how the Jews of Germany saw themselves and how they were viewed by the general population that caused so much disillusionment among German Jews.

When the Nazis came to power and began their ruthless persecution of the Jews, the Jews who perceived themselves as Germans first and Jews second received a shock that was often too much to bear. There were numerous suicides among the German-Jewish citizens of the Reich.

---

1. Peter Gay, *Freud, Jews, and Other Germans: Masters and Victims in Modernist Culture* (New York: Oxford University Press, 1978), 187.
2. Ibid., 156.
3. Ibid., 155–56, 161.
4. Ibid., 201, 203, 208.
5. Ibid, 186.

111

...IBM helped Nazis find and keep track of Jews

In 1884, a German immigrant to the United States named Herman Hollerith, working for the US Census Bureau, invented a machine that could eliminate the tedious task of hand counting. The new invention could perform rapid tabulations using a system of punched cards fed into the machine. Punches in the card in certain places were answers to the forms filled out by people responding to the census.[1] Hollerith's system was adopted by the United States Census Bureau, and the machines were leased from Hollerith for the census. Soon many countries and businesses were leasing machines and buying punch cards from Hollerith.

When Hitler came to power in 1933, the Great Depression was at its zenith, and Hollerith's company, now called International Business Machines,[2] was being run by a man named Thomas Watson.

Hitler began rearming Germany in violation of the Treaty of Versailles obligation imposed on Germany *not* to rearm.[3] Hitler's wanton killing and persecution of Jews and establishment of concentration camps brought revulsion to much of the world, and boycotts against trading with Germany were put into force by many firms. Not so with IBM. IBM's technology was useful to Hitler in efficiently tracking down Jews, and Watson was willing to oblige him. Watson's company supplied the Nazis with genealogical search engines capable of tracking people with only one-sixteenth Jewish blood![4]

Although many businesses were suffering due to the depression, IBM began to make a great deal of money by dealing with Nazi Germany. That Watson knew how his machines were being used, there can be no doubt. Finally feeling the pressure, Watson felt constrained to write a personal letter to Hitler entreating him to practice the "Golden Rule" in dealing with minority populations.[5]

While all this was going on, Watson was enjoying a close personal relationship with President Roosevelt. He was often called upon to advise the president, was an overnight guest in the White House, and was even offered a cabinet position.[6]

---

1. Edwin Black, IBM *and the Holocaust: The Strategic Alliance between Nazi Germany and America's Most Powerful Company* (New York: Crown, 2001), 24–26.
2. Ibid., 40–41.
3. Ibid., 68.
4. Ibid., 108.
5. Ibid., 147.
6. Ibid., 71.

...fifteen thousand Jews couldn't be right

The German occupation of Poland during World War I proved to be rather benign. It appeared as though the German army was going out of its way to show friendship toward the Jews. General Ludendorff summarily repealed the czar's anti-Jewish statutes, and even dedicated synagogues, saying things in Yiddish like *"Meine liebe Yidden in Poilen* (my dear Jews in Poland)."[1]

When the Germans came again to Poland in World War II, the *shtetl* (small town) of Eishyshok saw some fifteen thousand refugees stream through their town as they fled eastward before the advancing German army. The stories they told of atrocities committed against Jews stunned those who remembered fondly the German soldiers occupying their town during World War I and generously sharing their candy with the children of the villages. Many dismissed these horror stories. They could not believe that the sons of the soldiers of the previous occupation could be guilty of such monstrous behavior.[2]

Most of the townspeople chose not to flee and were soon systematically murdered by the sons of those Germans who befriended them almost thirty years before! What a tragic tale of failure to recognize living proof that times had changed!

1. Howard M. Sachar, *The Course of Modern Jewish History* (New York: Vintage Books, 1990), 348.
2. Yaffa Eliach, *There Once Was a World: A Nine-Hundred Year Chronicle of the Shtetl of Eishyshok* (Boston: Little, Brown, 1998), 59.

...France had concentration camps *before* Hitler came to power

Between 1918 and 1930 France experienced a large influx of foreigners. Having lost 1.4 million men in World War I and experiencing a low birth rate, France was suffering from a shortage of workers and began to attract guest workers and immigrants. The humanitarian approach by the government made France a haven for refugees, mainly from Eastern Europe but also from Germany.

With the onset of the depression, production took a precipitous plunge and unemployment rose sharply. As competition for jobs increased, resentment toward foreigners began to rise. Among the foreigners were substantial numbers of Jews. Soon anti-Semitic diatribes began to fill the newspapers. Jews were job stealers, a population not able to be assimilated into French society, and at the same time, polluters of French bloodlines. As the rhetoric heated up, longtime Jewish-French citizens began to be grouped with the immigrants.

Soon there began a discussion of a "Jewish problem," and there was talk of a special statute for Jews. Jews were also being depicted as warmongers complicating French efforts to get along with the Germans. The French writer Céline wrote, "If you really want to get rid of the Jews, then...racism! That's the only thing the Jews are afraid of: racism! And not a little bit, with the fingertips, but all the way! Totally! Inexorably! Like complete Pasteur sterilization."[1]

Finally, the French took the last step and established concentration camps for further sorting and disposition of the refugees. When the German army defeated the French forces in the summer of 1940 and established the Vichy[2] government in southern France, the infrastructure and the mindset for persecution and terror were already in place. By the end of 1940, 70 percent of the unrepatriated concentration camp residents were Jews, and many more were on the way.[3]

---

1. Michael R. Marrus and Robert O. Paxton, *Vichy France and the Jews* (New York: Basic Books, 1981), 42.
2. The Vichy French government was a puppet government dominated by Nazi Germany. Their army fought the Americans and the British in North Africa.
3. Marrus and Paxton, *Vichy France and the Jews*, chapter 2.

...the United States War College taught Nazism before Hitler

When the United States Army War College conducted classes for rank-ing officers, their purpose went far beyond what one might expect in an army war college. For some reason, the war college was deeply in-volved in political indoctrination, including undisguised racism. The army lecturers posited the thesis that war is an inevitable clash between "higher-order" human beings against "lower-order" humans. At stake was control of limited resources, in an ever more populated world.

Like the Nazis, the war college's curriculum claimed the superiority of the "Nordic race" over all others. This group is comprised of people from Scandinavia, Germany, and the British Isles. The undesirables are classified as the Southern and Eastern Europeans, especially Russians and Russian Jews. Like the Nazis, the war college presented "Orientals" and "Negroes" as inferior to the whites. Like the Nazis, the war college used cranial shapes as a racial identifying criterion. Like the Nazis, the war college warned of the dangers presented to the race by mixing with people of "substandard" races.

Singled out for special consideration by the war college were the Jews. They were cited as capitalistic oppressors of the poor, while at the same time being Socialists and Bolsheviks attempting to upset the existing order of economic activity. Jews were heavily censured for their unwillingness to assimilate into the larger culture of the countries in which they lived. At the same time, they represented a threat to the purity of the Nordic race, and by extension, the American way of life.

The war college continued to preach the threat posed by interna-tional Jewry to take over the world as set forth in the notorious *Protocols of the Elders of Zion*, even after the publication had been unmasked as a scurrilous fraud given wide currency by auto manufacturer Henry Ford.[1]

The war college's dogmatic teachings contributed to the passage of the National Origins Act of 1924, in which the bulk of the immigration slots were allocated to the so-called Nordic race at the expense of the less desirable Southern and Eastern European peoples. This played a major role in the failure of the Americans and the other Allies to mount any sort of rescue effort and/or relaxation of the restrictive immigration quotas during the Holocaust.[2]

---

1. Rafael Medoff, *Jewish Americans and Political Participation: A Reference Handbook* (Santa Barbara, CA: ABC-CLIO, 2002), 40; Jewish Virtual Library, "Henry Ford Invents a Jewish Conspiracy," http://www.jewishvirtuallibrary.org/jsource/anti-semitism/ford1.html.
2. Joseph W. Bendersky, *The Jewish Threat: Anti-Semitic Policies of the US Army* (New York: Basic Books, 2000), 121–66.

...US immigration laws doomed six million Jews

In 1921, alarmed by the flood of immigrants entering the United States, Congress passed the Emergency Quota Act, sometimes referred to as the Johnson Act. This law established a quota for each nationality group seeking entry to the country. The quota limited the number of immigrants to 3 percent of the number of people from each country in the United States as of the 1910 census.[1] The total number of immigrants was limited to 356,000.[2] In 1924, the Johnson Act was replaced by the National Origins Act. The new law limited the total number of immigrants to 2 percent of the number of people from each country residing in the United States as of the 1890 census. By changing the base year from 1910 to 1890, the law favored the Anglo-Saxon, Protestant population of America, since most of them had come before 1890, while the bulk of the immigration from Eastern and Southern Europe took place after 1890.[3]

The Jewish immigrants had come mostly from Russia, Poland, Lithuania, Romania, and other Balkan states. This meant that they fell into the nationality groups having the fewest eligible immigrants.[4] When the Nazis began to put pressure on the Jews in the 1930s and to physically exterminate them in the 1940s, the Jews were ready to flee. However, the National Origins Act was rigidly enforced, and only the miniscule quota numbers were allowed to enter the country. The rest were left to their fate under the Nazis.

Today, the United States still has laws that regulate the flow of immigrants into the country. However, when people's lives are in danger, they are declared refugees and are permitted into the country outside of the numbers fixed by law. Tragically, this legislation was not there to benefit the six million Jews who died in the Holocaust.

1. Adalberto Aguirre, *Racial and Ethnic Diversity in America: A Reference Handbook* (Santa Barbara, CA: ABC-CLIO, 2003), 22.
2. T.J. Hatton and Jeffrey G. Williamson, *Global Migration and the World Economy: Two Centuries of Policy and Performance* (Cambridge, MA: MIT Press, 2005), 185.
3. US Citizenship and Immigration Services, "Immigration Act of May 26, 1924 (43 Statutes-at-Large 153)," http://www.uscis.gov/files/nativedocuments/Legislation%20from%20 1901-1940.pdf.
4. Jewish Virtual Library, "Emanuel Celler," http://www.jewishvirtuallibrary.org/jsource/ biography/Celler.html.

...a Jewish athlete helped Nazi Germany get the Olympic Games

In 1931 the International Olympic Committee awarded the 1936 games to the democratically elected German Weimar Republic. When the totalitarian Nazi regime took power in 1933, many people began to regret the choice of the site of the 1936 games. Both the American ambassador to Germany and the head of the US Legation in Vienna opposed the Berlin Olympics. The National Council of the Methodist Church and the American Federation of Labor voiced opposition, and ten thousand people protested at Madison Square Garden. Seventy-five thousand German-American members of the German-American League for Culture asked for the removal of the games from Berlin, and the American Athletic Union (AAU) received more than 100,000 individual protests. But after a three-day argument, the convention voted by a narrow majority to keep the games in Berlin.[1]

Two people are credited with this decision: Avery Brundage, president of the International Olympic Organization, and Helene Mayer, the German-born Olympic gold-medal winner in the 1928 games, whose father was Jewish. Brundage worked for two years to get the Nazis to conform to world opinion and permit the German team to include at least one Jewish athlete. Helene Mayer, for her part, sealed the deal for Germany by agreeing to represent Germany in the games.

---

1. Richard D. Mandell, *The Nazi Olympics* (Champaign, IL: University of Illinois Press, 1987), 77.

...a Jewish athlete represented Nazi Germany

The 1936 Olympic medal ceremony in women's fencing was an exercise in irony. The gold medal went to Ilona Schacherer-Elek of Hungary, whose father was Jewish. The silver medal went to Helene Mayer of Germany, and the bronze went to Ellen Preis of Austria.[1] Who was Helene Mayer?

She was born in 1912 of a Jewish father – a physician – and a Christian mother. Helene was registered as Jewish and the family attended a synagogue. Their next-door neighbors were also Mayers and Helene's family was known as "the Jewish Mayers."

Helene Mayer was a natural athlete. By the age of twelve, she had proven her mettle in horseback riding, skiing, swimming, dance, and her ultimate arena, fencing.[2] In 1928, Helene, at the age of seventeen, won the gold at the Amsterdam Olympic Games. In 1932 Helene came in fifth at the games in Los Angeles and stayed on to study at the exclusive Scripps College. In 1933, after the Nazis had assumed power in Germany, her stipend was withdrawn, but Scripps immediately gave Helene a scholarship.[3]

Helene had studied law at the Sorbonne and had ambitions to work in a German foreign embassy. Realizing that the Nazis would never hire her, she switched her major to foreign languages.

Under an order from the International Olympic Committee, Germany had to agree not to discriminate in its selection of athletes for their 1936 team. This meant that they had to field at least one Jewish athlete. Helene Mayer was selected.

Having been deprived of her citizenship and kicked out of the Offenbach Fencing Club in absentia, because she was Jewish, Helene bargained with Hitler's government, indicating that she would accept the invitation to the German team in exchange for having her citizenship reinstated, a move supported by the German consul in San Francisco.[4]

As the medals were placed around the necks of Schacherer-Elek and Preis, the two women stood immobile. Not so Helene Mayer, who proudly offered the Nazi salute and later shook hands with Hitler.

---

1. There is a photograph of the three of them receiving their medals in Kay Schaffer and Sidonie Smith, *The Olympics at the Millennium: Power, Politics, and the Games* (Piscataway, NJ: Rutgers University Press, 2000), 58.
2. Milly Mogulof, *Foiled: Hitler's Jewish Olympian; The Helene Mayer Story* (Oakland, CA: RDR Books, 2002), 30.
3. Ibid., 71–72.
4. Ibid, 221–22.

Helene Mayer continued to compete in fencing and in 1937 defeated Schacherer-Elek to win the world title. As her train stopped in Frankfurt on her way home, Helene asked a friend if the press had carried news of her victory. When the friend replied in the negative, Helene finally faced reality and said, "Then I have to remain in America."[1]

The tragedy of Helene Mayer was her failure to face the reality early on. She slept through the loss of her citizenship, the loss of her membership in the fencing club, the loss of her college stipend, and the steady degradation of her fellow Jews. What finally woke her up was the refusal of the Nazi press to acknowledge her latest athletic achievement!

---

1. Carol Levy, "The Olympic Pause: 1936 Olympic Games in Nazi Germany," *The Jewish Magazine* (autumn 2000), http://www.jewishmag.com/36mag/olympic/olympic.htm.

...the Jewish catcher was also a spy

Morris (Moe) Berg was born to a Jewish family in New York in 1902. He grew up to be a gifted athlete with a precocious intellect. He was a star baseball player for Princeton and graduated cum laude with a degree in modern languages. He studied Latin, Greek, French, Spanish, Italian, German, and Sanskrit. After college, Berg signed a contract to play professional baseball and soon after enrolled in Columbia University Law School.

Although he was admitted to the bar and briefly practiced law, Berg's first love was baseball. His playing career lasted over fifteen years, and in 1932 he was one of three major-league players to go to Japan to teach baseball.[1]

In 1934 Berg made a second trip to Japan with an all-star team of American League baseball players. He acted as interpreter for the players, made speeches in Japanese, and carried with him a letter of introduction from President Roosevelt's Secretary of State Cordell Hull requesting that Berg be given every courtesy by the ambassador. The ambassador, however, had other plans for Berg.

The story goes that one day Berg was absent from the baseball field. Dressed in a kimono, Berg went to the hospital where the ambassador's daughter had just given birth. He was carrying a bouquet of flowers and asked the location of the patient. Instead of going to her room, Berg proceeded to the top floor carrying a camera hidden under his kimono.

Since the hospital was one of the tallest buildings in Tokyo, Berg was able to film "industrial complexes and armament plants, oil refineries and railroad lines...the Imperial Palace and warships in Tokyo Bay."[2]

Four months after Pearl Harbor, Berg's films were used to help guide the carrier-based bombers that made the first air raid against the Japanese home islands. The films were also used in subsequent raids.[3]

After retiring from baseball, Berg was recruited for another mission. With World War II raging, the Americans were hard at work on developing an atomic bomb. Thinking that perhaps they were in a race

---

1. Peter C. Bjarkman, *Diamonds around the Globe: The Encyclopedia of International Baseball* (Westport, CT: Greenwood, 2005), 123.
2. Louis Kaufman, Barbara Fitzgerald, and Tom Sewell, *Moe Berg: Athlete, Scholar, Spy* (Boston: Little, Brown, 1974), 27.
3. Nicholas Dawidoff however refutes claims that Berg's films were used and says there is no evidence that Berg was involved in espionage in 1934. See Dawidoff's book *The Catcher Was a Spy: The Mysterious Life of Moe Berg* (New York: Random House, 1994), 135, 386.

with Germany to see who would get the first bomb, the Americans turned to Moe Berg to try to find out the status of the German project.

Working through Swiss physicist Paul Scherrer, Berg was able to arrange for the eminent German physicist Werner Heisenberg to deliver a talk in Switzerland. Berg's instructions were to attend the lecture and to kill Heisenberg if he felt that the scientist was on the verge of supplying the Nazis with the bomb.

With his knowledge of German and having studied atomic physics in preparation for his assignment, Berg was able to understand the technical nature of the lecture. Berg also attended the dinner party following the lecture carrying a pistol in his pocket.[1]

During the course of the evening, Berg concluded that that the Germans were indeed far behind the Americans in their progress toward an atomic bomb, in spite of Nazi propaganda promising a new super weapon very soon. The German physicist Heisenberg would live to see another day.

1. Kaufman, Fitzgerald, and Sewell, *Moe Berg*, 196.

...Germany's best high jumper didn't get to jump

When the Nazis took power in Germany, every facet of German life, including sports, was pressed into service to promulgate Nazi ideology. Minister of Propaganda Joseph Goebbels announced on April 23, 1933, "German sport has only one task: to strengthen the character of the German people, imbuing it with the fighting spirit and steadfast camaraderie necessary in the struggle for its existence."[1]

Germany then began the systematic exclusion of non-Aryans, i.e., Jews, gypsies, and others, from athletics in Germany. Among those affected was world-class high jumper Gretel Bergmann. She was expelled from her sports club in Ulm in 1933, because she was Jewish.

In May 1933, the International Olympic Committee awarded the 1936 games to Germany to be held in Berlin. As the games approached, Propaganda Minister Goebbels had to deal with the problem of the half-Jewish fencing star Helene Mayer. He issued the following order to the press on February 19, 1936: "No comments should be made regarding Helene Mayer's non-Aryan ancestry or her expectations for a gold medal in the Olympics."[2] On July 16, 1936, two weeks before the start of the games, he again addressed the non-Aryan issue: "Press coverage should not mention that there are two non-Aryans among the women: Helene Mayer [fencing] and Gretel Bergmann [high jump and all-around track and field competition]."[3]

Bergmann's name appears as a competitor, because she had attained a height in the high jump identical to that which was to win the Olympic gold medal. Shortly after Goebbels's order to the press, Bergmann was informed that she would not be permitted to compete. By dismissing Bergmann, Germany sacrificed an almost sure gold medal.

In 1937 Gretel Bergmann immigrated to the United States to avoid further persecution in Germany.

---

1. Quoted in Anton Rippon, *Hitler's Olympics: The Story of the 1936 Nazi Games* (Barnsley, South Yorkshire, UK: Pen and Sword, 2006), 17; see also Jewish Virtual Library, "The Nazi Olympics," http://www.jewishvirtuallibrary.org/jsource/Holocaust/olympics.html.
2. Quoted in Jeremy Schaap, *Triumph: The Untold Story of Jesse Owens and Hitler's Olympics* (New York: Houghton Mifflin, 2007), 154.
3. Ibid.

...a Jew saved Winston Churchill's political career

One of Winston Churchill's favorite Americans was Bernard Baruch. In addition to being a wealthy financier, Baruch served for a long time as a trusted advisor and confidant to President Roosevelt. Another of Baruch's attributes was the ability to discern that Winston was a great statesman but an extremely inept investor.

On a trip to America in 1932, Churchill paid a visit to Baruch in his office. While there, Churchill decided to do some trading on his own. At the end of the day, a distraught Churchill sought out Baruch and told him that he was a financially ruined man. He had squandered so much of his family fortune that he would have to sell everything, including his beloved estate, Chartwell. He bemoaned the fact that his ill-fated foray into the market would mean that he would have to resign from the House of Commons to enter business. No longer a young man, Churchill would probably have to spend the rest of his life paying back the enormous losses he had incurred.

Baruch gently informed Churchill that he had lost nothing. Knowing how notoriously bad an investor Churchill was, Baruch had left instructions to his employees to watch Churchill's transactions as he went about his trading. Every time Churchill sold, Baruch's employees were to buy the same securities. Every time Churchill bought, Baruch's people were to sell. By the end of the day, Churchill was back where he started. Baruch's firm had even absorbed the commissions.

Thus it was that Winston Churchill was able to stay in politics and to guide England and much of the free world through the difficult times that lay ahead in World War II.[1]

---

1. William Manchester, *The Last Lion: Winston Spencer Churchill*, vol. 2, *Alone, 1932–1940* (Boston: Little, Brown, 1988), 14–15.

...206,000 Jewish soldiers fought for Hitler

When the Nazis took power in Germany in 1933, they inherited an army that contained tens of thousands of *Mischlinge*, men of mixed Jewish-German marriages. According to historian Bryan Rigg's research, about 140,000 quarter-Jews served in the Wehrmacht between 1935 and 1945. Added to this were another 60,000 half-Jews and another 6,000 full Jews.[1] How did this situation come about?

When the Nazi hierarchy began to debate the issue of what to do about these *Mischling* soldiers, it was argued that if the government labeled half-Jews as Jews, the Wehrmacht would lose about 45,000 soldiers.[2] Hitler himself never got around to declaring half-Jews as Jews, possibly out of reluctance to alienate the Aryan families of the *Mischling*.[3] Even the Jewish families of these soldiers received much favorable consideration because of the service being rendered by their sons. Indeed, many soldiers remained in the army specifically to protect their families. More amazing still is the fact that Hitler himself intervened to help the families of part-Jews.[4]

Another factor in the retention of part-Jews in the armed forces was the unwillingness of commanders to discharge experienced soldiers in their units. When a soldier trains for months and even years in the same company, a certain loyalty develops and the unit becomes a sort of surrogate family for the soldier. Even after discharge from the service, a mechanism was established whereby half-Jews could petition to remain in the army.[5]

Finally, distance from the headquarters sometimes played a role in the non-implementation of the racial policies. General Rommel, fighting fierce battles in North Africa, apparently did not concern himself with the racial decrees, and Admiral Raeder was tardy in implementing the racial laws on ships at sea.[6]

It must be pointed out that most of the racially motivated discharges were directed at half-Jews. Nevertheless, many half-Jews remained in the armed forces by simply lying about their "Aryan" status, and the bureaucracy was too far stretched to do the necessary research to expose the half-Jews. Quarter-Jews were far less affected, although many were denied promotions and/or medals on account of their ancestry.[7]

---

1. Bryan Mark Rigg, *Hitler's Jewish Soldiers: The Untold Story of Nazi Racial Laws and Men of Jewish Descent in the German Military* (Lawrence, KS: University of Kansas Press, 2002), 63–65.
2. Ibid., 96.
3. Ibid., 96
4. Ibid., 105, 108, 114, 120, 123, 124, 129, 140.
5. Ibid., 119.
6. Ibid., 131–32.
7. Ibid., 118.

In a sea of racism, the German army stands out as an island of tolerance.

Part of the Nazi concentration camp system intricately involved supplying slave laborers for the German war effort. A typical inmate was first examined by a doctor to determine his fitness for work, and a medical file on him was established. Then his registration form was completed including all pertinent information. The third step would be to check his name against the indices of the Political Section (lists of people associated with political groups incompatible with Nazi philosophy) to see if he should be subjected to special tortures. Finally, the prisoner would be assigned a five-digit number coded to correspond to the worker's particular skills.

In the Auschwitz complex, each prisoner's forearm was tattooed with this number; it would follow the inmate from one work assignment to another and was tracked by the ss Economic Administration, which oversaw all slave labor assignments. In this way the prisoners who were to be kept alive for work were efficiently tracked and assigned to areas where their services were most needed.

The German war effort was significantly aided by this system supplied by IBM.[1]

1. Ibid., 352.

...Germany honored Moses Mendelssohn – 200 years too late

Anti-Semitism in Germany was prevalent in all ages and in the reigns of most rulers. In an effort to limit the numbers of Jews and their activities, Frederick II of Prussia issued a charter, which the French liberal Mirabeau referred to as "worthy of a cannibal."[1] At the time of the charter, the Jews of Prussia were divided into categories according to their value to the state. There were a very few *General Privileged Jews* not bound by the charter and enjoying all economic and residential rights. Next were the *Regular Protected Jews*. They had limited rights and residence which they could transmit to the oldest son only. *Special Protected Jews* could not transfer their rights to even a single child. All Jewish communal officials, the younger children of the *Specials*, and all domestic servants were only classified as *Tolerated*.[2]

The charter, containing more than thirty articles, severely limited the numbers and types of Jews who could service the Jewish community. It also put harsh restrictions on the types of occupations Jews could pursue and who could buy a house. In a city as large as Berlin, only forty Jewish-owned houses were permitted. Where there were five Jewish families in a town, only one was permitted to buy a house.[3] Any Jew intending to live outside these regulations had to leave his jurisdiction and reside elsewhere.

The foremost German Jew of this time was the intellectual Moses Mendelssohn, who gained almost universal acceptance into German society. So prominent was Mendelssohn that his status was raised from a *Tolerated Protected Jew* to a *Special Protected Jew*. However, this change in status was still not high enough for him to transfer his status to any of his children, to settle a child in business, or to marry off a child.[4] When Mendelssohn was elected to membership in the Prussian Royal Academy of Sciences, Frederick failed to ratify his election.[5]

The severe restrictions placed upon all phases of the lives of Mendelssohn's children proved too much for them to tolerate, and all six of them converted to Christianity.

When World War II started, Mendelssohn's descendents were well represented in the German armed forces by one full Jew, eleven

---

1. Jacob R. Marcus, *The Jew in the Medieval World: A Source Book, 315–1791* (New York: Atheneum, 1938), 85.
2. Ibid., 84–85.
3. Ibid., 94.
4. Ibid., 87.
5. "Moses Mendelssohn," *Encyclopedia Judaica*, CD-ROM Edition (Jerusalem: Keter, 1995).

half-Jews, six 37.5-percent Jews, fifteen quarter-Jews, and six 12.5-percent Jews.[1] It was only due to Germany's manpower needs that these Jews were able to escape the gas chambers. Had German arms prevailed, it is fairly certain that these army veterans would have joined their brethren in the toll of the Holocaust.

It is ironic that in 1979, the 250th anniversary of Mendelssohn's birth, the Berlin city government announced a ninety-pfennig commemorative stamp to be issued in Mendelssohn's honor and a new twenty-thousand-deutschmark annual award (today's equivalent of around thirty thousand dollars), the Moses Mendelssohn Prize to Promote Tolerance.[2] Moses Mendelssohn's now mostly Christian descendents lived to see their illustrious Jewish ancestor honored with a prize in his name, a prize for promoting tolerance, something he only partially enjoyed and his children even less.

---

1. Bryan Mark Rigg, *Hitler's Jewish Soldiers: The Untold Story of Nazi Racial Laws and Men of Jewish Descent in the German Military* (Lawrence, KS: University of Kansas Press, 2002), 287.
2. "Moses Mendelssohn," *Encyclopedia Judaica.*

...Hitler promoted part-Jews to Aryan status

When the Nazis ascended to power in 1933, they immediately began to single out Jews for persecution. Full Jews were not a problem, but mixed-blood Jews, *Mischlinge,* needed special attention. When the racial laws began to be enforced in 1933, the effects were immediately felt in the army. Some soldiers were immediately discharged, some were permitted to remain in the army but were to be denied promotion, and still others had their status changed.

To effect these status changes, Hitler established three new categories. The first two categories were called *Genehmigungen,* approval or authorization. The lowest-level category simply allowed a soldier to remain in the army until the end of the war.[1] The second category allowed the soldier to remain in the army and be promoted. The third category allowed the soldier to describe himself as *deutschblütig,* of German blood. This conferred on the soldier all the rights of an Aryan except the privilege of joining the Nazi party and owning farmland.

Most of the soldiers fell into categories one and two. They usually had a clause written into their exemptions that after the war, Hitler himself would review their cases. If they fought well, they would be considered for elevation to *deutschblütig.* [2]

Another type of exemption was to declare the soldier an Aryan. This was most often accomplished by declaring that the Jewish father was not the real father. This process often entailed some conspicuous lying, but in many cases the deception was successful.[3]

---

1. Bryan Mark Rigg, *Hitler's Jewish Soldiers: The Untold Story of Nazi Racial Laws and Men of Jewish Descent in the German Military* (Lawrence, KS: University of Kansas Press, 2002), 111.
2. The permit for one such case read as follows: "I approve Private First Class Wilhelm v. Gwinner in 3rd Panzerjäger Company, Section 32, to be allowed to be promoted to ranks of authority during the war according to the exemption clause of Paragraph 15 (2) of the military law. After the war, I will decide whether to declare Wilhelm von Gwinner of German blood, according to his performance as a soldier. Führerhauptquartier, 5 March 1941. Signed: Adolf Hitler." Ibid., 19.
3. Ibid., 31.

...Mussolini's Italians did not make very good Nazis

When World War II began, Benito Mussolini, the Italian fascist dictator, fell into the orbit of Hitler's anti-Semitism. Laws were passed limiting Jewish participation in a variety of professional and business endeavors. However, there were loopholes in the system. Exempt were "favored war veterans, old Fascists, their children, grandchildren, parents, and grandparents." Moreover, lax enforcement of the laws permitted more potential victims to evade arrest.[1] In general, Italians were not following Mussolini's lead regarding persecution of Jews. With the Final Solution in full swing, the Jews of Italy were comparatively safe.

All this was to change. Having led the Italian nation into disastrous defeats in World War II, Mussolini was forced out of power in 1943. The German army then came in to occupy the country, and the roundup of Jews began for transport to the death camps.

It is a tragic irony that a leader who could not get his country to persecute Jews was removed from power paving the way for the Holocaust to reach Italy.

---

1. Elliot Rosenberg, *But Were They Good for the Jews? Over 150 Historical Figures Viewed from a Jewish Perspective* (Secaucus, NJ: Carol, 1997), 223.

...German soldiers rescued the Lubavitcher Rebbe

In the fall of 1939, after the German army had occupied Poland, members of the Lubavitcher movement in the United States began a concerted effort to get the Rebbe and his entourage out of Europe to a safe haven in America. Working through members of Congress, Secretary of State Cordell Hull, the Latvian embassy, the Swedish government, and prominent Jewish citizens, they were able to appeal successfully to the German government to facilitate the rescue of the Rebbe, his family, and his close advisors.

At that time, relations between the US and Germany were somewhat strained and the Nazis were anxious to improve relations with the United States by cooperating with the rescue of selected people whom the government would specify.[1]

Once the decision had been made to rescue the Rebbe, the task was delegated to Admiral Canaris, the head of the Abwehr, the Nazi intelligence services. Canaris then assigned a half-Jewish soldier, Major Ernst Bloch, to find the Rebbe. Also in the group were quarter-Jew Johannes Hamburger, knowledgeable in French, Russian, and Polish, half-Jew Klaus Schenk, and Major Johannes Horatzek, head of the Abwehr office in Warsaw.[2]

Then ensued a most remarkable search of Jewish areas of Warsaw. Four uniformed German soldiers were attempting to explain to terrified residents that they had come to rescue their spiritual leader! When the word finally reached the Rebbe that these soldiers were telling the truth, he came out of hiding.[3]

The trip out of Europe was itself fraught with danger. Several times they were stopped by ss and other soldiers demanding to know why these Jews were traveling first class and where were they headed. Using a combination of threats and bluster, Major Bloch was able to get the Jews to the Latvian border, and the group was soon on its way to America on a Swedish ship.[4]

During their relationship with Major Bloch, the Lubavitchers came to believe that Bloch was either a Jew masquerading as a German or a guardian angel sent by God.[5]

1. Bryan Mark Rigg, *Rescued from the Reich: How One of Hitler's Soldiers Saved the Lubavitcher Rebbe* (New Haven: Yale University Press, 2004), 59–70.
2. Ibid., 84–85.
3. Ibid., 123.
4. Ibid., 123–28, 148.
5. Ibid., 127–28.

...a Japanese diplomat sacrificed his career to save Jews

Chiune Sugihara became Japan's vice-consul general to Lithuania in September of 1939.[1] With the onset of the war, Sugihara's office was deluged with desperate people, most of them Jews, seeking transit visas out of the country. The lines literally snaked around the block.

From his early days as a student and diplomat, Sugihara was sensitive to the contrast drawn between the East and the West. Indeed, he displayed a keen desire to compete with the Americans to demonstrate who was more civilized. Early on in his rescue efforts, Sugihara noticed that most of his "clients" did not have the necessary details required to successfully complete their applications. The Japanese government was divided on the issue, but people were in need of immediate assistance.[2] Sugihara processed the applications anyway.

For the most part, the six thousand Jews aided by Sugihara were able to reach Japan, from where they traveled on to various destinations, mainly to Shanghai. The students of the Mir Yeshiva were among those saved by Sugihara.[3]

At the end of the war, the Sugiharas were held in a Russian prison camp in Romania with other Japanese members of the diplomatic corps.[4] When Sugihara finally returned home, he was asked to resign from the diplomatic service. Sugihara, an expert in the Russian language and culture, spent some of his remaining years as a translator of Russian reports for a Japanese radio station and about fifteen years working in a trade mission in Moscow to revive trade between the Soviet Union and Japan.[5]

In 1984 Chiune Sugihara was recognized as Righteous among the Nations by Yad Vashem, the Holocaust Martyrs' and Heroes' Remembrance Authority, and a park in Jerusalem was named in his honor.[6]

1. Hillel Levine, *In Search of Sugihara: The Elusive Japanese Diplomat Who Risked His Life to Rescue 10,000 Jews from the Holocaust* (New York: Simon and Schuster, 1996), 3.
2. Ibid., 259.
3. Ibid., 37, 242, 244, 255.
4. Ibid., 275.
5. Ibid., 277.
6. Yad Vashem; Mitchell Geoffrey Bard, *The Complete History of the Holocaust* (San Diego, CA: Greenhaven Press, 2001), 333.

In 1939, German General Johannes Blaskowitz was in charge of the troops who invaded Poland. Following closely on his heels were the ss Death's Head units assigned to liquidate undesirables, foremost among them Jews. As a member of the old school of soldiers who held to standards of decency, Blaskowitz was shocked by what he saw and ordered the court-martial of a number of members of the ss troops involved in the killings. This was an unpardonable sin in Nazi ideology, and the convicted ss men received speedy amnesties.

Blaskowitz continued to compile dossiers on those committing atrocities. Soon it became necessary for Himmler himself to speak to high-ranking officers about what the Third Reich was attempting to accomplish. Blaskowitz, however, kept up his agitating and was soon removed from his command.[1]

---

1. Elliot Rosenberg, *But Were They Good for the Jews: Over 150 Historical Figures Viewed from a Jewish Perspective* (Secaucus, NJ: Carol, 1997), 220–21.

...a Jew made possible US help to Britain at the start of World War II

At the start of World War II, President Roosevelt was morally committed to helping Great Britain. However, his efforts were severely limited by the Johnson Debt Default Act, which attempted to protect the United States by forbidding US government lending to any country that had previously defaulted on such loans. Great Britain met this criterion, having defaulted on nearly $3.5 billion in US loans made during World War I, and therefore Roosevelt could not legally extend any more credit to his ally nation.[1]

At this point, Jewish business man Armand Hammer stepped forward with an idea. He met with President Roosevelt and presented a plan whereby England would lease aviation and naval bases to the United States in exchange for wiping out England's debt. This would clear the way for England to receive additional ships, planes, and other matériel needed to stay in the war.

The plan was adopted by the United States and Great Britain, and soon it came to include the Soviet Union. Roosevelt's aides consulted with Hammer several times on the implementation of the plan soon to become famous as the "lend-lease" plan.[2]

---

1. Edward Jay Epstein, *Dossier: The Secret History of Armand Hammer* (New York: Carroll and Graf, 1996), 151.
2. Ibid., 151–55.

...only Christians could get visas during the war

In the early part of World War II, the stunning successes of the German army caused concern for the plight of war refugees in Europe. Eleanor Roosevelt, the president's wife, took a special interest in their difficult situation. After trying and failing to get the immigration quotas raised, she tried getting temporary visitors' visas for people seeking to escape. The plan worked out very well for British children, whose parents wanted them out of harm's way should the Germans invade England.[1] Later on, the program was extended to selected adults from various countries. This program didn't work out very well for the Jews, most of whom were from Germany. It was found that the Germans had made extensive use of spies in the target countries prior to the invasion by the army, and the United States was afraid that among the German refugees would be spies.[2]

While the British children brought over were mostly Christian, the ones from Germany were mostly Jewish, and Congress would not extend the visitors' visas to this group. This attitude was not limited to Congress. In a poll that asked what kind of people you most dislike, 35 percent listed Jews. The next year another poll showed that "53 percent said Jews were different from other people and that these differences should lead to restrictions in business and social life."[3]

---

1. Doris Kearns Goodwin, *No Ordinary Time: Franklin and Eleanor Roosevelt: The Home Front in World War II* (New York: Simon and Schuster, 1994), 100.
2. Ibid.
3. Ibid., 102.

...Adolf Eichmann helped rescue some Jews

By early 1939, the Nazis knew that they wanted to get rid of the Jews in the areas under their control. The Final Solution, the total extermination of the Jews, had not yet been decided upon, and the task of arranging the emigration of the Jews fell to Adolf Eichmann. At the same time, the Jewish secret service, the Mossad, was busy trying to affect the rescue of Jews from Nazi-dominated areas of Europe.

It was Eichmann's plan to move Jews out of Austria through the Slovak Republic. At one point, the Mossad agent Ehud Avriel was driven from Bratislava, the new capital of the Slovak Republic, to Vienna in a luxurious limousine driven by a uniformed SS chauffeur. Avriel was there to negotiate a transfer of Jews out of Europe.

In late 1939, Eichmann issued 1,100 visas to Jews who were to travel down the Danube River to Bratislava and on to Yugoslavia. There they were to meet a Mossad ship to transport the Jews to Palestine. Unfortunately, nobody was willing to sell a ship to the Jews, and nine months later, these same passport-carrying Jews were caught by the Nazi death squads. Tragically, it turned out that the Jews *did* have a ship, but the Haganah, the Jewish military forces, had sold the ship to the British for intelligence missions.

The Mossad-Eichmann relationship continued, and several small shipments of Jews were successfully taken out of Europe. This also marked the beginning of active participation of the Joint Distribution Committee in the illegal smuggling of Jews from Europe.

The Eichmann-Mossad relationship could have been a much greater success had it not been for the active interference of the British government. The British would not permit any Jewish refugees to enter areas under their control.[1]

While Winston Churchill is generally regarded as having been a friend of the Jews, this blatant abetting of mass murder happened on his watch. The British let people die rather than upset the Arabs.

---

1. Tad Szulc, *The Secret Alliance: The Extraordinary Story of the Rescue of the Jews since World War II* (New York: Farrar, Straus and Giroux, 1991), 27–31.

...Hitler couldn't pass the Aryan test

Nazi bureaucracy included many laws and decrees defining whether a given person was an Aryan. People who wanted to establish an official Aryan identity – including those who wanted to apply for or keep government jobs, get married, and certainly to receive official citizenship in the Reich – were required to produce documentation proving that all four of their grandparents were Aryan.[1] It is at this point that Hitler would have failed the test, because he could not definitively identify an Aryan as his maternal grandfather.[2]

The story goes that Hitler's grandmother, at age forty-two, was a domestic for a Jewish family, the Frankenbergers (or Frankenreiters) when she became pregnant. There is not much doubt that the Frankenbergers paid child support for the child, but Hitler maintained that it was merely a way to extort money from the Jewish family. The real father was an Aryan, he claimed, named George Heidler. Whatever the truth may be, it is certain that Hitler searched diligently for his family records. His own nephew Patrick claimed that Hitler said that the public "must not know where I came from and who my family is."[3]

---

1. Bryan Mark Rigg, *Hitler's Jewish Soldiers: The Untold Story of Nazi Racial Laws and Men of Jewish Descent in the German Military.* (Lawrence, KS: University of Kansas Press, 2002), 21; Gerald E. Markle, *Meditations of a Holocaust Traveler* (Albany, NY: SUNY Press, 1995), 79–82; Paul R. Mendes-Flohr and Jehuda Reinharz, *The Jew in the Modern World: A Documentary History* (New York: Oxford University Press, 1980), 642.
2. Rigg, *Hitler's Jewish Soldiers*, 174.
3. Ibid., 173.

...saving Jews cost a US diplomat his job

In 1940, Hiram Bingham IV was already a veteran diplomat, having been posted to Japan, China, Poland, and England. His latest assignment was as vice-consul to Vichy France in charge of issuing visas. The Vichy regime was the puppet government set up by the Germans in July of 1940. With the Nazis bringing their anti-Semitic crackdown to France, Bingham's office in Marseilles was literally besieged by visa seekers, mostly Jews, desperate to escape from the Nazis. In this humanitarian endeavor, Bingham was only too happy to oblige.

Since the United States was not yet at war with Germany and since the granting of escape visas was contrary to Vichy law, Bingham was clearly operating outside of his area of jurisdiction. Nevertheless, knowing the fate of those who would not be able to get visas, Bingham willingly broke the law.[1]

Before long Bingham's activities got the attention of both the United States State Department and the government of Vichy France. In the summer of 1941, Bingham was transferred to Lisbon, Portugal, and later to Argentina. With his career stagnating due to his disfavor within the foreign service because of his actions, he resigned in 1945.[2]

Bingham's story was a tightly guarded secret until he shared some of it with his granddaughter, who was writing a paper for school. More of Bingham's story surfaced when his son found a bundle of letters among his things.[3]

For his heroic efforts in the rescue of perhaps two thousand people, Hiram Bingham has been honored by the State of Israel, the United Nations, the United States, and the State of Connecticut.

---

1. *Connecticut State Register and Manual* (Hartford, CT: Secretary of the State, 2001), viii; also available at "Hiram Bingham IV," http://www.ct.gov/sots/cwp/view. asp?a=3188&q=392620.
2. Robert Kim Bingham, *Courageous Dissent: How Harry Bingham Defied His Government to Save Lives* (Greenwich, CT: Triune Books, 2007), 135.
3. *Connecticut State Register and Manual*, viii; see also the book written by Bingham's son, Robert Kim Bingham, *Courageous Dissent*.

...German scientists had to "Aryanize" Einstein's physics

With the rise to power of the Nazis, the work of Jewish scientists in general and Albert Einstein in particular were denigrated as "Jewish physics" and often committed to the flames of the book-burning orgies.

In November of 1940, German physicists gathered at a Reich-organized meeting that would later come to be called the Munich synod, to answer challenges by members of the Aryan Physics movement, which sought to sanitize the discipline from Jewish contributions.[1] The physicists were successful in rebutting the challengers' claims, and the following conclusions were issued as a summation of the meeting:

1. Theoretical physics is an indispensable part of physics.
2. Einstein's Special Theory of Relativity belongs to the experimentally verified facts of physics.
3. The theory of relativity has nothing to do with a general relativistic philosophy. No new concepts of time and space have been introduced.
4. Modern quantum theory is the only method known to describe quantitatively the properties of the atom. As yet, no one has been able to go beyond the mathematical formalism to obtain a deeper understanding of the atomic structure.[2]

In 1942 a second meeting was held. This time it was to soften the idea that relativity had to be accepted. The meeting concluded that "before Einstein, 'Aryan' scientists like Lorentz, Hassenohrl, Poincaire, etc., had created the foundations of the theory of relativity, and Einstein merely followed up the already existing ideas consistently and added the cornerstone."[3]

By this clever sleight-of-hand, the Germans were able to utilize "Jewish physics" by switching the credit for the discoveries to their own scientists.

---

1. Klaus Hentschel, *Physics and National Socialism: An Anthology of Primary Sources* (Basel: Birkhäuser, 1996), 290.
2. Ronald W. Clark, *Einstein: The Life and Times* (New York: Avon Books, 1984), 701–2.
3. Ibid., 702.

...hunted Jews took refuge on the Riviera

When France capitulated to the German invasion in 1940, the Nazis set about their goal of annihilating the Jews of the defeated nation. From the start, the French were reluctant to surrender their native French Jews to deportation to the death camps. As the war dragged on and German victory seemed more doubtful, the French began to put more and more obstacles in the path of German attempts to send their Jews to the death camps. Moreover, the Italian government began to waver in their alliance with Germans.

As part of the German defense against the expected Allied invasion of France, Italian troops were stationed in the south of France. It is to this area that the hunted Jews began to gravitate. All the luxury hotels were empty and the owners were happy to get any tenants who showed up.[1]

At the start of the war, Jews who could afford it went to Nice in Vichy France, where the German army was not an occupying force. As the war continued, the luxury hotels began to empty out and more and more refugee Jews began to occupy the space. Relief agencies provided money for many of the refugees.[2]

A truly odd scene began to unfold in the Hotel Roosevelt. The large hall was rented out to serve as a synagogue and a study room. Rabbis walked the streets in their traditional garb, and one could hear Talmudic discussions while fanatical Jew-haters were beside themselves with rage.[3]

As the Nazis began to step up the pressure on the Italians, the government officials and the army continued to stall. By then Mussolini had been deposed, and the new Italian government virtually ceased to cooperate with the Nazis. While the rescuers could no longer maintain the Jews on the Riviera, the underground successfully dispersed some fifty thousand Jews to the countryside, to Switzerland, and to Spain.[4]

---

1. Nora Levin, *The Holocaust: The Destruction of European Jewry, 1933–1945* (New York: Schocken, 1973), 450.
2. Ibid., 450–51.
3. Ibid., 451.
4. Ibid., 454–55.

...World War II Jewish GIs had more than one Jewish reason to fight

Immediately after the surprise attack on Pearl Harbor, American young men flocked to recruiting offices to fight against the Japanese. While this outpouring of rage against the Japanese affected Jewish youth, the Jewish recruits also had a separate list of incentives to serve in the armed forces. The wrath against the Japanese was quite new, but Jewish GIs had had two or more years to build up hatred for the Nazis as they continued to learn daily about the atrocities committed against their coreligionists in Europe. Most Jewish GIs preferred to fight the Germans.[1]

Another reason for Jews to get into the fight was to refute the widespread belief that Jews were physically unfit for combat. They were alleged to have "flat feet, bowed legs, asthmatic lungs, and stunted stature."[2] Also included in the list of Jewish infirmities was "verbal skill."[3]

GI Jews were also out to expunge the US Army's belief that Jews were likely to seek exemptions, or once in the military, to try for softer jobs.[4] As late as 1918 an army manual states, "The foreign born, and especially Jews, are more apt to malinger than the native born."[5]

Many army officers subscribed to the notion regarding Jews that "assimilation could be a monumental mistake, since it would dilute and bastardize the pure American stock they wanted to preserve."[6]

Zionist Jews had an additional reason to fight. By acquiring technical skills and combat experience, these GIs planned to form the nucleus of a new Jewish army in Palestine. They would train other Jews to defend themselves against invading Arabs once the new Jewish state became a reality.[7]

All of these incentives helped improve the performance of Jewish GIs in World War II and to eradicate the racial misconceptions regarding Jews' willingness and ability to fight.

1. Deborah Dash Moore, *GI Jews: How World War II Changed a Generation* (Cambridge, MA: Harvard University Press, 2004), 27–28.
2. Ibid., 28.
3. Ibid.
4. Ibid., 32.
5. Joseph W. Bendersky, *The Jewish Threat: Anti-Semitic Politics of the US Army* (New York: Basic Books, 2000), 38–39.
6. Ibid., 39.
7. Moore, *GI Jews*, 44.

...Japan couldn't build a bomb because Germany's Jews were gone

On December 17, 1941, a meeting of Japanese scientists and naval technicians met at the Naval Officers' Club in Tokyo. The topic was the building of a Japanese atomic bomb. Those in attendance soon realized that German scientists would be needed to assist the Japanese in their quest for the bomb.

When the matter of soliciting German scientists to assist in the project was raised, Tsunesaburo Asada, the chief physicist at Osaka University, remarked that not much help could be expected from the Germans. "Most of Germany's atomic scientists happened to be Jewish, and they've been expelled from the country. Some of them have gone to the United States. In my opinion, only the United States has the potential to build an atomic weapon."[1]

This prescient statement is significant for two reasons. The first is that it came only ten days after Pearl Harbor, when the Japanese were riding a wave of military success. The second is that it was a recognition of the potential contributions that Jews could make to the research into atomic energy.

---

1. Dan Kurzman, *The Day of the Bomb: Countdown to Hiroshima* (New York: McGraw-Hill, 1986), 142.

...mothers can either help or kill

A mother's lie cost her soldier son his life

Klaus Menge was the son of a German mother and a Jewish father. Because of his classification as a half-Jew, Klaus was discharged from the German army in October of 1940. In order to be reinstated in the army, Klaus had his mother swear out a statement that Klaus's father was an Aryan with whom she had an adulterous affair. The army accepted her story, and Klaus was returned to active service in April of 1941. In September of 1941, Klaus died in battle.[1]

A mother's lie made her son the number-two man in the German air force

Erhard Milch was a member of the German air force in 1935 when he was denounced to Luftwaffe head Herman Göring as being a Jew. Milch's mother went to her son-in-law, the police president in Hagen, with an affidavit stating that the father of her six children was her late uncle Carl Bauer. Göring approved the letter and Hitler issued instructions to have Milch's records revised to declare him of pure Aryan descent. Milch went on to receive Germany's highest rank, that of field marshal, and virtually commanded the Luftwaffe in major areas such as planning, production, and strategy.[2]

A mother's truth kept her son out of harm's way

In 1943, half-Jew Wolfgang Ebert received his draft notice ordering him to report for military service in the German army. His mother, Sonja Ebert nee Himmelstein, a Russian Jew, unwilling to lose her son in battle, immediately went to the recruiting office in Potsdam and convinced the recruiters that she was Jewish. She argued that according to Nazi race laws, her half-Jewish son should not be drafted. The recruiter was convinced and wrote "not to be used" on Ebert's papers and assigned him to the reserves. As a parting shot, Frau Ebert said to the recruiters, "and besides the war is over so you should just write my son sick."[3]

---

1. Bryan Mark Rigg, *Hitler's Jewish Soldiers: The Untold Story of Nazi Racial Laws and Men of Jewish Descent in the German Military* (Lawrence, KS: University of Kansas Press, 2002), 30.
2. Ibid., 29–30.
3. Ibid., 145.

...coded letters leaked word of the Holocaust

In the early days of the Holocaust, the news of what was actually going on was too horrible to contemplate. Surely, those bringing such reports must be exaggerating! However, as more evidence from a variety of sources began to come in, the enormity of the crime began to penetrate the benumbed minds of the world at large.

One such bit of evidence was brought in semi-coded letters as shown below. The letters were written in German and bore stamps indicating they had passed the German censors. The most telling words are transliterated Hebrew (in italics). The words in parentheses are translations added later to make the code intelligible.

> I spoke to *Mr. Jager* (hunter, thus the Germans). He told me he will invite all relatives of the family *Achenu* (our brethren, thus the Jews), with the exception of *Miss Eisenzweig* (apparently ironworkers, thus heavy industry workers), from Warsaw, to his countryside dwelling *Kewer* (tomb). I am alone here: I feel lonely... Uncle *Gerusch* (deportation) works also in Warsaw; he is a very capable worker. His friend *Miso* (death) works together with him. Please pray for me.[1]

This letter was followed by another repeating the news of the wholesale extermination. It begins: "I too was in sorrow, for I am now so lonely. Uncle *Achenu* has died."[2]

The writer has expressed, in a few words, a volume of tragic text.

---

1. David S. Wyman, *The Abandonment of the Jews: America and the Holocaust, 1941–1945* (New York: New Press, 1984), 50.
2. Ibid.

...beets, dumplings, and fine linen can be lethal

During World War II, many Jews turned to non-Jews for sustenance and shelter from the Nazi dragnets that were set out for their capture.

In one instance, a Jewish woman was admonished by her Polish hostess that by slicing the beets so evenly, she might give herself away if anyone noticed that the beets were being prepared "Jewish style." In another instance, a member of a hostile Polish guerilla group, the AK, responsible for the murder of countless Jews, was eating soup with dumplings in the home of a family sheltering Jews. The hungry killer was heard to exclaim, "These dumplings could only have been cooked by a Jewess." That night, the dumpling maker was again on the run.

In yet another instance, a Polish woman sheltering Jews spread her freshly spun linen on the grass for drying. A passing Polish farmer remarked, "That's Jew linen, very fine." The Polish woman bluffed her way out of the situation by telling the farmer that the sun was blinding him, and that the linen was indeed her own.[1]

---

1. Yaffa Eliach, *There Once Was a World: A 900-Year Chronicle of the Shtetl of Eishyshok* (Boston: Little, Brown, 1998), 617.

...a conference to save Jews was held to do nothing

As news of the Holocaust began to become more common knowledge, pressure on the Allies to do something to rescue those still alive began to mount. In order to still the outcry, the Americans and the British decided to convene a conference, ostensibly to devise a plan to aid the millions marked for death at the hands of the Nazis. The venue chosen for the conference was the island of Bermuda, which served to keep the conference out of the public eye; travel to the area was restricted due to military activity.[1]

When a State Department representative was asked the purpose of the meeting, he replied that it "was to be simply a preliminary meeting to put in motion the Executive Committee of the Intergovernmental Committee on Political Refugees." He said this in 1943, but the committee had been in existence since 1938![2]

Although the reason for calling the conference was the outcry over the systematic slaughter of Jews, the conference rules "prohibited any emphasis on Jews. And no steps were to be taken exclusively for Jews."[3] The State Department further stated that "no commitment regarding transatlantic shipping space can be made."[4] It should be noted that many supply ships were returning to the United States empty.[5]

Delegates were further cautioned that the administration "had no power to relax or rescind [the immigration] laws." What was left unsaid was that the administration *did* have the power to bring in refugees to fill the almost untouched *legal* immigration quotas.[6]

When the conference finally got around to the problem of finding space for refugees on empty ships, fourteen refugees actually were permitted to come to America. It was then that the us State Department closed the loophole by creating a convenient catch-22. The new regulation stipulated that shipping would not be granted to anybody without a quota number. It further stipulated that no quota numbers could be issued unless shipping was guaranteed. As expected, nobody qualified to go.[7]

The list of failures goes on and on, but the fact was that the conference was organized for failure, and it succeeded splendidly. If corroboration of the obvious is necessary, it was provided by Richard Law, a member of the British delegation. Many years later he said that "the process was no more than 'a façade for inaction.'"[8]

---

1. David S., Wyman, *The Abandonment of the Jews: America and the Holocaust* (New York: New Press, 1984), 108.
2. Ibid., 108–109.
3. Ibid., 113.
4. Ibid.
5. Ibid., 114.
6. Ibid.
7. Ibid., 128.
8. Ibid., 122.

...famous architecture is worth more than human lives

During the Holocaust, many people and organizations in the United States pleaded with the Allies to bomb the gas chambers and crematoria at Auschwitz. Their reasoning was that it would prevent the rapid killing and disposing of vast numbers of people. Without their death factories, to continue the extermination of the Jews would have required a lot of personnel at a time when the Germans were hard-pressed for manpower in many areas. The government's answer to these pleas was that the best way to save the remaining Jews was to bring the war to a speedy conclusion. The official line was that diverting bombers to destroy the death mechanisms at Auschwitz would slow down the war effort,[1] even though bombers were regularly attacking the industrial complexes in Auschwitz, often within five miles of the killing facilities.[2]

In an answer to a plea from the World Jewish Congress pleading for the bombing of Auschwitz,[3] John J. McCloy, a high-ranking member of the United States War Department, wrote back saying in part that "such an operation could be executed only by the diversion of considerable air support essential to the success of our forces now engaged in decisive operations elsewhere..." and that "such an action, even if practicable, might provoke even more vindictive action by the Germans."[4]

At a later date, Secretary of War Stimson said to this same John J. McCloy, "Would you consider me a sentimental old man if I removed Kyoto from the target cities of our bombers?" McCloy agreed to this, *even over the objections of the Air Force command!* McCloy himself prevented the bombing of Rothenburg, a German town known for its medieval architecture.[5] While the Allies could not spare the resources to destroy the death mechanisms, they were willing to refrain from attacking viable German cities.

During this time, a pathetically ironic drama was being played out in the Auschwitz death camp itself. Jewish women slave laborers working at making munitions in the camp managed to pass tiny amounts of gunpowder, little by little, to the Sonderkommando (Jewish men forced to man the death works). Their heroic efforts culminated in the starving, imprisoned Jews achieving what the mighty Allies claimed they could not do: in a prisoner uprising on October 7, 1944, the Sonderkommando blew up Crematorium IV. In recognition of this accomplishment they were summarily executed.[6]

1. David S. Wyman, *The Abandonment of the Jews: America and the Holocaust, 1941–1945* (New York: New Press, 1994), 353.
2. Ibid., 302.
3. Ibid., 295.
4. One might wonder how much more vindictive the Germans could have gotten than thousands of murders per day!
5. Wyman, *The Abandonment of the Jews*, 305.
6. Ibid., 307; Emily Taitz, *Holocaust Survivors: A Biographical Dictionary*, vol. 1 (Westport, CT: Greenwood Press, 2007), xxx.

...Holocaust mentality took German lives

When the Germans penetrated deep into Russia during World War II, they assumed major tasks in rail transportation in order to keep their army supplied. Sometimes, when traffic was heavy, trains carrying Jews headed for the death camps were shunted off onto sidings until clear tracks could be allocated.

In one incident, a trainload of German soldiers wounded in the battle was parked on a siding. The train was sealed and its markings had been removed in order that the train would not become an inviting target for the roving bands of partisans who were constantly harassing German shipping. Unfortunately for the train's occupants, the transit orders had been destroyed in a bombing raid. The stationmaster did hear sounds coming from within the train pleading for fresh air and water. However, he assumed that the train was carrying Jews bound for extermination, and the cries he heard were coming from German-speaking Jews. When the train was finally unsealed, they found that more than 200 German soldiers had perished.[1]

So indoctrinated was the German population that the people they were dealing with were a subhuman species, that they caused their own soldiers to suffer the fate decreed for others.

---

1. Alan Clark, *Barbarossa: The Russian–German Conflict, 1941–1945* (London: Weidenfeld and Nicolson, 1995), 193–94.

...Jews were forced to counterfeit Allied currency

During World War II, the Nazi government employed Jews in an effort to destabilize the British economy. For at least 150 years, it had been the policy of warring nations to attempt to wreak havoc on the economy of their enemies by counterfeiting their currency. Such was the plan of Germany against England.

Their plan was to counterfeit massive quantities of British currency and to drop the fake money from bombers flying overhead. Once the five-pound notes were found by the citizens of the British Isles, they would immediately begin to spend the money. This would cause a dramatic increase in currency in circulation, and the resulting rise in prices would damage the English economy and seriously hamper their war effort against Germany.

In order to carry out their scheme, the Nazis searched the Auschwitz concentration camp for Jews who were skilled artists, engravers, or printers, or had any other talents that would be useful in counterfeiting currency. The Jews were put into an isolated area of the camp where they could not communicate with any other inmates. If a prisoner became ill, he was brought to the medical center for treatment under guard until he was cured.

When the first bills were produced, they were almost identical to authentic British five-pound notes. Unfortunately for the Germans, the Luftwaffe was so depleted by losses suffered during the *Blitzkrieg* of England that they had to postpone plans to send bombers over England to drop the money. However, the Nazis successfully used the currency throughout the war for a variety of other purposes, but on a much smaller scale than originally intended. This story is featured in a 2001 documentary film.[1]

This was not the only Jewish counterfeiting group working for the Nazis. In early 2007, a movie about Jews counterfeiting Allied currency was made by an Austrian filmmaker, Stefan Ruzowitzky. The movie, *Die Falscher* (The counterfeiters) begins with the apprehension of Jewish printer Adolf Burger while he was counterfeiting baptismal certificates for Jews attempting to avoid the death camps. Burger was initially incarcerated in Birkenau but was soon transferred to Sachsenhausen, where he was put into a group of 140 Jewish printers, fine artists, and bankers.

1. "Making a Buck," *Time Machine*, History Channel, 2001.

Conditions in Sachsenhausen were much better for the prisoners, and they were put to work counterfeiting British pounds. The group produced 134 million British pounds and caused a 75 percent loss in the value of the British currency. Swiss banks eventually refused to accept the notes, but they floated freely on the black market. Some of it even financed illegal Jewish immigration to Palestine!

After a time, the counterfeiters turned their attention to American dollars. They were able to produce acceptable currency, but the end of the war prevented any widespread circulation of the dollars.

At the age of 89, Burger embarked on a speaking tour of Germany. While not blaming Germany's young people for what happened so many years ago, he wanted young Germans to beware of becoming neo-Nazis.[1]

It is ironic that a group of "subhuman" people would be singled out for a highly technical operation so critical to the Reich.

---

1. Katharina Goetze, "Hitler's Jewish Counterfeiter," *The Forward* (February 16, 2007), http://www.forward.com/articles/10099/.

...Russian Jews were unfit to live but too valuable to be killed

When the German army invaded Russia in 1941, they conquered vast territories including a large population of Russian Jews. Following closely behind the army were two competing organizations, the Generalbevollmächtige für den Arbeitseinsatz (GBA, meaning "general plenipotentiary for manpower") and the ss (the Schutzstaffel, or "elite guard"). The GBA was charged with conscripting slave labor for the Reich. The ss was charged with rounding up candidates for internment in concentration camps, most of whom would soon be killed. Each group was responsible for supplying its own quota of prisoners.

When the new director of the GBA assumed office, he issued the following directive: "I must ask you to exhaust all possibilities for speedily shipping the maximum number of men to the Reich; recruitment quotas are to be trebled immediately."[1] The requirements of the GBA immediately conflicted with those of the ss. Each group felt that the other was hindering the meeting of its quota. In one instance an ss general, when asked why not enough Jews in his jurisdiction had been killed, replied, "the Jews form an extraordinarily high percentage of specialists who cannot be spared because of the absence of other reserves."[2]

The Germans faced a dilemma; the Jews should be killed immediately, but their labor was indispensable to the Reich. While it may seem obvious that the needs of the GBA would override those of the ss, such was not always the case. One regional commissar pleaded that executions be postponed, citing the fact that the Jews were working as skilled laborers and specialists. He pointed out that there were no White Russian mechanics, and that the only ones available were Jews. His plea was ignored and the executions proceeded.

Vehicles loaded with ammunition for the troops fighting desperately at the front were left standing in the streets, because the Jewish drivers had been sent off to be killed. Workshops that once produced wooden carts, soap, candles, leather, and soap were left idle, because the Jews had been hauled off to the killing fields. German soldiers were freezing for lack of adequate shoes and German civilians were walking around with cardboard soles in their shoes, because the Jewish workers had been shipped off to the death camps.[3]

Such stories were repeated ad infinitum. It might be said that the victims of the mass murders, by their absence from the workplaces operating for the German Army, contributed as much to the Allied war effort as many of the soldiers who died on the battlefield.

---

1. Alan Clark, *Barbarossa: The Russian-German Conflict, 1941–1945* (London: Weidenfeld and Nicolson, 1995), 317–18.
2. Ibid., 318.
3. Nora Levin, *The Holocaust: The Destruction of European Jewry, 1933–1945* (New York: Schocken, 1973), 252–53, 257.

...murdered Jews' assets are a bigger prize than Jews themselves

When the Nazi-allied government of Hungary had its Jews deported to the death camps during the Holocaust, the confiscated assets of the victims attracted local, national, and international attention.

The first predators to be attracted to the loot were high-ranking Hungarian government officials. They skimmed the most portable and valuable property for themselves.[1] What they could not carry with them, they cached in hiding places in the Austrian countryside before the Russian army could complete its occupation of the country.[2]

Next in line were various governments. The United States was eager to get its hands on the stolen loot. The Americans wanted to turn the money over to the Jewish agencies involved in resettling the remnants of the European Jewish population who had survived the Holocaust. The American government was eager to get out from under the burden of paying most of the cost of caring for the refugees.[3]

The French government, which found itself in possession of most of the Jewish assets, was interested in using the loot to coerce the Hungarian government to return some three thousand French railroad cars that Hungary had acquired during the war. The British, while ostensibly siding with the Americans in favor of using the treasure to help resettle Jews, were quietly encouraging the French not to follow the Americans' wishes. Their purpose was to try to limit the number of Jews who might attempt to make their way to Palestine and complicate matters for the Arab-leaning English government.[4]

The Hungarian government was pushing for the return of the looted assets to their own country. While expressing their desire to assist the few surviving Jews in Hungary,[5] they really wanted the money to restart their banking system and curb the ruinous inflation that was crushing the economy.[6]

Last in line were the few surviving Hungarian Jews. In a pathetically misguided plea, they asked that the gold, jewelry, and other items of value be returned to Hungary, so that they might be compensated for their losses.[7]

In the end, the French got back their rolling stock; the Hungarians got enough treasure to restart their banking system; the British were able to measure their success by how many Jews did *not* get to Palestine; and only fifteen to twenty Hungarian Jews out of a wartime Jewish population of 800,000 received some compensation.

---

1. Ronald W. Zweig, *The Gold Train: The Destruction of the Jews and the Looting* *of Hungary* (New York: HarperCollins, 2002), 85.
2. Ibid., 115.
3. Ibid., 173.
4. Ibid., 175–76.
5. Ibid. 149.
6. Ibid., 152.
7. Ibid., 188.

...the American atomic bomb was a largely Jewish project

When Einstein's famous equation $E=mc^2$ was published, the scientific world was not long in grasping the potential residing in the atom. Scientists from many nations began to delve into the problem of releasing this enormous potential. Among these scientists was a Hungarian Jew named Leo Szilard. Szilard was employed by the prestigious Kaiser Wilhelm Institute in Germany, but he was forced to flee when the Nazis took over.

While working in England, it occurred to Szilard that, if he could "find an element which is split by neutrons and which would emit *two* neutrons when it absorbed *one* neutron, such an element, if assembled in sufficiently large mass, could sustain a nuclear chain reaction."[1]

Szilard wrote up his thesis, took out a patent on it in 1934, and promptly assigned the patent to the British Admiralty, because the only way to keep a patent secret was to assign it to the government. Curiously, neither the British War Office nor the Admiralty exhibited much interest in Szilard's findings.[2] Eventually, Szilard immigrated to the United States, where he was granted the use of laboratory facilities by Columbia University.[3]

In the meantime, other scientists were also at work on the atom. Lise Meitner, an Austrian-born Jewess and twenty-year head of the physics department at the Kaiser Wilhelm Institute for Chemistry, was working on the problem of atomic energy with Otto Hahn and Fritz Strassman. The Nazi Anschluss in Austria caused Meitner to flee Germany, first to Denmark and then to Sweden. While in Sweden in 1938, Meitner received a letter from Hahn telling her that he and Strassmann had split a uranium atom with an accompanying release of tremendous

---

1. Ronald W. Clark, *Einstein: The Life and Times* (New York: Avon Books, 1984), 603.
2. Ibid., 604.
3. Maurice Goldsmith, "Leo Szilard," *Encyclopedia Judaica*, CD-ROM *Edition* (Jerusalem: Keter, 1997).

energy. Meitner discussed the finding with her nephew Otto Frisch, a scientist in his own right. At that time Frisch was working at Neils Bohr's Copenhagen Institute. Realizing the significance of the German finding, Meitner and Frisch decided to inform Neils Bohr, then preparing for a trip to America.

Neils Bohr, a Danish-Jewish physicist and Nobel laureate, was scheduled to speak at the fifth Washington Conference on Theoretical Physics, where he described the German breakthrough. The news that Bohr was carrying would launch the scientific community into a frenzied period of experimentation to understand and harness the properties of nuclear fission.[1]

By now, Leo Szilard was settled in at Columbia University and immediately set out to duplicate the Germans' findings. Alarmed that the Germans could be so close to producing an atom bomb, Szilard and Hungarian-Jewish refugee scientist Eugene Wigner met with a Jewish refugee scientist named Albert Einstein and drafted a letter to President Roosevelt urging him to begin an American effort to become the first to have a nuclear bomb. The letter was to be presented over the signature of Einstein. At a second meeting with Einstein, Szilard was accompanied by another Jewish-Hungarian scientist, Edward Teller, who would later be credited with being the father of the hydrogen bomb.

In order to avoid bureaucratic delays, Szilard and Wigner enlisted the aid of Alexander Sachs, a Jewish economist and a confidant of Roosevelt. After several drafts, Einstein signed the letter, and Sachs made sure it went directly to Roosevelt. Thus was born the history-making Manhattan Project, culminating in the war-ending explosions at Hiroshima and Nagasaki.

1. James Gleick, *Genius: The Life and Science of Richard Feynman* (New York: Pantheon Books, 1992), 94; Daniel S. Greenberg, *The Politics of Pure Science* (Chicago: University of Chicago Press, 1999), 72; Herbert L. Anderson, "Early Days of the Chain Reaction," *Bulletin of the Atomic Scientists* 29, no. 4 (April 1973): 8–12.

...a German ally saved most of its Jews

In August of 1943, a fateful meeting was held between Germany's dictator Adolf Hitler and Bulgaria's King Boris. At this meeting, Hitler put forth two demands. One was that Bulgaria should surrender its Jewish population for deportation to the death camps. The other was that Bulgaria should honor its alliance with Germany by declaring war on Russia and sending its troops to the Eastern front to fight the Russians.

In an amazing act of courage, King Boris did not give in to Hitler's screaming tirade of accusations and threats. He would neither commit his troops to the battle, nor would he surrender his country's fifty thousand Jews to deportation.[1]

When the Iron Curtain fell over Bulgaria after the war, the Communist government claimed the credit for saving the Jews. However, when the Communists were ousted in 1989, and the truth began to filter out, it became clear that the credit goes to King Boris, who was not without allies in his lonely struggle. The Holy Synod of the Bulgarian Orthodox Church unanimously asked the Bulgarian parliament to prevent the deportation. Also adding their voices to the protest were prominent Bulgarian politicians representing *all* the branches of Bulgarian politics.

In true manifestations of Christian charity, Bulgaria's Bishop Stefan threatened to "open the doors of all Bulgarian churches to them [the Jews] and then we shall see who can drive them out."[2] Stefan's colleague Bishop Kyril of Plovdiv sent King Boris a telegram indicating he would refuse to cooperate with deportations and would actively oppose the government unless they were canceled.[3]

---

1. R. J. Crampton, *A Concise History of Bulgaria* (Cambridge, UK: Cambridge University Press, 1997), 176.
2. Christo Boyadjieff, *Saving the Bulgarian Jews in World War II* (Ottawa: Free Bulgarian Center, 1989), 125.
3. Benjamin Arditi, *Yehudei Bulgaria bi-shnot hamishtar hanatzi, 1940–1944* [Bulgarian Jewry under the Nazi regime] (Holon, 1962), 289.

Who Knew?!

HOLOCAUST: Perpetrators, Bystanders, Rescuers

In January 1943, President Roosevelt visited Casablanca for consultations with US Allies. One of his conversations was with General Auguste Nogues, a French colonial administrator who had served as governor general of Morocco. In the course of the conversation, Nogues told Roosevelt and other high-ranking American officials that "it would be a sad thing for the French to win the war merely to open the way for the Jews to control the professions and the business world of North Africa."[1]

In answer to Nogues, Roosevelt suggested that "the number of Jews engaged in the practice of the professions (law, medicine, etc.) should be definitely limited to the percentage that the Jewish population in North Africa bears to the whole of the North African population."[2] Roosevelt went on to say that "his plan would further eliminate the specific and *understandable* [italics mine] complaints which the Germans bore toward the Jews in Germany, namely, that while they represented a small part of the population, over fifty per cent of the lawyers, doctors, school teachers, college professors, etc. in Germany were Jews."[3]

1. Michael R. Marrus and Robert O. Paxton, *Vichy France and the Jews* (New York: Basic Books, 1981), 196.
2. Ibid.
3. Ibid.

...Jewish musicians helped demoralize German soldiers

As part of its propaganda effort during World War II, the Americans and British jointly operated a radio program entitled *Soldatensender West*. The program was directed primarily at the German army. It operated from 8:00 PM to 8:00 AM and broadcast music and news, which contained, as might be expected, Allied propaganda. The British provided the news, and the Americans provided the entertainment. German lyrics were provided to songs by George Gershwin, Rodgers and Hart, Irving Berlin, Kurt Weill, and Jerome Kern, among others.

Operating under the utmost secrecy, the group did not tell the artists about what the real purpose of the music was. Only performer Marlene Dietrich knew that they were working for the government propaganda machine. This work was considered so important that the copyrights to the songs were waived, so that the broadcasts might continue.

Between July of 1944 and April of 1945, the group produced 312 recordings. Among the songs produced in German translation were "I'll Get By," "My Heart Stood Still," "I Couldn't Sleep a Wink Last Night," and the haunting "Lili Marlene." As the war dragged on, more and more German soldiers became listeners, as was attested to by numerous German prisoners of war. This, of course, was the whole idea for the project.[1]

---

156   1.   Elizabeth P. McIntosh, *Sisterhood of Spies: The Women of the OSS* (New York: Dell, 1998), 71–75.

...England wouldn't let Jews fight the Nazis

In 1939 the British government issued its White Paper, Command 6019. It provided for fifteen thousand Jews to be admitted to Palestine for the next five years. After that, no Jews would be permitted to enter Palestine without full Arab approval. This meant that the Jews would always be a minority in Palestine. This action by the British prompted David Ben-Gurion to issue his famous statement "We will fight the war as though there were no White Paper and the White Paper as if there were no war."[1] To back up Ben-Gurion's words, eighty-five thousand Jewish men and fifty thousand Jewish women signed up to help the British war effort.[2]

In 1940, Chaim Weizmann and Ben-Gurion visited Colonial Secretary Lord Lloyd. Among other things discussed was the idea of two Jewish divisions for the British army. One division would be comprised of Palestinian Jews and the other of Jews from the Diaspora. Lord Lloyd turned down the offer and asked why the Jews didn't join the British army without a "Jewish" designation. Ben-Gurion asked Lloyd why he didn't ask that of the French, Poles, or Czechs, who all had separate units in the British army.[3]

By 1942, after the Germans had been stopped in North Africa, the British no longer felt so threatened that they would antagonize their Arab clients by fielding a Jewish fighting force. The oil revenues were more important, and they saw through the Zionists' plan to use this military force against the Arabs in a later conflict they felt was sure to come.[4] (Indeed, these trained soldiers *did* form the nucleus of the soon-to-be Israel Defense Forces.)

Finally, in 1944, Winston Churchill persuaded the British army to incorporate a Jewish fighting force of twenty-five thousand men. The soldiers were committed to combat, but their main contributions, ironically, came in their participation in rescue efforts of European Jews *after* the war.[5]

1. Robert St. John, *Ben-Gurion: A Biography* (New York: Doubleday, 1971), 78.
2. Ibid. 79.
3. Ibid., 84.
4. Paul Johnson, *A History of the Jews* (New York: Harper and Row, 1987), 520–21.
5. Tad Szulc, *The Secret Alliance: The Extraordinary Story of the Rescue of the Jews since World War II* (New York: Farrar, Straus and Giroux, 1991), 12, 63, 68, 77–80, 82, and more.

...Wallenberg swam the icy Danube to rescue Jews

In the pantheon of heroes who rescued Jews from the Holocaust, no name shines more brightly than Raoul Wallenberg. The Swedish diplomat is credited with saving 100,000 Jews by issuing them Swedish passports, thereby preventing their deportation to the death camps. Wallenberg's achievements in this area are well documented.

What is not so well known is a story that took place in the winter of 1944. The Germans, in an effort to save on the cost of bullets, devised a fiendish scheme to tie Jews together in threes, shoot the person in the middle, and throw the trio into the river. Wallenberg and two associates, witnessing all this one cold morning, jumped into the freezing water, untied the Jews, and swam them to shore. In all, they rescued eighty would-be victims of the Nazis.

One of the Wallenberg assistants who helped in the rescue was a Jewish woman named Agnes Adaci, a former competitive swimmer in high school, who was willing to risk her life to help others.[1] In addition to issuing passports, Wallenberg bought buildings and draped them in Swedish flags as diplomatically protected territory. He dressed Aryan-looking Jews in ss uniforms to protect these Jewish hideouts and even had the audacity to intimidate Nazi soldiers to open the doors of cattle cars to free the intended deportees.[2]

While Raoul Wallenberg was risking his life saving Jews, his cousins Jacob and Marcus Wallenberg were taking a different route. As operators of Sweden's largest commercial bank, they were instrumental in helping the Nazis dispose of gold and jewels taken from murdered Jews in the concentration camps. They also helped shield the assets of major German corporations from confiscation by Allied governments.[3]

When the Russian army entered Hungary, Raoul Wallenberg was taken into custody. For some years, he was reported to have been sighted in Russian gulags, but he was never heard from again.[4]

1. Kathleen F. Falsani, "Wallenberg Aide Shares Tale of Rescuing 80 Jews," *Chicago Sun Times* (November 12, 2004): 40.
2. George F. Will, *The Morning After: American Successes and Excesses, 1981–1986* (New York: Macmillan, 1986), 325.
3. John Loftus and Mark Aarons, *The Secret War against the Jews: How Western Espionage Betrayed the Jewish People* (New York: St. Martin's Griffin, 1994), 62.
4. Will, *The Morning After*, 325.

...Heinrich Himmler saved Jews at the end of the war

As it became obvious that Germany was going to lose World War II, high-ranking Nazis began to plan their escapes from the inevitable war crimes tribunals. Among these was Heinrich Himmler, probably the number-two or number-three man in the Nazi hierarchy. Himmler concocted a scheme whereby he could acquire sufficient funds to flee Germany and start a new life elsewhere by ransoming trainloads of Jews bound for concentration camps. Negotiations were handled by high-ranking ss officers including Adolf Eichmann, the Swedish government, the Red Cross, the Swiss government, and the World Jewish Congress.[1]

A price was set at about seven hundred Swiss francs per head. One trainload of Jews was delivered into Switzerland in August of 1944 and another in December of 1944. Deliveries then stopped, because the Nazis claimed they had received no payments. The World Jewish Congress was reluctant to release the funds pending further guarantees from the Germans. The problems were finally solved, the first five million francs were paid over by the Swiss, and a third trainload of Jews was dispatched to Switzerland.[2]

Soon after all of these events, the Third Reich fell. Eichmann escaped to Argentina until the Israelis captured him years later. Himmler shaved off his distinctive mustache and donned a private's uniform. He was, however, apprehended by the British, and in a fit of panic, bit into the poison capsule wedged between his gums and died.[3]

In a curious coincidence, the price of seven hundred Swiss francs per Jew is roughly equivalent to the forty talents paid for a slave during the Roman Empire and the two hundred Confederate dollars paid for a slave before the Civil War.[4]

---

1. Alan Clark, *Barbarossa: The Russian German Conflict 1941–1945* (London: Weidenfeld and Nicolson, 1995), 450–51.
2. Ibid., 450–51.
3. Ibid., 461.
4. Ibid., 450.

...Jewish death squads stalked Nazis

As World War II ended, the Allies realized that their main challenge in the years to come would be the Soviet Union. They also viewed West Germany as a crucial element in containing communist expansionism. As a result, the search for and will to prosecute Nazis began to wane.[1] This angered the Jews, who wanted some measure of justice to be meted out to those who had participated in the Holocaust.

At the end of the war, some members of the Jewish Brigade (a group of Jewish soldiers from then Palestine who enlisted to fight for England but were not committed to battle until 1944), some Holocaust survivors, and several officers of the Haganah (a Jewish defense group in Palestine which was ultimately to become the Israel Defense Forces) formed themselves into a group called *Nokmim* (Avengers). They wore British army uniforms and used British military documentation, equipment, and vehicles, although they were operating independently and did not have official British sanction for their actions. Operating in Italy, Austria, and Germany, they hunted down and systematically killed several hundred Gestapo, ss, and other Nazi officials.[2]

After the postwar Nuremberg trials and the subsequent dying down of the punishment of Nazi war criminals, the issue was revived with the Israeli capture of Adolf Eichmann, chief administrator of the Holocaust.

During Eichmann's pretrial incarceration and during the trial, he received mail from many people. Many of those anonymous letters urged Eichmann to commit suicide, and some even included razor blades. Because he knew too much, ex-Nazis were afraid he might expose them. Some of these former Nazis managed to gain entry into Israel, and a few even got in to see the trial!

While all this was going on, Shin Bet, the Israeli internal security service, was busy uncovering the true identities of these seemingly innocuous visitors. Soon there began to appear in the Israeli newspapers accounts of "automobile accidents" involving the deaths of foreign nationals. Nobody seemed to think that these deaths were anything but highway accidents.[3]

1. John Loftus and Mark Aarons, *The Secret War against the Jews: How Western Espionage Betrayed the Jewish People* (New York: St. Martin's Griffin, 1994), 131.
2. Ian Black and Benny Morris, *Israel's Secret Wars: A History of Israel's Intelligence Services* (New York: Grove Weidenfeld, 1991), 188.
3. Howard M. Sachar, *Israel and Europe: An Appraisal in History* (New York: Random House, 1998), 125.

A second group also calling itself the Avengers came into being at the end of the war. It was led by Abba Kovner, a charismatic ghetto denizen, sewer rat, and resistance fighter. Having spent the war years sneaking in and out of the Warsaw ghetto and marauding across the Russian countryside, disrupting German lines of communication and supply, Kovner was just getting started.

Kovner's plan was for his group to hunt down and kill Germans without regard to age, sex, or any other criteria. The plan was to become familiar with the sewer systems of five German cities, shut off certain valves, release poison gas into the system, and have death flow from every faucet.[1]

However, from the outset, Kovner began to experience difficulties. Having successfully reached Palestine (soon to be Israel) he found that the people were more interested in getting the United Nations to vote for the establishment of a Jewish state. Indiscriminate killing of Germans would hurt the Jewish cause in world public opinion. He was arrested and incarcerated in a jail in Cairo.[2]

Upon his release, Kovner received an audience with Chaim Weizmann, one of the preeminent architects of the Jewish state and its first president. Weizmann was so moved by Kovner's story that he wrote out a letter of introduction to a chemist who could help further Kovner's plan. Nevertheless, Abba Kovner realized that his plan for poisoning the sewers would never come off, and he switched to an alternative plan. His group would infiltrate the bakery at Stalag 13, an American POW camp near Nuremberg where German prisoners were being held, and poison the bread. This plan succeeded and over two thousand Germans were sickened or died.[3] However, Kovner was finally convinced that his best course of action was to move to Israel and fight in the war that was sure to come. He convinced some of the other Avengers to join him in going to Israel, where they fought in the army, married, and raised families.

The time for vengeance had passed and the time for nation building had arrived.

---

1. Rich Cohen, *The Avengers* (New York: Random House, 2000), 203.
2. Ibid., 203.
3. Ibid., 201, 212. Exact figures about the number of casualties are difficult to obtain, since officials kept information under wraps to avoid inciting panic after the incident. Local news accounts at the time indicate that none of the sickened prisoners died, but the Avengers claimed that as many as seven or eight hundred were paralyzed or died due to the poisoning. Jonathan B. Tucker, *Toxic Terror: Assessing Terrorist Use of Chemical and Biological Weapons* (Cambridge, MA: MIT Press, 2001), 36.

...non-Jewish GIs attended Yom Kippur services

A few days after the war in Europe ended, three hundred German prisoners of war were assembled in a large public area to hear a pep talk from one of their officers. This officer asked permission from General Huebner, the officer in charge, if he might give his men a "*Sieg Heil*" and a "*Heil Hitler*." The general declined the request.

As soon as the German officer concluded his speech, General Huebner announced to the five hundred assembled American soldiers from the Big Red One, the American First Division, that Yom Kippur services would be held immediately in the cathedral across the field. As the Jewish GIs began to file toward the cathedral, the gentile sergeant of one of the Jewish soldiers turned around and began to walk to the cathedral. He was followed by virtually all the American soldiers present.

The German POWs certainly couldn't believe that they were seeing an all-Jewish outfit. What they *were* seeing was "a bold message to Nazi anti-Semites and an extraordinary demonstration of American solidarity with Jews."[1]

---

1. Deborah Dash Moore, *GI Jews: How World War II Changed a Generation* (Cambridge, MA: Harvard University Press, 2004), 242–44.

...kosher is not always kosher

Following the end of World War II, Jewish organizations were engaged in massive efforts at ameliorating the physical conditions of refugees, finding them places for resettlement, and transporting them to safe destinations. Feeding the refugees, of course, was a monumental task, and Jewish relief agencies were heavily involved in the work. To make sure that the food for the refugees was prepared according to the laws of keeping kosher, the Mizrachi, a religious Zionist group, was engaged to oversee the preparation of food in a camp outside of Prague in Czechoslovakia.

All went well until a group of ultra-Orthodox rabbis and their followers arrived in the camp. Seeing that the Mizrachi was in charge of the kitchen, they threatened to "tear the place down if we didn't get those 'Reform Jews' out of the kitchen."[1] They insisted on setting up a "glatt kosher" kitchen to feed their members. "Glatt" kosher, derived from the Hebrew word *glatt*, meaning "smooth" (indicating that the lungs of kosher-slaughtered animals have been carefully inspected to ensure that they are unquestionably kosher, free from any blemish that could indicate the animal had been ill) is a system of food preparation that requires the most meticulous care. Those who are exacting in their observance of Jewish dietary laws only entrust food preparation to people who they are confident share their level of religious concern.

Thus we find that the Jewish organizations, attempting to rescue and resettle Jewish refugees from war-torn Europe, were beset with solving factional disputes between contending groups of Jews within their jurisdictions. The most remarkable thing is that they did![2]

---

1. Tad Szulc, *The Secret Alliance: The Extraordinary Story of the Rescue of the Jews since World War II*. (New York: Farrar, Straus and Giroux, 1991), 162.
2. Ibid., 161–62.

...the Jews meant more to the German leader than to the American

After World War II, the West German Bundesrepublik began its road to recovery. Helped by the Marshall Plan, West Germany rapidly regained much of its economic strength. About this time, the victor nations began to speak of reparations from Germany for waging an aggressive war. East Germany, under Soviet domination, would not cooperate, so all attention focused on West Germany. The State of Israel put forth its claim to reparations due the Jewish people from all over Europe.[1]

German Chancellor Adenauer took a special interest in the question of reparations for Israel and individual Jewish survivors or their heirs and gave them priority over other claimants. Without undue haggling over amounts or arguments over methods of payment, a figure of one billion dollars for the State of Israel and half a billion for individuals was agreed to by Germany and Israel.[2]

During the Suez crisis of 1956, President Eisenhower invoked sanctions against England, France, and Israel. As part of the sanctions, Eisenhower demanded that Germany cease its reparations payments to Israel. Adenauer refused, saying that the reparations were not subject to political issues.[3]

An interesting sidelight to this story of Conrad Adenauer's friendly overtures to Israel dates back to prewar Germany. After 1933, the Nazis drove Adenauer from his position as mayor of Cologne. Reduced to poverty, Adenauer had to rely on dollar remittances from two Jewish friends, Otto Kraus and Daniel Heinemann, who had emigrated from Germany to the United States.[4]

---

1. Howard M. Sachar, *Israel and Europe: An Appraisal in History* (New York: Random House, 1996), 41.
2. Ibid., 45.
3. Ibid., 52.
4. Ibid., 37.

...Jews laundered money for the cardinal

In postwar Europe, two of the organizations helping resettle Jewish survivors of the Holocaust were the Mossad and Brichah. In order to finance their activities, they were given money by the Joint Distribution Committee. This money was used to buy local currency purchased at the legal exchange rate. Eventually, one of their members suggested using dollars instead in order to lessen the expense.

Once a month, a courier traveled to Switzerland from Budapest or Prague to smuggle in three or four hundred thousand dollars to pay for maintaining the displaced Jews in their care in Czechoslovakia, Hungary, Romania, and Austria. Since the smuggling was risky, they turned to the head of the Roman Catholic Church in Hungary, Cardinal Mindszenty. The cardinal gave the Brichah the money in pengos (local Hungarian currency) and the Brichah deposited the dollars in the Church's Swiss bank account less a 15 percent commission.

This enabled the Church to get their money out of Hungary before the Communist government could confiscate it and the Brichah to have the local currency to finance their operations. Thus it was that a cardinal laundered Church money using Jewish relief organizations as a conduit.[1]

HOLOCAUST: Perpetrators, Bystanders, Rescuers

---

1. Tad Szulc, *The Secret Alliance: The Extraordinary Story of the Rescue of the Jews since World War II* (New York: Farrar, Straus and Giroux, 1991), 135.

...anniversary flowers sealed Adolf Eichmann's fate

After the defeat of Nazi Germany in World War II, many Nazi war criminals went into hiding. Among these was Adolf Eichmann, the person in charge of the systematic annihilation of six million Jews. Eichmann's first hideout was a German farm. From there he was smuggled out to Italy and then to Argentina, where he assumed the name of Ricardo Klement.

After two years, Eichmann sent for his family. His small children had been told that their father was dead. When the family arrived in Argentina, they met "Uncle Ricardo," who subsequently "married" their mother.

When the State of Israel was founded in 1948, one of the agencies the new country established was the Mossad, an overseas network of agents assigned to carry out clandestine operations. One of their functions in the late 1950s was the search for escaped Nazis. A break in the Eichmann case came when an Austrian newspaper carried an obituary for Eichmann's father; among the mourners listed was "Vera Eichmann, née Leibl." She was still using her original married name![1]

Then a tip in the form of a postcard from Argentina came from an associate of Nazi-hunter Simon Weisenthal: "I saw that dirty pig Eichmann." It was now evident that Eichmann was in Buenos Aires, Argentina.

Then another bit of information surfaced. Lothar Hermann, a Jewish former inmate of Dachau concentration camp, had settled in Argentina, and incredibly, his daughter Sylvia became romantically involved with Klaus Klement, Eichmann's son. Soon she informed her father that Klaus had boasted of his father's Nazi party membership and participation in the Holocaust. Her father then sent her on a fact-finding mission. Sylvia knocked at the door of the Klement home asking for Klaus. The man who answered the door informed her that Klaus was not home. She then inquired whether Klement (Eichmann) was his father. The answer was affirmative. When she told her father what she had learned, Hermann informed West German authorities, who contacted the Israelis.[2] Agents from the Mossad quickly located the "Klement" home and put it under surveillance.

A telephoto snapshot of Ricardo was taken and sent to Israel for comparison. It seemed to be a good likeness. The agents, however, did not make their move but continued their surveillance. Several weeks later, their patience was rewarded. On March 21, Ricardo was observed coming home carrying a bouquet of flowers. Ordinarily, this gesture would have had little significance. However, the Mossad knew that the Eichmanns had been married in Austria on March 21, 1935. They had their man!

---

1. Howard M. Sachar, *Israel and Europe: An Appraisal in History* (New York: Random House, 1998) 120–21.
2. Zvi Aharoni and Wilhelm Dietl, *Operation Eichmann: The Truth about the Pursuit, Capture and Trial* (Hoboken, NJ: John Wiley and Sons, 1997), 82.

Who Knew?!

AMERICA:
Finding a Home and Contributing

...Yuchi Indians celebrated the Feast of Tabernacles (Sukkot)

In his scholarly work entitled *Before Columbus: Links between the Old World and Ancient America*, Professor Cyrus H. Gordon presents a convincing case for there having been extensive interaction between Europe and America long before Columbus's arrival. Citing archeological, artistic, cultural, and linguistic evidence, Professor Gordon documents a great deal of contact between Europe and America dating back more than a thousand years.

With this introduction in mind, we visit the Yuchi Indians of Georgia and more recently of Oklahoma. One of the Yuchi Indians' agricultural festivals is highly reminiscent of the Jewish Feast of Tabernacles as described in Leviticus 23.

Professor Gordon describes the similarities between the Yuchis' festival and Sukkot: "The Yuchis celebrate (1) an eight-day festival (2) that starts on the fifteenth day (or full moon) of the holy harvest month; throughout the holiday they (3) live in 'booths.'"[1]

Is this a coincidence or is there a true historical link?

---

1. Cyrus H. Gordon, *Before Columbus: Links between the Old World and Ancient America* (New York: Crown Publishers, 1971), 89.

...Puritans relived the Israelite experience

When the Puritans came to America, they brought with them their great attachment to the Hebrew Bible. They were noted for giving their children Pentateuchal names like Daniel, Jonathan, Rachel, Esther, Ezra, and Enoch. Towns were routinely given names like Canaan, Zion, Hebron, Jericho, Shiloh, Gilead, and Eden. However, the Puritans' attachment to Israelites and the Hebrew Bible went far deeper.

King James I was their Pharaoh and England was their house of bondage. Crossing the Atlantic Ocean was crossing the Red Sea and America was the New Canaan.[1] When it came time to establish laws for the colonies, the Mosaic Law was adopted in the Connecticut Code of 1650. While half the statutes in the Code of 1655 for the colony of New Haven contain references to the Hebrew Bible, only 3 percent refer to the latter part of the Christian Bible.[2] During the battle for independence, the Puritans saw the British as Amalekites and Philistines.[3]

Washington and Adams were Moses and Joshua,[4] to whom others were likened as well. Prominent New England Puritan minister John Cotton, who expended great effort in defending the government's right to enforce religious rules, has the following inscription on his tombstone:

> But let his mourning flock be comforted,
> Though Moses be, yet Joshua is not dead;
> I mean renowned Norton; worthy he
> Successor to our Moses is to be,
> O happy Israel in America,
> In such a Moses, such a Joshua.[5]

And in exhorting his Puritan flock to obey the laws of God, John Winthrop stated, "If wee keep this covenant, wee shall finde that the God of Israell is among us, but if wee deal falsely with our God...wee are consumed out of the good land wither wee are goeing."[6]

So overt were the Puritans in modeling their lives on the story of the Israelites that a man named Peter Folger was moved to write,

> New England they are like the Jews
> As like, as like can be.[7]

1. Dagobert D. Runes, ed., *The Hebrew Impact on Western Civilization* (New York: Philosophical Library, 1951), 16.
2. Ibid..
3. Ibid., 13.
4. Ibid., 16.
5. Ibid., 17.
6. Ibid., 15.
7. Ibid.

...a doctor healed the colony and the Jews could stay

In 1733 the *William and Sarah* set sail from England bound for the colony of Georgia in America. Aboard were forty-two Jews, most of them refugees from the Portuguese Inquisition. One of these Jews was Dr. Nunez-Ribeiro, formerly a physician at the Portuguese court.

When the ship arrived in what is now Savannah, Georgia, the newcomers found that a yellow fever epidemic was raging in the colony. When the colonists learned that there was a Jewish physician among the newcomers, the doctor was pressed into service. The epidemic was quelled and the colony was saved.

James Oglethorpe, the head of the colony, suggested to the colonial directors that the usual Jewish disabilities to settlement be waived. All the Jews were admitted, and they were granted full rights as citizens of the colony. Families of the original settlers continue to live in Savannah to this day.[1]

---

1. Aaron Lichtenstein, "Nunez-Rubiero," *Encyclopedia Judaica*, CD-ROM *Edition* (Jerusalem: Keter, 1997).

...a Revolutionary War pirate was president of his synagogue

Isaac Moses was an immigrant who fled persecution of Jews in Germany in 1764. He succeeded in almost every commercial endeavor in which he was involved. During the Revolutionary War, Moses, unlike many other men of means, threw in his lot with the patriot cause. At that time, Robert Morris was in charge of financing the Continental Congress. Moses helped finance the French army fighting for the colonies and was one of the underwriters for a proposed bank to establish the necessary credits for carrying on the war. Moses also crossed paths with another famous Jewish fund-raising patriot, Haym Solomon.

In addition to his other enterprises, Moses was outright owner or partner with Robert Morris in eight ships. As the war dragged on, it became obvious to the Continental Congress that the fight must be waged on the sea as well as on land. In order to disrupt British shipping, Moses put his ships into the fray as pirates against the British. We do not know how many ships Moses' little flotilla captured, but we do know that the British had about seven hundred of their ships taken at a loss of some eighteen million dollars. This caused the English merchants to pressure their government to end the war.

Besides giving assistance to the fledgling United States government, Isaac Moses was also involved in Jewish affairs. While he was on the run from the British, he helped found the Mikveh Israel Synagogue in New York and served as its president. When he returned to Philadelphia, he also served as *parnass* (president) of the famous Shearith Yisrael Synagogue in Philadelphia, probably the only pirate in Jewish history to claim the title of president of two synagogues.[1]

---

1. Harry Simonhoff, *Jewish Notables in America, 1776–1865: Links of an Endless Chain* (New York: Greenberg, 1956), 121–24.

...a Jew helped the American revolutionaries defeat the British

Haym Salomon was a Polish-Jewish immigrant who had many linguistic and financial talents. Although coming from a largely Yiddish-speaking background, he was somehow able to acquire a knowledge of French, German, Dutch, Russian, Italian, and Polish. He made his success in Colonial America as a merchant, and when the Revolutionary War started, he joined a patriotic group called the Sons of Liberty and was soon arrested by the British. He was released when the British found out he could act as an interpreter for the German-speaking Hessian mercenaries fighting in the British army.

This did not last long, because some of the Hessians began to desert the army, and suspicion was centered on Salomon. He was tried and sentenced to be executed, but was apparently rescued by the Minutemen and fled to Philadelphia.

There he became a broker to the Continental Congress and is best remembered as having been instrumental in raising money to keep Washington's army well supplied in the field.

During this time in Philadelphia, a young man serving in Congress was hard pressed for expense money and confided his needs to a colleague. The colleague told him of "a certain Haym Salomon on Front Street who often helped out a fellow in distress."[1]

The delegate to the Continental Congress wrote home saying, "I have been for some time a pensioner of Haym Solomon, a Jew broker." He later wrote a letter to John Randolph expressing "his annoyance at the Jew moneylender who refused to take interest."[2]

The needy letter writer was James Madison, destined to become the fourth president of the United States.

---

1. Harry Simonhoff, *Jewish Notables in America, 1776–1865: Links of an Endless Chain* (New York: Greenberg, 1956), 23.
2. Ibid.

...a famous quote of George Washington's came from a rabbi

As George Washington was approaching his inauguration as the first president of the United States, representatives of various minority groups took a keen interest. At the time, each colony had an established church, and Jews, Catholics, and dissenting Protestants did not enjoy equal rights.

When the Jews representing six synagogues got together to draft a congratulatory message to Washington, there was a disagreement between New York and Rhode Island, and Rabbi Moses Mendes Seixas decided to write his own letter representing the Newport Congregation. The Seixas letter reads in part,

> Deprived as we hitherto have been of the invaluable rights of free citizens, we now – with a deep sense of gratitude to the Almighty Disposer of all events – behold a government erected by the majesty of the people – a government which to bigotry gives no sanction, to persecution no assistance, but generously affording to all liberty of conscience and immunities of citizenship, deeming every one of whatever nation, tongue or language, equal parts of the great governmental machine.[1]

Washington replied to the letter:

> It is now no more that toleration is spoken of as if it were by the indulgence of one class of people that another enjoyed the exercise of their inherent natural rights, for, happily, the Government of the United States, *which gives to bigotry no sanction, to persecution no assistance*, requires only that they who live under its protection should demean themselves as good citizens in giving it on all occasions their effectual support.[2] [Italics added]

It is significant to note that Washington, in his reply, chose to incorporate Seixas's phrase "which gives to bigotry no sanction, to persecution no assistance." This phrase can be found in *Bartlett's Familiar Quotations* under the heading of quotations of George Washington, labeled "Letter to the Jewish Congregation of Newport, Rhode Island."[3]

---

1. Harry Simonhoff, *Jewish Notables in America, 1776–1865: Links of an Endless Chain* (New York: Greenberg, 1956), 72–73.
2. Ibid., 73.
3. John Bartlett and Justin Kaplan, *Bartlett's Familiar Quotations* (New York: Little, Brown, 1992), 337.

...Benjamin Franklin donated to a synagogue building fund

Benjamin Franklin was raised as a Christian and believed in God, but he did not wish to subscribe to any particular denomination. Offended by the "intolerant orthodoxy"[1] of Boston, he moved to Philadelphia, where people of diverse religions could live in harmony. Tolerance was the cornerstone of Franklin's ideology, and he promulgated the concept his entire life. As he so aptly put it, "I think vital religion has always suffered when orthodoxy is more regarded than virtue."[2]

In an era when whole colonies were organized on religious grounds, Franklin is recorded as having donated money to every denomination represented in Philadelphia, including Congregation Mikveh Israel. He also contributed to the building of a meeting hall in Philadelphia "expressly for the use of any preacher of any religious persuasion who might desire to say something."[3]

During the Fourth of July celebration in 1788, Franklin was too ill to leave his bed, but he arranged for the parade to pass under his bedroom window, and as he had stipulated, "the clergy of different Christian denominations, with the rabbi of the Jews, walked arm in arm."[4] At his death, all the clergymen of every faith in the city accompanied his casket to his grave.

AMERICA: Finding a Home and Contributing

---

1. Walter Isaacson, "Citizen Ben's 7 Great Virtues," *Time* (July 7, 2003): 40–53.
2. Ibid.
3. Ibid.
4. Ibid.

175

...obeying a biblical law saved the life of a slave owner

Abraham Moise was a successful Jewish planter on the Island of Santo Domingo. Mindful of the biblical injunctions that masters were supposed to treat their slaves kindly, Moise's treatment of his slaves was far better than was the norm for the island.[1]

In 1791 there was a bloody slave uprising. The Moise family was awakened in the middle of the night by the ringleader of the slave uprising and hustled off to a departing ship in the harbor. This same slave leader later took his master's last name and became known as the distinguished General Moise. His leadership resulted in the establishment of the "Negro Republic" of Haiti.[2]

Abraham Moise's kindly treatment of his slaves undoubtedly saved him from the grisly fate of many of the other slaveholders on the island. He reached South Carolina safely and began life anew.

---

1. Rabbi Dr. Joseph H. Hertz, *The Pentateuch and Haftorahs* (London: Soncino Press, 1952), 207, 306, 396, 537, 767, 813, 872, 924.
2. Harry Simonhoff, *Jewish Notables in America, 1776–1865: Links of an Endless Chain* (New York: Greenberg, 1956), 251–52.

...a Jewish naval officer tried NOT to shoot his enemy in a duel

In 1816 Jewish naval officer Uriah Levy was attending a ball. A fellow officer, Lieutenant William Potter, apparently seeking to provoke a fight, deliberately bumped into Levy three times. Levy slapped Lieutenant Potter. Enraged, Potter called Levy a "damned Jew." Levy responded, "That I am a Jew, I neither deny nor regret." The next day Levy received a written challenge from Potter.

Levy, an expert marksman, arrived at the appointed place and attempted to persuade Potter to call off the duel. Potter called Levy a coward, and Levy in turn called Potter a fool. They paced off twenty steps and Potter turned and fired. He missed and Levy fired into the air. Three more times Potter fired and three more times Levy fired into the air. On the fifth shot, Potter nicked Levy's ear. Potter then began to reload, shouting, "I mean to have his life." This time Levy fired his pistol at Potter, killing him instantly.[1]

---

1. Donovan Fitzpatrick and Saul Saphire, *Navy Maverick: Uriah Phillips Levy* (New York: Doubleday, 1963), 65.

...the navy hated the sailor but presidents loved him

Uriah Phillips Levy suffered six navy courts martial, yet achieved the highest rank possible. Uriah Levy was a committed Jew and a dedicated sailor who stood up for himself in all circumstances.

In 1817 Uriah Levy fought with a marine who called him a damned Jew. Both were court-martialed and reprimanded by the navy. Nevertheless, in that same year President Monroe signed Levy's commission as a navy lieutenant, only the second Jew to be so honored.[1]

In 1818, while serving aboard the uss *United States*, Levy was court-martialed for a petty offense and was sentenced to be dismissed from the service. President Monroe ordered the decision reversed.[2]

In 1819 Levy was court-martialed for rebuking a fellow officer in offensive language. He was sentenced to be dismissed from the navy, but President Monroe again reversed the decision.[3]

Levy was revolted by the inhumane naval punishment of flogging and abolished the practice aboard his ship. For this offense, in 1844 he was court-martialed and sentenced to be dismissed from the service. President Tyler reduced his sentence to a one-year suspension. While the suspension was running, Tyler promoted Levy to the rank of captain.[4] Congress abolished the practice of flogging in 1850.[5]

In 1855, a group of naval officers, charged with eliminating some officers from the navy, included Levy on their list. So thorough was Levy's defense of his record that the decision was reversed, much to the embarrassment of the navy.[6]

In February of 1860, President Buchanan gave Levy command of the Mediterranean fleet and raised him to the rank of commodore, the highest rank in the navy. Levy retired from the navy in July of 1860, but President Lincoln, in an act of extreme irony, appointed Levy to be president of the navy court-martial board.[7]

---

1. Donovan Fitzpatrick and Saul Saphire, *Navy Maverick: Uriah Phillips Levy* (New York: Doubleday, 1963), 70.
2. Ibid., 89.
3. Ibid., 97.
4. Ibid., 173.
5. Sol Scharfstein, *Jewish History and You* (Jersey City, NJ: Ktav, 2003), 77.
6. Fitzpatrick and Saphire, *Navy Maverick*, 209.
7. Ibid., 244.

...Chapman Levy helped Andrew Jackson crush nullification

When South Carolina in 1832 promulgated its theory of nullification of any laws of the United States government it deemed unfit, not everybody in the state agreed. Among those dissenters was Chapman Levy, a Jewish resident of Camden, South Carolina.

The first thing Levy did was to arrange for the printing and dissemination of President Jackson's *Proclamation Regarding Nullification.* Since his cohorts did not supply enough of the money for the printing, Levy paid the balance himself. The next task that Levy undertook was the organization of meetings to publicize the resistance to nullification.[1]

In later correspondence, President Jackson himself expressed his personal appreciation of the efforts Chapman Levy had exerted on behalf of Jackson and the nation.

---

1. Joseph L. Blau and Salo W. Baron, eds., *The Jews of the United States, 1790–1840: A Documentary History* (New York: Columbia University Press, 1963), 376–80.

...a Jewish family's good deeds were as important as Gettysburg

Joseph Seligman was a German-Jewish immigrant who came to America in 1837. As he was attempting to get started in business in Selma, Alabama, Seligman was involved in an altercation in which a man was killed. Seligman's trial was not going well, and it looked like he was about to get a long prison sentence. However, a fifteen-year-old lad who had witnessed the event came forward and offered testimony that exonerated Seligman. Joseph Seligman and other family members went on to become successful bankers.[1]

Following the Civil War, the State of Alabama, sorely in need of funds, sent one of its state supreme court justices to New York's financial district seeking loans for his state. Anti-South sentiment was still running high, and the judge was having no luck at all – until he met with Joseph Seligman, now a New York banker. Recognizing the man as the boy who had come to his rescue so many years before, Seligman immediately granted the loan that his benefactor so richly deserved.

While Seligman was willing to help the State of Alabama *after* the war, his sentiments were strongly in favor of the Union *during* the war. When the Civil War came, Joseph Seligman and another Jewish banker, August Belmont, went to work to help the Union cause financially. Belmont went to England in 1861 and urged the bankers to support the ethical principles of the Lincoln administration. He was also successful in putting pressure on the banking houses in France, England, Germany, and Holland not to help the South even if they were not inclined to help the North.

Seligman, for his part, toured Europe and sold more than two hundred million dollars in United States securities, mostly in Germany and Holland, where Seligman was fluent in the languages. This was such a significant sum that historian W.E. Dodd expressed the opinion that Seligman's effort with the bonds was worth as much as the Battle of Gettysburg.[2]

What made the feat of these Jewish bankers more remarkable was the fact that the European upper classes, those most likely to have money to invest, were generally in favor of the South gaining its independence.

Good deeds were not limited to the American branch of the Seligman family. After the death of President Lincoln, his wife Mary Todd

---

1. Harry Simonhoff, *Jewish Participants in the Civil War* (New York: Arco, 1963), 84–85.
2. Ibid.

Lincoln began to suffer from delusions. Although she was provided for in Lincoln's will, she imagined herself to be in need of money, and she went so far as to sell her clothes.

Unable to recover from her grief, she moved to England with her son Tad. It was there that she was found by Henry Seligman, who was in Frankfurt as head of the family banking business. Seeing that Mrs. Lincoln was living in poverty and that her son was ill, Henry Seligman wrote letters to several senators and his brother Joseph used his influence with Congress and with President Grant. Soon Mrs. Lincoln was awarded an annual pension of three thousand dollars, later raised to five thousand.

This family of immigrant Jews certainly made significant contributions to their adopted country.

AMERICA: Finding a Home and Contributing

...an anonymous Jewish donation helped shorten the Civil War

In 1863, US intelligence services learned that the British government was building two ironclad ships for the Confederacy to use against the Union blockade, which was preventing the South from selling its cotton for badly needed cash to help fund the war.

Because the metal ironclads would be so hard to sink, the Union feared that they would be able to open gaps in the blockade to permit Confederate ships to resume their trade with England. The British, for their part, were anxious to receive the cotton, so that they could reopen their shuttered textile mills and put their people back to work. The French were also desirous of seeing the blockade fail, so that they could pursue their own commercial interests with the South.

When the American government raised the issue with the British, the latter denied that the ships were for the Confederacy and demanded to see definitive proof of the allegations that they were helping the South. They further demanded that the witnesses against the Crown be made available for cross-examination and that the United States Government post a five-million-dollar deposit in gold coin to indemnify the British of any losses incurred by them due to the delay.

Since the American ambassador had no authorization to post such a bond, and since the sailing date of the ironclads was imminent, the cause appeared to be lost. At this point, a Jewish banker came forward with a no-conditions-attached offer to put up the money with the proviso that his name was never to be revealed. Questioned as to why he would make such a magnanimous gesture, he replied that it was in gratitude for the US government's granting of full citizenship to Jews, and it was his way of repaying the kindness. The offer was accepted, the Confederacy never received the ships, and the South was beaten into submission much more rapidly than if they had been able to market their cotton to pay for the war.

The story was known only to a few people until 1890, when it was published in *Recollections of President Lincoln and His Administration*, written by L.E. Crittendon, a former official in the Lincoln administration. Other people corroborated the story, but the name of the benefactor was never revealed.[1]

---

1. Harry Simonhoff, *Jewish Participants in the Civil War* (New York: Arco, 1963), 47–52.

...Yale University's emblem and motto are Jewish in origin

The official emblem of Yale University depicts an open Bible on whose pages are the Hebrew words *urim v'tumim*. Below the Bible is the Latin phrase *Lux et veritas*.[1]

In ancient times, the high priest (Kohen Gadol*)* of the Israelites wore on his outer garment a breastplate (ephod*)*. Mounted on the breastplate were twelve precious stones, one for each of the twelve tribes descended from the patriarch Jacob. In times of stress or momentous events, the king or the prophet would go to the high priest to view the stones on the breastplate in order to ascertain God's will in the matter at hand.[2]

When the elders of Yale University were seeking an emblem that would best exemplify the purpose of their university, they decided on an image of the open Bible with the words *urim v'tumim*. Knowing that many people did not have a knowledge of Hebrew, they added the Latin translation of *urim v'tumim*, "light and truth,"[3] which is really the goal of any institution of higher learning.

---

1. For an image and discussion of the emblem, see http://www.yale.cdu/emeritus/yale shield.html.
2. Yehoshua M. Grintz, "Ephod"; also "Oracle," *Encyclopedia Judaica*, CD-ROM *Edition* (Jerusalem: Keter, 1977).
3. Dagobert D. Runes, ed., *The Hebrew Impact on Western Civilization* (New York: Philosophical Library, 1951), 24.

...a soldier's heroism spawned a word

In the late 1800s, Galveston rabbi Henry Cohen was puzzled by the word *fronthall*, which he had often heard in reference to a person of unusual courage. He investigated and found that the word described a Jewish Confederate soldier named Max Frankenthal. Enlisted as a drummer boy, Frankenthal fought in many battles, the most memorable being the one known as the Bloody Acute Angle.

In 1893 Colonel A.T. Watts, a participant in the battle, wrote a description of the battle in a letter to the Galveston *Daily News*. After describing the battle, Colonel Watts, by this time a prominent judge, ended his letter with the following:

> In conclusion, I cannot forego the mention of one individual, Fronthall, a little Jew, though insignificant in appearance, had the heart of a lion. For several hours he stood at the immediate point of contact, amid the most terrific hail of lead, and coolly and deliberately loaded and fired without cringing. After observing his unflinching bravery and constancy, the thought occurred to the writer – I now understood how it was that a handful of Jews could drive before them the hundred kings; they were all Fronthalls![1]

Thus, a word, albeit a short-lived one, was born.

1. Harry Simonhoff, *Jewish Participants in the Civil War* (New York: Arco,1963), 263–64.

...a Jewish woman ran a Jewish school using a Christian Bible

In the mid 1800s, Rebecca Gratz spent her life doing good deeds for others. When she noticed that Jewish children had little or no opportunity to learn about their faith, she became concerned. Impressed by the Christian Sunday schools, Rebecca decided to start a Jewish Sunday school. Since the only Bible in print at that time was the King James Version, Rebecca taped over the portions she did not want the children to read. Much of the early text materials were also Christian in nature. Nevertheless, the school was a success and served as a prototype for similar Jewish schools on the east coast of the United States.[1]

It is widely believed that the heroine of Sir Walter Scott's famous novel *Ivanhoe* was modeled after Rebecca Gratz. Scott's novel tells of a Jewish maiden who refused to marry out of her faith. How did Scott in England get to know Rebecca Gratz? When Washington Irving's fiancée Matilda Hoffman was ill, it was Rebecca who nursed her back to health. On a subsequent trip to England, Irving recounted the story to his friend Sir Walter Scott. Scott was so impressed with the narrative about Rebecca Gratz that he made her the heroine of his book. In later correspondence with Irving, Scott is alleged to have written, "How do you like your Rebecca? Does the Rebecca I have pictured compare well with the pattern given?"[2]

Although Rebecca Gratz raised her sister's nine orphaned children, she herself never married. Another persisting legend is that she did indeed fall in love with a non-Jew named Ewing. Ewing was the lawyer son of a prominent Christian clergyman. The story goes that he proposed marriage to Rebecca, but she refused to marry out of her faith. He eventually married someone else, but he died at the age of thirty-nine.[3]

Rebecca lived to the age of eighty-eight and contributed to the formation and operation of important Jewish social service and educational institutions in Philadelphia.

---

1. Elinor Slater and Robert Slater, *Great Jewish Women* (New York: Jonathan David, 1994), 113.
2. Ibid., 113–14.
3. Ibid., 112–13.

...the pants were Levi's

In 1850, Levi Strauss came to California during the gold rush. He didn't intend to mine for gold, but he did hope to mine a few dollars from the miners by selling rough cloth for tents and wagon covers. When some of the miners told Strauss that they were in need of pants that could withstand incredibly hard wear, Strauss came up with the idea of sewing the tent material into pants. The pants were strong enough, but the rough material tended to chafe the miners' skin. Strauss then substituted a softer but still tough material called *serge de Nimes* (twill fabric from the French city of Nimes), which came to be known as *denim*. As the miners began to notice the durable pants some other miners were wearing, they would ask, "Whose pants are these?" The reply would be, "These are Levi's," and thus a name was born.[1]

---

1. Milton Moskowitz, *Everybody's Business: An Almanac; An Irreverent Guide to Corporate America* (New York: Harper and Row, 1980), 153; Mary Bellis, "Levi Strauss: The History of Blue Jeans," http://inventors.about.com/od/sstartinventors/a/Levi_Strauss.htm.

...a Jew rode with abolitionist John Brown

When he was fifteen years old, Anshel Bondi, a Viennese Jew, joined an unsuccessful effort to free Hungary from Austrian rule. His family fled to America and settled in Saint Louis, Missouri. Anshel enlisted in a revolutionary movement to free Cuba from Spanish rule, but that plan never materialized. Eventually he got a job as a store clerk in St. Louis but moved to Kansas when his employer decided to open a store there.

At that time, Kansas was the scene of violence between pro-slavery and anti-slavery forces, with Southern sympathizers leading the way. To assist the anti-slavery forces, abolitionist John Brown came to Kansas and soon Anshel (now August) Bondi and his employer Theodore Weiner joined his band, and for the next two years rode with him on his escapades.

When the Civil War came, Bondi joined the Fifth Kansas Cavalry and fought in all their engagements. Following the war, Bondi returned to Salina, Kansas, and became a farmer, a real estate broker, and a lawyer. He held the offices of township trustee and clerk of the district court. He also served as a director of the Kansas Historical Society and presented to them the musket that John Brown had given to him.[1]

---

1. Harry Simonhoff, *Jewish Notables in America, 1776–1865: Links of an Endless Chain* (New York: Greenberg, 1956), 344–47.

...a Jew ran the Civil War for the South

One of the most prominent people of the Civil War era was Judah Benjamin. An outstanding lawyer, he was offered but declined a seat on the United States Supreme Court at the age of forty-one. He was elected to both houses of the Louisiana legislature, helped draft their constitution, and went on to serve in the United States Senate. His Southern sympathies caused one of his colleagues to tag him as "an Israelite with the principles of an Egyptian."[1]

At the outbreak of the Civil War, Benjamin resigned his Senate seat and was appointed attorney general of the Confederacy. He soon became a confidant of Jefferson Davis and was thereafter appointed to be secretary of war.

He then went on to become secretary of state for the Confederacy. In that office, he reasoned that Lincoln could hardly recognize Southern independence if foreign nations were not willing to grant recognition. In an effort to win support for the Southern cause, he offered the French duty-free imports and a hundred thousand bales of cotton free of charge. He tried to get European businessmen to buy Southern products to be stored in Southern ports due to the blockade. Finally, he pledged abolition of slavery in exchange for recognition of the Confederacy. Since slavery was arguably the major cause of the war, this was an astounding concession for Secretary Benjamin to make. His offer was not accepted.

With the defeat of the South, Benjamin fled to England and enrolled in law school at age fifty-five to fulfill the requirements for the English bar. After six months, the English courts waived the three-year residency requirement for him, and he quickly became one of England's foremost attorneys, arguing major cases in England's highest courts. At his retirement he was honored as the only lawyer to be so distinguished at the bar of two different countries.[2]

---

1. Harry Simonhoff, *Jewish Participants in the Civil War* (New York: Arco, 1963), 161.
2. Ibid., 161–71.

...Ulysses S. Grant did *teshuva* (repentance)

During the Civil War, Southern planters were having a difficult time selling their cotton either in the North or overseas. There soon developed an active black market in which speculators bought cotton cheaply and resold it in the North at high prices. False charges exaggerated the magnitude of Jewish participation in the scheme, prompting General Grant to issue his infamous Order No. 11 expelling all Jews from his jurisdiction. No mention was made of the non-Jewish dealers.[1] When word of Order No. 11 reached President Lincoln, he promptly rescinded the order. In 1868, when Grant was running for president, many prominent Jews, mindful of Order No. 11, campaigned actively for his defeat.[2]

Upon assuming the presidency, Grant repented of his earlier error and proved to be a good friend of the Jews. During his administration, Grant appointed more Jews to public office than any president before his time. In 1869, when the Russians were contemplating the expulsion of twenty thousand Jews from southwestern Russia, Grant intervened with the czar, and the expulsion was rescinded. When the Jews of Romania needed help, Grant appointed a Jewish consul to Romania to monitor the situation.[3]

Grant tried to appoint another Jewish supporter to a cabinet-level post, but the supporter preferred to lend his assistance from outside the government.[4]

1. David G. Dalin and Alfred J. Kolatch, *The Presidents of the United States and the Jews* (New York: Jonathan David, 2000), 87–88.
2. Ibid., 88–89.
3. Ibid., 89.
4. Ibid., 90.

...Jews make great Indian fighters

In 1868, General Philip Sheridan of the US Army ordered the formation of a band of fifty scouts to seek out and engage marauding Indians who were terrorizing the frontier. The group stood at forty-nine when Sigmund Shlesinger, an out-of-work, out-of-funds Hungarian-Jewish immigrant showed up to join the scouts. Short of stature, of scrawny build, with almost no training in firearms and horsemanship, Shlesinger seemed to be an unpromising recruit. Nevertheless, he was the needed fiftieth man, and his signing enabled the group to move out on its mission. The young recruit was generally not well received by the scouts, but he was befriended by two of its members, Jack Stillwell and Jack Peate.

After eight days, the scouts encountered the Indians and the battle was joined. On the first day of fighting, the Indians, numbering about a thousand, killed all the scouts' horses. Outnumbered twenty to one, the scouts established a defensive perimeter on a sandbar in the Republican River. Firing from their dug-in positions, they managed to repulse repeated attacks by the Indians. Realizing the hopelessness of their position, Colonel Forsyth assigned two scouts to slip out at night to go for help.

During the battle, Colonel Forsyth, although twice wounded, kept his command and noted the great courage and skill showed by Shlesinger. In addition to his part in the fighting, Shlesinger took three Indian scalps and shot a coyote to provide much-needed food for the starving scouts. On the fifth day, help arrived and the scouts were saved.

Shlesinger soon returned to the East and settled in Ohio, where he became a prominent member of his synagogue and was very active in philanthropic causes. He also kept up lifelong correspondence and exchanges of visits with members of the scouts. Shlesinger was very proud of his part in the battle, but he was frustrated that nobody would believe his stories. This all changed when soldier-historian General James B. Fry wrote about Shlesinger in an account of the battle as related by Colonel Forsyth. He even appended a short poem lauding Shlesinger's courage. It reads as follows:

When the foe charged on the breastworks
With madness and despair,
And the bravest souls were tested,
The little Jew was there.

When the weary dozed on duty
Or the wounded needed care,
When another shot was called for,
The little Jew was there.

With the festering dead around them,
Shedding poison in the air,
When the crippled chieftain ordered,
The little Jew was there.

When Shlesinger died in 1928 at the age of seventy-nine, an elderly stranger came to Cleveland to pay his respects. The grizzled octogenarian was the last surviving member of the scouts, Jack Peate.[1]

---

1. M.L. Marks, *Jews among the Indians: Tales of Adventure and Conflict in the Old West* (Chicago: Benison Books, 1992), 15–28.

...the *New York Times* cut its price to one cent and made millions

When Adolph Ochs's father went broke in 1869, eleven-year-old Adolph went to work for twenty-five cents a day to help put food on the table. All his jobs were with newspapers, and by the age of nineteen, he decided he wanted to publish his own paper.[1]

The *Chattanooga Times* was going broke, and Ochs was able to borrow $250 to buy half interest in the newspaper. Ochs made a great success of the paper, and by the time he bought the other half of the paper at its face value, he paid $5500.[2]

There was a huge upsurge in Tennessee real estate at the time, and Ochs went in with a group of investors. When the bottom dropped out of the market, the others filed for bankruptcy, but Ochs refused to do so. Borrowing against his flourishing newspaper and floating a substantial bond issue, Ochs realized he would need even more money to repay his debts. He went to New York to try to recoup his fortune.[3]

At that time, the famous *New York Times* was losing money and was heading into bankruptcy. The stockholders, with little to lose, sold the paper to Ochs. Within two years the circulation climbed from nine thousand per day to twenty-five thousand.

Competing against New York daily newspaper publishers Hearst and Pulitzer proved to be difficult indeed. Their tabloid newspapers were selling for one cent, while the classier *New York Times* was selling for three cents. Ochs decided that the *Times*, too, would sell for one cent. Immediately the circulation soared to seventy-five thousand. Sales of advertising space increased greatly, and the *New York Times* achieved financial security. Without sacrificing any of its renowned quality, the paper was on its way to becoming arguably one of the world's greatest newspapers and has remained so for many years.[4] (As of this writing, the *New York Times* has come upon hard times and is on the verge of bankruptcy again.)

Unusual Stories in Jewish History

---

1. Harry Simonhoff, *Saga of American Jewry, 1865–1914: Links of an Endless Chain* (New York: Arco, 1950), 290.
2. Ibid., 290.
3. Ibid., 291.
4. Ibid., 292–93.

...a Jew improved what Edison and Bell invented

Emile Berliner's formal education ended at age fourteen, and he went to work in a dry goods store. Without scientific training, he nevertheless showed inventive genius, and at age sixteen, he built a weaving machine. When a family friend offered him a job in Washington, Emile took the opportunity to leave Germany.

After experimenting with a number of low-paying jobs, Emile wound up in New York working in a laboratory analyzing sugar. At night he began taking courses at the Cooper Union, which was founded in 1859 for the advancement of Sciences and Art. About this time, a druggist in his neighborhood gave him a book on physics written in German. This proved to be a turning point in his life.

At the American Centennial Fair in Philadelphia in 1876, Alexander Graham Bell's telephone was on display. Berliner was fascinated and began to experiment with it. Noticing how imperfectly the machine transmitted sound, he worked on eliminating the deficiencies. Eventually his efforts proved successful and he sold the patents. Berliner had invented what is now called the microphone, which made the telephone practical for long-distance use.

Alexander Graham Bell had begun to rent out his imperfect equipment when Western Union became interested in marketing the telephone. Using a patent from Thomas Edison, Western Union was able to put out a device superior to Bell's. About this time, an agent for Bell came across Berliner's device. Bell Telephone Company eventually acquired Berliner's patent, an improvement which was critical to the fledgling company's success.

Berliner then became interested in Edison's phonograph. Edison was selling the devices with the recorded material on a soft wax cylinder. Berliner changed the wax cylinder to a hard rubber disc with the needle in a shallow groove. The new machine was a great improvement over Edison's. Berliner's patent was bought by the Victor Talking Machine Company with the familiar trademark of the dog listening to "His Master's Voice."

Between 1926 and 1929, Berliner built and tested three helicopters. He was also interested in public health and founded the Society for the Prevention of Sickness to help promote the pasteurization of milk.[1] In his later years, Berliner supported the rebuilding of Palestine.[2]

1. Harry Simonhoff, *Saga of American Jewry, 1865–1914: Links of an Endless Chain* (New York: Arco, 1959), 269–74.
2. Grete Leibowitz, "Emile Berliner," *Encyclopedia Judaica*, CD-ROM Edition (Jerusalem: Keter, 1997).

...a Jew became an Indian chief

Solomon Bibo was a Prussian-Jewish immigrant who went to New Mexico to seek his fortune. Around 1882, Solomon established a trading post on the Acoma Indian Pueblo in New Mexico. He soon learned to speak the Acoma language and earned the trust of the inhabitants.

In 1884 Solomon Bibo signed a thirty-year lease for the Acoma lands. In exchange, Bibo agreed to pay the Indians three hundred dollars per year for the first ten years, four hundred per year for the second ten years and five hundred per year for the third ten years. In addition, Bibo agreed to pay the Indians a royalty on any mineral ores extracted from the land. He also agreed to keep squatters from settling on Acoma lands and to protect the Acoma's cattle.

When word of the deal reached the Indian agent Sanchez, he wrote to Hiram Price, the commissioner of Indian affairs, accusing Solomon Bibo of defrauding the Indians and seeking to have Bibo's trading license revoked. Bibo demanded a hearing before Commissioner Price.

At the hearing, Bibo presented evidence that he had only leased the land to prevent Sanchez and some partners from defrauding the Indians. Their lease was drawn up to pay the Acoma one cow per year for leasing all their lands, but Solomon Bibo offered the Acoma a much better deal. Furthermore, nearly all the members of the pueblo signed a letter endorsing Bibo as an honest and trustworthy trader.

The case was referred to General Whittlesly, a member of the board of Indian commissioners. Whittlesly was so impressed with the evidence that he wrote that revocation of Solomon Bibo's trader's license was not in the best interests of the Indians. Sanchez was replaced and the new agent, W.D. Williams, appointed Bibo as governor of the pueblo.

A year later, Solomon Bibo married an Acoma woman named Juana, in a church ceremony. In 1898, Bibo moved his wife and children to San Francisco so that his children could have a Jewish education. Juana converted to Judaism, and Solomon Bibo started a new business in San Francisco. Bibo is the only white man in the history of the Acoma to hold the title of chief.[1]

It is a curious coincidence that the names of Solomon Bibo and Hiram Price correspond to those in a biblical story. When King Solomon was building the Temple in Jerusalem, he contracted with King Hiram of Tyre for building materials and later for funding.[2] Just as Solomon and Hiram cooperated to build the Temple, so it was that another Solomon and Hiram cooperated to bring good government to the Acoma.

---

1. M.L. Marks, *Jews among the Indians: Tales of Adventure and Conflict in the Old West* (Chicago: Benison Press, 1992), 107–25.

2. "Hiram," in Geoffrey Wigoder, ed., *Illustrated Dictionary and Concordance to the Bible* (Jerusalem: Jerusalem Publishing House, 1986).

...paying debts can pay off big

Following the Civil War, southern businessman Lazarus Straus went about the business of repaying his creditors. Even though the statute of limitations had run out, Straus insisted on making good his pre-Civil War debts. One of his creditors was a man named George Bliss who was amazed that Straus still wanted to pay.

Twenty years later, when Lazarus's son Isidor came to the United States Trust Company for a loan, the same George Bliss was one of the directors of the bank. He gave Isidor the loan, saying, "If the old man is still with the firm, he is good for anything he will put his name to."[1]

Another grateful creditor who received his money was a crockery dealer named Cauldwell. Cauldwell said that the Straus debt was the only prewar debt paid to his firm after the war. Straus and Cauldwell were friends, and one day Cauldwell offered to sell the business to Straus. So it was that the Straus family got into the crockery and glassware business.

By now, another son, Nathan, was working in the business, and he managed to place some of the crockery and glassware with Macy's department store. Soon they became partners with the Macys, and eventually Isidor and Nathan became the sole owners. Under their leadership, Macy's became the world's largest department store, renowned for its honesty and fair dealings.

Isidor Straus was active in many other civic and philanthropic ventures. He was a close friend of President Cleveland and served one term in Congress but refused to run again. Together with his brothers, Isidor was a founder of the American Jewish Committee, was a guarantor of *The Jewish Encyclopedia*, contributed generously to the Jewish Theological Seminary, and helped organize the Educational Alliance as a cultural center for New York's Jewish intelligentsia.

In 1912, the sixty-seven-year-old Isidor Straus and his wife were aboard the *Titanic* when it struck the iceberg. Straus declined to accept a seat in a lifeboat as long as there were women and children aboard who had no seats. His wife refused to leave his side and they were both lost in the terrible disaster. Their story is told in the book and the movie *A Night to Remember*, which depicts the sinking of the *Titanic*.[2]

---

1. Harry Simonhoff, *Saga of American Jewry, 1865–1914: Links of an Endless Chain* (New York: Arco, 1959), 241.
2. Ibid., 241–43.

...the Guggenheims proved that fair play is good business

In April of 1899, the Smelters Association of Colorado was organized "to fix prices [of copper] and stifle competition."[1] The prospectus stated that their intention was "to combine all the principal smelting works in the United States with the exception of the Guggenheims," a family in the smelting business.[2]

In the meantime, the Colorado General Assembly passed a law prohibiting employers from working their men more than eight hours without paying overtime. The Guggenheims accepted the new law, but the Smelters Association of Colorado changed their payment method to an hourly wage carefully calibrated to require eight hours of straight time and four hours of overtime in order to earn the same pay workers were earning before the eight-hour day was passed into law. The Western Federation of Miners answered by going on strike against every smelter of the association.

Since all the other smelters were shut down, the mine owners took their business to the Guggenheim-owned Philadelphia Smelter in Pueblo, Colorado. The strike lasted two months; eventually the eight-hour-day law was declared unconstitutional and the twelve-hour day returned. But many miners stayed with the Guggenheims, because they seemed like a better company to deal with.

Obstinately, the association raised processing prices for the small mine owners, and lowered the price it paid miners for gold, thus driving more of them to do business with the Guggenheims.[3]

Eventually, the association had to come to the Guggenheims, and after some complex negotiations, the Guggenheims took control of the association.[4] Of course, trusts were eventually declared illegal on the grounds of restraint of trade, but the Guggenheims proved that fair dealings could also mean good business. They went on to become very philanthropic especially in the field of aeronautics.

In an amazing irony, the Guggenheims sponsored Charles Lindbergh's cross-country aviation tour after the epic flight across the Atlantic Ocean. Lindbergh turned out to be a Nazi sympathizer who opposed the United States' involvement in fighting Hitler and the Third Reich.

---

1. Edwin P. Hoyt Jr., *The Guggenheims and the American Dream* (New York: Funk and Wagnalls, 1968), 116.
2. Ibid.
3. Ibid., 120, 128.
4. Ibid.

...Guggenheim thought of the New Deal twenty years before Roosevelt

The early part of the twentieth century was critical for workers in America generally and for miners and smelters in particular. The owners ruthlessly exploited their workers, and anybody who complained could be easily replaced by newly arrived immigrants from Poland, China, or perhaps from the Balkan countries. But the workers did complain, and there were major strikes in the metals industry in 1911, 1912, and 1913.[1]

It was in this atmosphere that Daniel Guggenheim decided that there had to be a better way. The Guggenheim-controlled American Smelter and Refining set up their own bureau of labor relations in order to care for any labor problems that might arise. In 1915 the Wilson administration's United States Industrial Relations Commission was holding hearings and Daniel Guggenheim was called to testify.

His response to the commission was an astounding statement considering that at that time there were no child labor laws, and management routinely opposed independent unions. Guggenheim stated:

> There is today a great difference between the rich man and the poor man. To remedy this is too big a job for the state or the employer to tackle single-handed. There should be a combination in this work between the Federal government, the state, the employer, and the employee. The men want more comforts – more of the luxuries of life. *They are entitled to them. I say this because humanity owes it to them.*[2] [Italics added]

He went on further to state:

> I think the State should furnish work for the men who lack employment. You may call me Socialistic if you like, but it is a job of the United States to look after its people. Were it not for the philanthropic work, there would be a revolution here. But sufficient help is not given in this case. People won't give up the money they make easily, even if they have more than they need. *So the government must raise the money – raise it by taxing the estates of the rich, if you will – but the United States must raise it some way.*[3] [Italics added]

This prophetic statement was uttered almost two decades before Roosevelt's New Deal attempted exactly what Daniel Guggenheim was proposing!

---

1. Edwin P. Hoyt Jr., *The Guggenheims and the American Dream* (New York: Funk and Wagnalls, 1968), 235.
2. Ibid., 234–35.
3. Ibid., 235–36.

...Jews were heavily involved in prostitution

At the turn of the twentieth century, when masses of immigrants were flooding into America, it was only a short time before the long hours in the sweatshop, the grinding poverty of a system designed to exploit cheap immigrant labor, and the hopelessness of finding a way out of their misery began to take its toll on the lives of the Jewish newcomers to the *goldene medina,* the "golden land."[1]

Some immigrants turned to violent crime, some became professional boxers, still others turned to prostitution – most of them women but a few men as pimps and white slavers.[2]

From November 1908 to March 1909, the New York City magistrate's office listed foreign-born prostitutes as 154 French, 64 German, 31 Italian, 29 Irish, 10 Polish, and 225 Jewish.[3] Of course, not much can be inferred from raw figures. However, the problem was not limited to New York City. A visiting rabbi from the Transvaal province in South Africa reported widespread Jewish prostitution in Johannesburg, Pretoria, Lourenco Marques, Beira, and Salisbury. A schoolmaster reported trafficking of Jewesses by Jews in Alexandria, Cairo, and Port Said in Egypt.[4]

The condition spread as far as Calcutta and the free ports of China. Other reports emanated from Constantinople, where the traffickers were reputed to have their own synagogue. Of the 199 licensed brothels in Buenos Aires, Argentina, 102 had Jewish madams and fully half of the prostitutes were Jewish.[5]

In a relatively short time, improved economic conditions, the effectiveness of the legendary Jewish social services programs, and a corresponding curtailment of immigration from Southern and Eastern Europe all contributed to the virtual eradication of a disgraceful blight on the Jewish immigrant community.[6]

---

1. Melvin Konner, *Unsettled: An Anthropology of the Jews* (New York: Viking Penguin, 2003), 335.
2. Ibid., 336–37.
3. Ibid., 336.
4. Ibid., 337.
5. Ibid.
6. For more on the subject see Rich Cohen, *Tough Jews* (New York: Simon and Schuster, 1998), and Allen Bodner, *When Boxing Was a Jewish Sport* (Westport, CT: Praeger, 1997).

...entering the wrong door can change a life

In 1900, four days after his arrival in America from Russia, nine-year-old David Sarnoff was hawking the Yiddish daily newspaper *Tageblatt*. So resourceful was young David that he earned as much in two hours as a sweatshop worker could earn in a day and had time for school.[1]

There David encountered a teacher who was using Shakespeare's *Merchant of Venice* to spew anti-Semitic venom in the classroom. When David objected, he was taken to the principal's office where the teacher delivered an ultimatum: he would resign if David was not expelled from his class. David countered that he had connections in the media, and that it would not look good for the school to be portrayed as fostering anti-Semitism. The principal accepted the teacher's resignation.[2]

After having purchased a newsstand for his family, David began to look for a job. He applied to be a bicycle messenger for the *New York Herald*, was accepted, and told to report to the personnel office. By mistake, David entered the wrong door and went into the offices of the Commercial Cable Company where he was given a job delivering telegrams.

In order to understand the priorities involved in delivering the telegrams, David taught himself Morse code. Soon he was tapping out coded messages with a counterpart across town. David soon was promoted to the position of a telegrapher. He was still spending four hours a day picking up and delivering the newspapers to the family newsstand.[3]

When David asked for time off without pay to sing in the synagogue choir on the High Holy Days, he was immediately fired. To add to his woes, the choir director reduced his pay by a nickel, because he could no longer hit a high C. However, he landed a new job as a radio operator for the navy.

One night, back in New York at a special station atop Wanamaker's Department Store, David picked up a signal from the SS *Olympic*, one of the ships on the way to help rescue survivors of the sinking *Titanic*. David stayed at his post for seventy-two hours receiving and sending news of the tragedy. In that short period of time, Sarnoff became a media sensation. The instant fame and his rise in the organization culminated in his becoming general manager of the company, by that time known as the Radio Corporation of America, RCA.[4]

David Sarnoff's talents would have certainly made him a success in life, but had he not entered by the wrong door when he applied for the job, his life would have been much different.

1. Stephen Birmingham, *The Rest of Us: The Rise of America's Eastern European Jews* (Boston: Little, Brown, 1984), 93–94.
2. Ibid., 96.
3. Ibid., 98.
4. Ibid., 98–101.

...Harry Kane was a minor-league sensation but a major-league flop

Harry Kane (born Cohen) was a left-handed pitcher for Springfield in the Missouri Valley League. In the 1902 season, he won twenty out of twenty-one games including three no-hitters. That year he was promoted to the major-league St. Louis Browns, but his debut was undistinguished. His earned run average was 5.48, and in 1903 he was back to the minor league in Springfield.

That season he again pitched three no-hitters. He also pitched a double-header winning both games with three-hit shutouts. He was again promoted to the major leagues, this time to the Detroit Tigers, but the 1904 season found him back in the minors. In fifty-one innings he did not allow a single run. In 1905 he pitched for Savannah and pitched a thirteen-inning no-hitter which he lost 1-0.

In 1905, he was back in the major leagues, this time with Philadelphia. His record was 1-1 including a five-hit shutout of the St. Louis Cardinals. In 1906 he pitched in six games for the Phillies. He quit playing in 1906 leaving a record of fifteen major-league games played. He won two, lost seven, and had an earned run average of 4.81.

He became an umpire in 1906.[1]

---

1. Peter S. Horvitz and Joachim Horvitz, *The Big Book of Jewish Baseball: An Illustrated Encyclopedia and Anecdotal History* (New York: SPI Books, 2001).

...a Jewish girl went into business in order to buy a blouse

Josephine Esther (Esty) Mentzer was born in 1908 to an immigrant Jewish family in New York. She began to hone her marketing skills in her father's hardware store and in her half-brother's dry goods store. However, she found her real calling when she began to sell a face cream developed by her uncle, who was a chemist. Esty herself experimented with the cream for about twenty years before it was perfected.[1] She sometimes went to beauty salons where she gave free face cream treatments to women who were waiting for their hair to dry. She had a good product, and many women bought it.[2]

An incident in a beauty parlor proved to be a pivotal moment in Esty's life. An elegant-looking woman entered the salon wearing a blouse that Esty admired. When she asked the woman where she bought it, the woman replied, "What difference could it possibly make? You could never afford it." Esty was humiliated and vowed that some day she would be able to buy anything she wanted.[3]

At the age of nineteen, Esty married Joseph Lauter. They had two sons, but Esty continued to market cosmetics. She always carried samples of her products wherever she went. After a while, her husband quit his job to help Esty in her business. They got their big break in 1948 when Saks Fifth Avenue placed a sizable order. Esty and Joseph made up the creams in their factory, a converted restaurant. Esty personally worked the counter and Saks sold out their supply in two days.[4] Other stores including Bloomingdales, Marshall Field's, Neiman-Marcus, Harrods in London, and Galleries Lafayette in Paris began to carry their products. Esty and Joseph began to make their fortune and Esty now spelled her name "Estee," also changing Lauter to "Lauder."[5]

In 1998 Estee Lauder controlled 45 percent of the American market in cosmetics, and had sales of $3.6 billion in 118 countries. The Lauder family shares were worth more than $6 billion.[6] Estee Lauder could now buy the blouse she so admired and anything else she might desire!

1. Deborah G. Felder and Diana Rosen, *Fifty Jewish Women Who Changed the World* (New York: Kensington, 2003), 182.
2. CBS News, "Cosmetics Mogul Estee Lauder Dies," April 12, 2004; http://www.cbsnews.com/stories/2004/04/12/national/mail/main611403.shtml.
3. Todd G. Buchholz, *New Ideas from Dead CEOs: Lasting Lessons from the Corner Office* (New York: Collins, 2007), 86; Sara Alpern, "Estee Lauder," *Jewish Virtual Library*, 2007 http://jewish virtuallibrary.org/jsource/Lauder.html.
4. *The Economist* 371 (2004): 88.
5. CBS News, "Cosmetics Mogul Estee Lauder Dies."
6. CBS News, *People of the Century* (New York: Simon and Schuster, 1999), 261.

...a Jew put the brakes on Ford

Louis Marshall was the president of the American Jewish Committee from 1912 to 1929. During this time he proved his worth as a master negotiator. In 1912 he convinced the Taft administration to reject extension of the Russo-American trade treaty on the grounds that Russia refused to grant entry visas to American Jews wishing to visit Russia. Six years later he was successful in winning over the Wilson administration to back the granting of minority rights in Eastern Europe.

Perhaps the most surprising of Marshall's diplomatic successes was in his dealings with the rabidly anti-Semitic car manufacturer Henry Ford. Aside from his widespread distribution of the scurrilous treatise *The Protocols of the Elders of Zion,* Ford published his own newspaper, the *Dearborn Independent.* This paper was Ford's vehicle for disseminating anti-Semitism through the editorial page. Not only was Marshall able to convince Ford to cease publication of the paper, but he also convinced him to apologize for the tenor and content of the editorials.

Israel Zangwill once commented wittily that "American Jewry was living under Marshall Law."[1]

---

1. Howard M. Sachar, *The Course of Modern Jewish History* (New York: Vintage Books, 1990), 707.

...Jews are probably the most assimilated group in the world

During the period from 1919 to 1933, the United States Army War College was engaged in a particularly virulent campaign of racial anti-Semitism. Paramount among their racial conclusions about Jews was their congenital inability to assimilate into this country and become good Americans.[1] This is a strong statement, but Lothrop Stoddard, in his lectures at the war college, failed to explain himself. Moreover, Nazi Germany and its imitators adopted the mantra that it was impossible to assimilate Jews into their society.

The beginning of the answer to this wild allegation might be found in the days of the Roman Empire. During the reign of Claudius in the first century CE, the population of the empire was between 55,000,000 and 100,000,000. It was estimated that there were about 6,944,000 Jews in the empire and perhaps another million in the areas adjacent to it. This meant that the Jewish population of the empire was no less than 7 percent and perhaps as high as 10 percent.[2]

However, with the rise of Christianity, the Jewish population of Europe dwindled to about 1,000,000, a loss estimated at between 66 percent and 85 percent.[3] To what might the loss be attributed? While massacres certainly accounted for a percentage, they do not explain the decimation of the population. In an era of forced conversions and severe discrimination against those who tried to cling to their faith, conversion was often the only way to relieve the suffering.

Even in areas where persecution was minimal, the Jewish population continued to decline. In 1638 in Italy, the Jewish population was about one per thousand. Put another way, during this period, the Italian population quadrupled, while the Jewish population barely doubled.[4]

It is an extreme irony that Nazi Germany found 200,000 part-Jewish soldiers and 6,000 full Jews in the Wehrmacht during World War II. Among them were literally dozens of generals and one admiral. It was a monumental task to find and weed out these "undesirables." Hitler himself made numerous exceptions.[5]

The statement that the Jews do not assimilate into the larger society is not borne out by the facts.

1. Joseph W. Bendersky, *The Jewish Threat: Anti-Semitic Policies of the US Army* (New York: Basic Books, 2000).
2. Cecil Roth, *Personalities and Events in Jewish History* (Philadelphia: Jewish Publication Society, 1953), 39.
3. Ibid., 40.
4. Ibid., 44.
5. Bryan Mark Rigg, *Hitler's Jewish Soldiers: The Untold Story of Nazi Racial Laws and Men of Jewish Descent in the German Military* (Lawrence, KS: University of Kansas Press, 2002), 172–89.

...Brandeis was great *because* he was a Jew

In 1916 President Woodrow Wilson nominated Louis Brandeis to become the first Jewish justice on the United States Supreme Court. Wilson was quite surprised at the strength of the opposition to Brandeis's nomination. Brandeis was accused of being radical, liberal, pro-union, and Jewish. During the struggle, one of Wilson's advisors said to Wilson, "Isn't it a shame, Mr. President, that a man as great as Mr. Justice Brandeis should be a Jew?" Wilson responded, "But he would not be Mr. Brandeis if he were *not* a Jew."[1]

Brandeis was eventually confirmed and served on the court with distinction.

---

204   1.   David G. Dalin and Alfred J. Kolatch, *The Presidents of the United States and the Jews* (New York: Jonathan David, 2000), 136.

...Roosevelt's opponents called the New Deal "the Jew Deal"

When Franklin Roosevelt became president in 1933, Jews were still facing significant discrimination in American life. Many elite universities had admission quotas for Jews and promotion to the highest business and government positions was often denied to Jews. Major law firms and law schools routinely declined to hire Jews.

However, by 1932 Roosevelt was being opposed by most of the nation's Protestant elite and appointing them to high office seemed to be counterproductive. To fill the void, Roosevelt increasingly began to appoint Jews to positions in his administration.

One of Roosevelt's key aides was Samuel Rosenman, who coined the name "New Deal" to describe Roosevelt's program for economic recovery. Another key advisor to Roosevelt was Felix Frankfurter, later to become Roosevelt's appointee to the United States Supreme Court. Frankfurter channeled many young Jewish lawyers into government service. They soon became known as "Frankfurter's happy hot dogs."

Benjamin Cohen, one of Frankfurter's protégés, helped write key New Deal legislation. He coauthored the Securities Act of 1933, the Securities and Exchange Act of 1934, the Public Utility Holding Act of 1935, the Federal Communications Act, the Tennessee Valley Authority Act, and the Minimum Wage Act.

Supreme Court justice Louis Brandeis advised the administration how best to get the legislation past any challenges that would come before the courts. Henry Morgenthau Jr. became Roosevelt's secretary of the treasury. Isidor Lubin became head of the Bureau of Labor Statistics and doubled as FDR's chief economic advisor. Jerome Frank headed the Securities and Exchange Commission; David Lilienthal chaired the Tennessee Valley Authority, and the Housing Administration was headed by Nathan Straus.

Although Jews comprised only 3 percent of the nation's population, they occupied 15 percent of Roosevelt's appointed positions. It would seem that when Roosevelt's anti-Semitic detractors derisively referred to the New Deal as the *Jew Deal*, they may have been close to the truth.[1]

---

1. L. Sandy Maisel and Ira N. Forman, eds., *Jews in American Politics* (Lanham, MD: Rowman and Littlefield, 2001), 10–11.

...a kosher chicken killed part of Roosevelt's New Deal

In an effort to ease the economic hardships brought on by the Great Depression, President Roosevelt proposed many pieces of legislation. Among these was the National Industrial Recovery Act (NIRA). Its purpose was to promote fair competition, create jobs for unemployed workers, support prices and competition, and stimulate the United States economy to recover from the depression gripping the country. Because the act was quite complicated and contained three thousand administrative orders running to over ten thousand pages,[1] it was inevitable that a case involving the National Recovery Adminstration (NRA) would end up in the courts. One of the cases involved the Schechter Poultry Corp.[2] The Schechter brothers had been brought into the New York circuit court to face sixty violations of the NRA code. This number was eventually brought down to eighteen, among them the sale of diseased chickens and the sale of uninspected chickens. The Schechters were convicted but promptly appealed to the United States Supreme Court.[3]

In a unanimous decision, the Supreme Court ruled in favor of the Schechters, declaring that the National Recovery Administration's codes "provided excessive delegation of legislative powers" and that the NRA was therefore unconstitutional.[4]

The case came to be known as the "sick chicken case"[5] and destroyed a major piece of President Roosevelt's efforts to cope with the Great Depression.

---

1. Jason Togyer, *For the Love of Murphy's: The Behind-the-Counter Story of a Great American* (University Park, PA: Penn State Press, 2008), 55.
2. "Schechter" is a Jewish surname meaning "slaughterer" (i.e., "butcher").
3. Arthur M. Schlesinger Jr., *The Age of Roosevelt: The Politics of Upheaval* (Boston: Houghton Mifflin, 1960), 278.
4. Stanley L. Engerman and Robert E. Gallman, *The Cambridge Economic History of the United States* (Cambridge, UK: Cambridge University Press, 2000), 978; see also http://law.jrank.org/pages/13620/L-Schechter-Poultry-Corporation-v-United-States.html.
5. Schlesinger, *The Age of Roosevelt*, 277.

Who Knew?!

ISRAEL:
Building and
Defending a Nation

...Jews developed Palestine for Arabs

"Absorptive capacity" was a term used extensively by the British in administering the Palestine Mandate. As the name suggests, it deals with the capacity of the land to absorb new immigrants. The ostensible purpose of Britain's immigration policies for the territory of Palestine was to prevent working people in Palestine from losing their jobs to newly arrived immigrants, and to prevent unemployment resulting from admitting more immigrants than the local job market could handle.

The use of the term "absorptive capacity" was fraudulent on two counts. To begin with, in a land that was notoriously underdeveloped, the absorptive capacity for the foreseeable future was virtually unlimited. Secondly, the British showed no concern for overcrowding when it came to the influx of thousands of illegal Arab immigrants; they only applied this concept to Jews.

In practice, "absorptive capacity" was merely a device for severely limiting Jewish immigration. It worked something like this. Jews would apply for immigration under the quota system set by the Mandatory power. The British would then apply the "absorptive capacity" standard to limit their numbers. Then Jews would engage in developing more agricultural and industrial projects and attempt to bring in more Jews. However, news of better-paying jobs would attract masses of illegal-immigrant Arab laborers. Ignoring the origin of these illegal Arab immigrants, the British would then claim that if more Jews were allowed in, the Arab workers would be displaced. Under this system, Jewish immigration was constantly being curtailed.

Jews were put into the position of creating jobs for a few Jews and many Arabs, while needy Jews were kept out. On the other hand, if the Jews had stopped development, immigration might have been cut off altogether. Thus, the Jews were kept in a vicious cycle of expending energy and money with the Arabs being the main beneficiaries.

Perhaps the worst application of the "absorptive capacity" canard was during the Holocaust. The British would complain, "If all those Jews came in, where would we put them?" Of course, when the Jewish state was finally proclaimed, the land was able to accommodate the thousands of Jews from the displaced persons camps as well as the hundreds of thousands of Jews fleeing their former homes in Arab countries.[1]

---

1. Joan Peters, *From Time Immemorial: The Origins of the Arab-Jewish Conflict over Palestine* (Chicago: JKAP Publishing, 1984), 304–11.

...Jews of Palestine denounced Jews in the British army

As the number of Jews living in Palestine increased during the period from 1880 to 1914, most of them retained citizenship from their countries of origin. They did this to protect themselves from the capricious rule of the Turks who were then sovereign in Palestine.

With the outbreak of World War I, the Turkish government initiated a severe crackdown on foreign non-Muslims who were residing in Turkey but not citizens. This led to the rapid emigration of some seven thousand Jews. In order to stem the massive emigration threatening the viability of the Jewish community, the Jews immediately decided to apply for Ottoman citizenship. Some twelve thousand Jews did so, and the following year another twenty-four thousand applied. The threat to the Jews then seemed to subside.

By 1915, as the war dragged on, able-bodied Jewish young men, previously exempt from military service, began to be drafted into labor battalions. Some Jews even petitioned for the formation of a Jewish fighting force on the side of the Turks. This was denied. Moreover, the Turks even began a series of anti-Jewish measures designed to stymie Zionism in Palestine. They closed the Anglo-Palestinian Bank and banned Zionist newspapers, schools, and political offices.

Meanwhile, anti-Turkish resentment began to rise among the émigrés who had fled to Egypt. Able-bodied Jewish young men began to offer themselves as fighters on the British side. While the British were reluctant to arm Jewish troops in their own units, they did agree to allow them to form the Zion Mule Corps, a five-hundred-man unit charged with running supply mules to the front lines. The unit performed admirably while suffering casualties amounting to eight killed and fifty-five wounded.

When it became widely known that the Zion Mule Corps was serving in the British army, the Jews in Palestine began to worry that it would result in more unfavorable treatment of the Jews under Turkish rule. Many of them took to the streets denouncing the mule corps as "traitors." It all became moot when the British evacuated the Dardanelles and disbanded the Zion Mule Corps.[1]

This episode reflects the tenuous position of Jews without a country. Failure to support the British might have led to repatriation to places like Jew-hating Russia. Failure to support the Turks could have led to further persecution including invalidation of the Jewish land claims purchased dearly from Arab landlords. It was a no-win situation.

1. Howard M.Sachar, *A History of Israel from the Rise of Zionism to Our Time* (New York: Knopf, 1996), 89–93.

...one preposition cost Israel most of its territory

As Zionism gathered steam in the early part of the twentieth century, Chaim Weizmann was in England working hard at trading in Jewish support for Britain's political agenda in exchange for British support for the Zionist agenda. He and his colleagues submitted to key members of the British government a proposed draft of what was to become the Balfour Declaration, a document that expressed Britain's support for the Zionist program.[1] The Balfour Declaration is known today as a pivotal moment in the making of the modern State of Israel.

What many do not realize is that the Balfour Declaration went through many revisions and had to meet the approval of many politicians (including US President Woodrow Wilson[2]) before it was publicly issued. In the course of these political manipulations, the declaration underwent several important transformations. The original draft expressed British support for the idea that "Palestine should be reconstituted *as* the National Home of the Jewish people,"[3] but by the time the document was actually released, it had been watered down to endorse only "the establishment *in* Palestine of a national home for the Jewish people" (italics mine).

The original text implied support for a Jewish state comprising the *entire* territory then known as Palestine (which included the territory west of the Jordan River now known as the Kingdom of Jordan). The final version was a much more tepid endorsement that could be (and later was) construed to refer only to a *part* of the territory, which was subsequently carved up and given largely to the Arabs.

Thus, along with a change of the article from definite (*the*) to indefinite (*a*), and a downgrade of the concept of "national home" from capital letters to lower case,[4] a preposition proved to be very costly to the Zionist enterprise.

The news of the Balfour Declaration touched off celebrations throughout the Jewish world. Amid all the rejoicing and prayers of thanksgiving, few people noticed that the establishment of Palestine *as the* homeland was quite different from *a* homeland *in* Palestine.

---

1. Haim Hillel Ben-Sasson, ed., *A History of the Jewish People* (Cambridge, MA: Harvard University Press, 1976), 991.
2. Steven L. Spiegel, *The Other Arab-Israeli Conflict: Making America's Middle East Policy, from Truman to Reagan* (Chicago: University of Chicago Press, 1985), 11.
3. Quoted in Ben-Sasson, *A History of the Jewish People*, 991; see also Howard M. Sachar, *The Course of Modern Jewish History* (New York: Vintage Books, 1990), 447.
4. Fritz Liebreich, *Britain's Naval and Political Reaction to the Illegal Immigration of Jews to Palestine, 1945–1948* (London and New York: Routledge, 2005), 13.

...a Zionist Jew appointed a Nazi to high office

Sir Herbert Samuel, a Zionist and a Jew, was high commissioner of Palestine from 1920 to 1925. In an incredible act of appeasement of Arab agitation, Samuel appointed the murderous Hajj Amin el-Husseini as grand mufti of Jerusalem. So notorious was Husseini that he had to be brought back from exile to assume his post. He had fled to avoid prosecution for criminal activities.

When Hitler came to power, Husseini became an active collaborator with the Nazis. He spent much of the war years in Germany assisting the Nazis in putting out propaganda, mainly against Jews. In his broadcasts, he is quoted as saying: "Arise, o sons of Arabia. Fight for your sacred rights. Slaughter Jews wherever you find them. Their spilled blood pleases Allah, our history, and our religion. That will save our honor."[1]

He also organized a pro-Nazi coup in Iraq and mobilized thousands of Muslims in the Balkans to carry out atrocities against Yugoslav Jews, Serbs, and Gypsies. In 1944 he commanded a German-Arab commando unit that parachuted into Palestine to poison the wells in Tel Aviv.[2] He was instrumental in organizing Arab children into Nazi Scouts and was quoted as saying that "Muslims inside and outside Palestine welcome the new regime of Germany and hope for the extension of the fascist, anti-democratic, governmental system to other countries."[3]

The mufti's worst atrocity was convincing Adolf Eichmann, the ss officer in charge of implementing the Final Solution, to intervene with the Hungarian government to rescind its plan to save several thousand Jewish children from the gas chambers.[4] In the event of a German victory in the war, the mufti had plans to build an Auschwitz-like death camp near Nablus (Shechem) to dispose of the Jewish population of Palestine.[5]

Following the war, the Nuremberg tribunals branded the mufti as a war criminal, but he escaped punishment by fleeing to Egypt, where he was granted asylum, and continued to direct other Nazi sympathizers in terrorism against Israel.[6]

As late as 1992, Yasser Arafat, the chairman of the Palestinian Authority, in an interview reprinted in the Palestinian daily *Al-Quds*, referred to Husseini as "our hero" and boasted of being "one of his troops."[7]

1. Alan Dershowitz, *The Case for Israel* (Hoboken, NJ: John Wiley and Sons, 2003), 55.
2. Ibid.
3. Ibid., 54.
4. Ibid.,.57.
5. Ibid., 55.
6. Ibid., 56.
7. Ibid.

...a Jew saved Czechoslovakia and Czechoslovakia saved Israel

Jan Ludvik Hoch was born in 1923, the son of a Jewish farm laborer. When the Nazis occupied his native Czechoslovakia, Hoch fled to Hungary, where he was soon arrested and imprisoned by the Nazis.[1] He beat his guard to death and escaped to Syria where he joined the French Foreign Legion. Making his way to southern France, he joined the free Czech forces. At the fall of France, he was included in a contingent of Czech fighters transported to England, eventually winding up in the Somerset Light Infantry with the new name of Robert Maxwell. He served with distinction, won the Military Cross for bravery, was promoted from corporal to officer, and eventually was recruited by the British intelligence.[2]

His skill in languages won him a job as interrogator of prominent Nazis in Spandau Prison and later a job as a spy for the British. Posing as a purveyor of forged documents, he was instrumental in the capture of a number of Nazis in hiding.[3]

Recognizing his remarkable insights, the British secret service enticed Maxwell to leave the army to work for them. While in their employ, he increased his language skills by studying Russian.

In 1946, Maxwell discovered that the British M16 secret service agency was scheming to replace the free and democratic government of Czechoslovakia with a group of ex-Nazis they felt would be more cooperative with their aims. This was an affront to Maxwell, who had lost virtually his entire family in the Holocaust. He approached his former prison cellmate, the Czech leader Vladimir Clementis, and revealed the plot. The scandal was exposed, and in the ensuing elections, the ex-Nazis were defeated and Clementis became the Czech foreign minister.[4]

In the meantime, the Israeli leader David Ben-Gurion was faced with dire circumstances. Heavily armed Arab nations were massing to destroy his embryonic country, and nobody would sell the beleaguered Jews any arms with which to defend themselves. In desperation, Ben-Gurion turned to Robert Maxwell. Maxwell, in turn, went to a grateful Vladimir Clementis who readily agreed to massive arms and planes shipments to Israel. Stalin was furious with the Czechs' support of Israel, but Clementis defied him. The arms shipments were completed, and Israel won the war. Clementis and others later paid with their lives.[5]

Today Robert Maxwell's memory is honored in Israel. He is buried in Jerusalem on the Mount of Olives.[6]

1. David Cesarani, "Robert Maxwell," *Encyclopedia Judaica, CD-ROM Edition* (Jerusalem: Keter, 1997).
2. John Loftus and Mark Aarons, *The Secret War against the Jews: How Western Espionage Betrayed the Jewish People* (New York: St. Martin's Griffin, 1994), 201–3.
3. Ibid., 203.
4. Ibid., 203, 206.
5. Ibid., 207.
6. Ibid., 210.

...British interference continued after their Palestine Mandate ended

In December 1947, after the United Nations had voted to partition Palestine, David Ben-Gurion called on the British high commissioner in Palestine, Alan Cunningham, requesting land records for the soon-to-be-born State of Israel. Cunningham refused. When the UN commission arrived in Palestine to monitor the transition, Cunningham assigned the commissioners to an unventilated basement and made no provisions for feeding them. They were not able to accomplish anything.[1]

The British then nearly bankrupted the embryonic Jewish state by freezing the currency deposits of the Jewish Agency and private Jewish firms, banks, and other institutions with deposits in London.[2]

On May 14, 1948, the British Mandate for Palestine was terminated and five Arab nations attacked Israel. When UN mediator Bernadotte was assigned to go to Palestine in June, the British convinced him that the partition lines needed re-drawing and that the Israeli-assigned Negev should be transferred to the Kingdom of Transjordan. This point became moot when Israeli forces drove the Egyptian army out of the Negev.[3]

On January 7, 1949, Israeli pilots shot down five British fighter planes in an air battle with the Egyptians. President Truman summoned the British ambassador and told him: "I don't like what your people are doing. Your planes have no business over the battle area in Palestine."[4]

When the Mandate was in force, would-be Jewish immigrants were intercepted and interned. With Israeli independence, all the women and children detainees were released. However, a year and a half later, the British were still holding able-bodied Jewish male refugees, those capable of bearing arms.[5] Were they being kept out of the war against England's clients?

When Israel declared its independence, Arab oil ceased to flow to the refineries in Haifa, Israel. When the Israelis purchased crude oil elsewhere, the British-owned Anglo-Iranian Oil Company refused to refine the oil for Israel. When Ben-Gurion threatened to nationalize their facilities, the British finally agreed to refine the crude oil Israel had purchased.

---

1. Howard M. Sachar, *Israel and Europe: An Appraisal in History* (New York: Random House, 1998), 4.
2. Ibid., 5.
3. Ibid., 7–9.
4. Ibid., 11.
5. Ibid.

In June of 1949, Israel and England began negotiations regarding the frozen Jewish Agency (now Israeli) funds. The British contended that the funds would be used to indemnify England for their property, which the Israelis had sequestered. Much of the property in question was in the form of fortified positions. The Israelis countered by saying that England had lost title to these lands when they turned them over to the Arabs before they left. The Israelis had suffered much loss of life in conquering these positions, and they did not feel that they should have to purchase them again.[1]

The British behavior in Palestine was exacting a heavy toll; England was suffering much internal dissension at home and diplomatic pressure from abroad. In the end, they released the detainees, called off their armed forces, and worked out their financial claims against Israel. They accepted a nominal monetary settlement and gave the Israelis fifteen years to pay at 1-percent interest.

Thus ended a sad chapter in the relationship between Israel and Great Britain.

---

1. Ibid., 12.

...Zionists had to be resourceful to get UN votes for partition

In early 1947, the United Nations took up the question of partition of Palestine into separate Jewish and Arab states. As the time for a vote approached, the Zionists began to realize that they would have to employ resourceful techniques to achieve their goal.

Knowing that they lacked the necessary two-thirds of the voting UN members, the Jews had to keep the issue from coming to a vote before they were ready. To accomplish this, they resorted to the time-honored technique of filibuster. They lined up a number of friendly states to keep talking until assembly president Oswaldo Aranha, a good friend of the Zionists, gaveled the session to a close and postponed the vote for two days.[1]

One of the crucial votes was from the nation of Liberia. That government was originally for partition but had lately switched positions and was ready to cast a "no" vote. A call went out to Harvey Firestone, president of Firestone Tire and Rubber Company.[2] Firestone called his representatives in Liberia to exert pressure on the government, and they soon changed their vote back to a "yes."[3]

The next problem was Haiti. A Zionist investigator learned that the Haitians switched their vote to pressure the United States to grant them a five-million-dollar loan. The pro-Zionists soon persuaded the Haitians that they could get the loan approved more quickly if they voted "yes."[4]

The Philippine Islands posed a major obstacle. The Philippine president, Romulo, delivered a strong anti-Zionist speech while in New York. Shortly thereafter, Supreme Court Justices Murphy and Frankfurter visited the Philippine ambassador to the United States and reminded him that a "no" vote might jeopardize passage of seven bills in Congress dealing with the Philippines. New York Senator Robert Murphy and twenty-five senators signed a letter that was sent to Manila urging a "yes" vote. The Philippines switched their position.[5]

---

1. Dan Kurzman, *Genesis 1948: The First Arab-Israeli War* (New York: World, 1970), 19.
2. Firestone held a concession for one million acres of land in Liberia and had helped the government out of some financial difficulties.
3. Kurzman, *Genesis 1948*, 20.
4. Ibid.
5. Ibid., 20.

The pro-partition forces had to enlist the aid of the Jewish house detective in the hotel where the Syrian delegate was housed. A listening device was planted in the ventilator of the delegate's room, and the Zionists soon learned that the female delegate of a small Latin-American country was being assiduously courted by a delegate of the Arab contingent. So successful was his courtship of the lady that she was preparing to defy her country's order to vote "yes" on the partition plan. The Zionists informed her government, and she was replaced by a male delegate.[1]

There is also the story of a bugged conversation that took place in a vehicle belonging to the British delegation. Hearing the perfect English spoken by Abba Eban, the Israeli foreign minister, they were concerned that he had made a favorable impression on the audience at the United Nations when he made his first speech. One of their people was heard to say, "Who is that bloke? Where did he learn to speak the King's English?"

Another passenger replied, "He's a bloody don from Cambridge."[2]

The vote for partition succeeded in garnering the necessary two-thirds vote, and the Jews earned the right to fight to preserve the United Nations resolution, which the Arabs were attempting to negate by force.

---

1. Ibid., 18.
2. Ibid.

...a Swedish housewife made sure Israel got its machine gun

In the days following World War II, the Jews of Palestine were confident that they would be given a state. They were also confident that the Arabs would attack, and that they would have to defend themselves. With nations willing to sell arms to the Arabs and no one willing to sell arms to the Jews, a massive underground network was fashioned to overcome this disparity in armaments.

Haim Slavin, a Russian-born Jewish immigrant to Palestine with a background in engineering, was sent to the United States to work on arms procurement. Through an American contact, he was put in touch with a semi-retired Swedish immigrant gunsmith named Carl Ekdahl. Ekdahl agreed to design a light submachine gun for the Jews for seventeen thousand dollars.

Midway through the project, Ekdahl came to Slavin and reported that an Egyptian group was offering a hundred thousand dollars for the same job. Slavin told Ekdahl that he understood and that Carl was free to sell his expertise elsewhere, if it would help his modest financial situation. Ekdahl invited Slavin to his home to talk it over with his wife.

When Mrs. Ekdahl was apprised of the situation, she asked two questions. Did her husband have a contract, and was Slavin living up to the terms? Receiving two affirmative answers, she said that there was nothing to discuss, and that Carl should get on with the job and fulfill his obligations to the Jews.[1]

1. Leonard Slater, *The Pledge* (New York: Simon and Schuster, 1970), 56–57.

...a film about New Zealand pilots helped Israel win a war

After the end of the British mandate for Palestine, Israel was clandestinely searching all over the world for arms and fighter aircraft. Emmanuel Zur, an Israeli secret agent in London, had managed to obtain three Beaufighter bombers and was trying to figure out how to get them out of England from under the watchful eyes of the British. The answer came to Zur when a pilot he had hired introduced him to a New Zealand actress, who subsequently agreed to star in a "movie" Zur would produce "about New Zealand's role in World War II."[1]

Within a few days, Zur provided funds for the film "documenting" the courage exhibited by New Zealand pilots during the war. He then contacted people in the British film industry and organized a production company. The "actors" he hired were all real pilots. The final scene in the script called for a mass takeoff of the Beaufighters. The cameras rolled and the planes took off on a one-way trip to Israel.[2]

---

1. Dan Kurzman, *Genesis 1948: The First Arab-Israeli War* (New York: World, 1970), 486.
2. Ibid., 486.

...the Syrians lost the same cargo twice

In April of 1948, in anticipation of the coming war with the Arabs, the Jews sank the Syrian arms ship *Lino* in the Bari Harbor of Italy. A few months later, Ada Serini, the chief Israeli underground agent in Italy, received word from an Italian official that the Syrians were planning to retrieve the lost weapons from the bottom of the harbor. Ms. Serini saw an inviting prospect of getting the arms and having the Syrians pay the salvage bill.

Ms. Serini contacted a trusted and well-paid shipping agent who was engaged to "help" the Syrians locate a vessel and crew. Everything went according to plan, and the ship, the *Agira*, set out for Syria with the recovered arms and two crewmen chosen by Ada. She then dispatched a fishing boat with two Israelis in Syrian army uniforms. The fishing boat soon caught up with the *Agira*, told them that the ship was in danger, and asked to come aboard with some special communications equipment.

Once aboard, the Israelis took over the ship, transferred the cargo and crew,[1] and scuttled the ship.

Thus it was that the Syrians lost two ships, while all the arms that they had purchased went to Israel.

1. Dan Kurzman, *Genesis 1948: The First Arab Israeli War* (New York: World, 1970), 549–50.

During the 1948 war for Israeli independence, Israel had two armies in the field. One was the regular Israeli army, and the other was a force of irregulars called the Irgun. The Irgun was cooperating with the Israeli army while retaining much of its own autonomy. As part of their own war effort, the Irgun negotiated an arms deal with the French. The French were upset with the British government for forcing them out of Syria and Lebanon. They felt that if the Irgun came to power in Israel, their influence would be substantial.[1] So strongly did the French feel about the matter that they agreed to furnish the arms free of charge.

The *Altalena*, the ship bearing the arms for Israel, left France on its way to Israel, but a dispute arose between Irgun leader Menachem Begin and Israeli prime minister and defense minister David Ben-Gurion about jurisdiction over the arms. Begin insisted that a substantial portion be allocated to Irgun troops, while Ben-Gurion insisted that the Israeli army assume jurisdiction.[2] The dispute escalated, exchanges of fire took place between the two groups, casualties mounted, and the *Altalena* was sunk with its load of arms.

The tragic irony is that there soon would have been enough arms for all. So great was the French stockpile of arms for Israel that it was estimated the *Altalena* would have required four more trips to make the complete delivery.[3]

---

1. Dan Kurzman, *Genesis 1948: The First Arab-Israeli War* (New York: World, 1970), 458.
2. Ibid., 465.
3. Ibid., 458.

...the jailer asked the prisoner for a character reference

In Israel's 1948 War of Independence, the Jewish settlement of Kfar Etzion dominated the road needed by the Arabs to reinforce and resupply their troops besieging Jerusalem. With the help of Jordan's renowned Arab Legion, Arab troops attacked Kfar Etzion. The battle raged for several days until the outnumbered, outgunned, and out-of-ammunition Jews surrendered. The Arab makeshift soldiers went on a rampage killing almost all the prisoners who had surrendered.[1]

Among the prisoners was a female radio operator named Aliza Feuchtwanger. Two Arab irregulars, bent on raping the woman, were pulling her from either side, when suddenly a volley of shots rang out and both attackers fell dead. The shooter identified himself as Captain Hekmat of the Jordanian Arab Legion.[2] He took Aliza into his car and drove her in the direction of a prison in Hebron. On the way, the captain made a pass at her, but she rebuffed him saying that she thought that the officers of the Legion were gentlemen. Hekmat then offered marriage, but she lied and told him that she was already married.[3]

For the rest of the 1948 war, Aliza and her fiancé Moshe Beginsky, also a prisoner, remained in the prison. Treatment was good and Aliza and Moshe were granted some time together in their cells.[4]

When the war ended and the prisoners were repatriated, Captain Hekmat asked if Aliza would write a note stating that he had always acted like a gentleman. Aliza willingly wrote the note. Here was a prisoner writing a character reference for her jailer.[5]

Then she went off to Jerusalem to marry Moshe.

1. Dan Kurzman, *Genesis 1948: The First Arab-Israeli War* (New York: World, 1970), 229.
2. Ibid., 230–31.
3. Ibid., 231–32.
4. Ibid., 234.
5. Ibid., 233–34.

...a tank driver's poor English lost Jerusalem for the Israelis

During the 1948 Arab-Israeli War, the Israelis made two unsuccessful attempts to capture Latrun, the fortress controlling the main road to Jerusalem. As they set out upon their third attempt, the Israelis were confident of success. They had the defenders outmanned and outgunned. As the Israeli armored attack force approached the battle zone, the leader, a former English soldier, noticed that his main gun was jammed. Jumping out of his tank, he informed the second tanker to continue the attack while he went to the airport where he could find the tool to clear the jammed gun.

On his arrival at the airport, he happened to look behind him and saw the entire Israeli column following him. Furious, he descended on the hapless tanker and demanded to know why he had followed him rather than continue the attack as ordered. As it turned out, the man did not understand English.

Meanwhile, the infantry back at Latrun was unable to carry out the mission without the support of the tanks. Since the second United Nations cease-fire was to go into effect in a few minutes, there was no time to go back to renew the attack, and the Old City remained under Arab control for the next nineteen years.[1]

---

1. Dan Kurzman, *Genesis 1948: The First Arab-Israeli War* (New York: World, 1970), 534–35.

...Arab leaders admit that they created the refugee problem

Beginning in 1948, Arab policies contributed to the creation and perpetuation of the Arab refugee problem.

During the War of Independence, when the Arab nations attacked the fledgling state of Israel, one of the battles fought was in the village of Deir Yassin. Although it was a bloody battle with many civilian casualties, the Arabs exacerbated the situation by spreading a false rumor that the Jewish fighters were raping the women. This lead to massive flight by the Arab populace.

When confronted with the false rumor, Hussein Khalidi, an Arab leader, said, "We have to say this, so that the Arab armies will come to liberate us." Arab journalist Hazam Nusseibi admitted more recently to the BBC that the trumped-up charge "was our biggest mistake...as soon as they heard that women had been raped at Deir Yassin, the Palestinians fled in terror."[1]

Another contributing factor to the refugee problem followed the battle for the city of Haifa. "The Arab leaders, preferring not to surrender, announced that they and their community intended to evacuate the town...."[2] A somewhat similar situation occurred in Jaffa, where many of the town's populace fled. However, enough stayed so that Jaffa is still an Arab town.[3]

Another major cause of making Arabs refugees came from Arab threats. Azzam Pasha, secretary general of the Arab League, was quoted as saying, "This will be a war of extermination and a momentous massacre which will be spoken of like the Mongolian massacre and the Crusades."[4] When the war began to turn in favor of the Israelis, Arabs feared that the Israelis would do to the Arabs what the pasha had promised for the Jews, and a massive exodus took place.

The former prime minister of Syria, Khalid al-Azm, wrote in his memoirs in 1972, regarding the refugees,

1. Quoted in Alan Dershowitz, *The Case for Israel* (Hoboken, NJ: John Wiley and Sons, 2003), 82.
2. Benny Morris, quoted in Dershowitz, *The Case for Israel*, 83.
3. Dershowitz, *The Case for Israel*, 83.
4. Howard M. Sachar, *A History of Israel: From the Rise of Zionism to Our Time* (New York: Knopf, 1996), 323.

[I]t is we who made them leave.... We brought disaster upon... Arab refugees, by inviting them and bringing pressure to bear upon them to leave.... We have rendered them dispossessed.... We have accustomed them to begging.... We have lowered their moral and social level.... Then we exploited them in executing crimes of murder, arson, and throwing bombs upon...men, women, and children – all this in the service of political purposes.[1]

Alan Dershowitz, in *The Case for Israel*, shows that Palestinian Authority head Mahmoud Abbas reproached Arab armies for "forc[ing Palestinians] to emigrate," and cites a research study conducted by the Institute for Palestine Studies that determined that most Arab refuges left of their own will, without any contact with the Israeli army.[2]

The so-called "refugee" problem of the Arabs could have been solved in 1948.

Following the War of Independence, it seemed to the United Nations that the Arabs and the State of Israel would soon sign a peace treaty and conditions would become normal.

In order to bring this about, the United Nations General Assembly passed a resolution recommending that all the refugees who wanted to do so could return to their homes. All the Arab states voted against the resolution. To this day, the Arabs are demanding the "return" of four million "refugees" as a condition for any peace treaty.

Why was the original resolution turned down by the Arabs? Because it would have provided tacit recognition of Israel as a sovereign nation, something that they did not wish to accept then and still do not accept today.

---

1. Quoted in Dershowitz, *The Case for Israel*, 84.
2. Ibid.

...Israel limited immigration of Jews

In the early 1950s, the Israeli economy was not doing well. Faced with the financial burdens of settling droves of new immigrants, providing for defense against hostile neighbors, and developing a viable economy for the new nation, the country was close to economic collapse. In a desperate effort to stave off the disaster, the Israeli government and the Jewish Agency were forced to impose restrictions on the arrival of new immigrants.

Immigration was limited to Jews who would be at mortal risk if they stayed in their current locations abroad, and exceptions were made only for those who were well placed to contribute to the fledgling nation.[1]

Happily, the crisis did not last long. As the economy stabilized, unlimited Jewish immigration was soon resumed.

---

1. Howard M. Sachar, *A History of Israel from the Rise of Zionism to Our Time* (New York: Knopf, 1996), 415.

...Soviets gave Jewish jobs to Muslims

In the mid-1950s, Nikita Khrushchev, the Soviet dictator, was confronted with some troubling demographic data. The Muslim population of Soviet Central Asia and the Caucasus was burgeoning. Fearing an ethnic challenge to Slavic domination, the Soviets decided to placate the Muslims by compensating them with a virtual monopoly on second-level technocratic positions in their bureaucracies, professions, and universities.

Jews, as the best educated nationality in the Soviet Union, normally occupied these positions. To accomplish the change from Jews to Muslims, Khrushchev went on the all-too-familiar tirade against Jews as potentially disloyal and as an outpost for the "imperialistic West." Some trials were held for "financial corruption."

This occurred at a time when pressures for Jewish emigration were building in many other parts of the Soviet Union. The new tide of would-be emigrants was one the Soviet Union would be unable to stem.[1]

In the not-too-distant future, the Soviet Union would be faced with bloody Muslim insurrections. The group they tried to placate was seeking total independence, while the peaceful and productive population of Jews found life so intolerable that they were forced to emigrate in large numbers.

---

1. Howard M. Sachar, *Israel and Europe: An Appraisal in History* (New York: Random House, 1998), 257.

...Israelis look like Norwegians

Throughout the 1950s and 1960s, France was a major supplier of military hardware for the Jewish state. With the ascension to power of Charles de Gaulle, a reappraisal of French-Israeli and French-Arab relations took place. France decided to incline toward the Arabs and away from the Israelis.

An arms embargo began slowly on selected items, but Israel wasn't affected too badly. At the same time, the Israelis had contracted with West Germany for the construction of a dozen speedy coastal vessels to be named *Sa'ar*. Once delivered, the boats could be fitted with the Israeli-developed Gabriel missile, "an exceptionally accurate sea-skimmer capable of avoiding enemy radar."[1] However, news of the contract was leaked to the press, and political considerations caused the Germans to rescind it. It was at this point that the Israelis made a deal with the French to manufacture the boats.

Three of the *Sa'ar*s left for Israel in 1967 but too late to participate in the Six-Day War. Although de Gaulle's embargo on arms sales to Israel was supposed to be complete, French naval and marine officials ignored the ban, and work on the *Sa'ar*s proceeded. By December, three more boats were completed and left for Israel.

After new French elections, the incoming premier, Georges Pompidou, decided to strictly enforce the embargo.[2] But even as he did so, two more *Sa'ar*s slipped out of the harbor and cruised to Israel. Work proceeded on the other boats, but a new way had to be found to get them to Israel. Aware of the extreme necessity of having *all* these boats, Moshe Dayan, Israeli defense minister, devised a plan. The shipyard was to entertain offers from buyers wishing to purchase the remaining five boats. A Norwegian firm purchased the boats, allegedly for oil exploration in Alaska. A group of blond, blue-eyed "Norwegian" (really Israeli) sailors boarded the craft and readied them for departure.[3]

---

1. Howard M. Sachar, *Israel and Europe: An Appraisal in History* (New York: Random House, 1998), 188.
2. Ibid., 189.
3. Ibid., 190.

When Pompidou learned of the deception, he called a meeting of high officials to discuss the matter. It was determined at the meeting to avoid further international derision by putting out the story that the boats had been sold to a private firm and were no longer a matter for government concern.

The boats would ultimately prove their worth to the Israelis. During the Yom Kippur War they were used to great effect off the Egyptian and Syrian coasts.[1]

Another blow from the French to the Israeli war machine was the cancellation of all contracts to supply the Israeli air force with the French Mirage jet plane. Since the Mirage was manufactured in Switzerland, the Mossad, the Israeli intelligence agency, went to work to obtain the construction blueprints for the French fighter. By the time they had accomplished their mission, they had illegally acquired an astounding 200,000 blueprints for the Mirage plane and the specifications for the machine tools needed to build the plane. This enabled the Israelis to build their own versions of the Mirage, which they called the Nesher and the Kfir.[2]

Sometime later a Swiss national was convicted of stealing the blueprints and served four and a half years in prison.[3] It is interesting to note that, by contrast, Jonathan Pollard, the American Jew who gave some American secrets to Israel, was sentenced to *life* in prison.[4]

---

1. Ibid., 192.
2. Ian Black and Benny Morris, *Israel's Secret Wars: A History of Israel's Intelligence Services* (New York: Grove Weidenfeld, 1991), 234–35.
3. Ibid., 235.
4. Meron Medzini, "The Pollard Affair," *Encyclopedia Judaica*, CD-ROM Edition (Jerusalem: Keter, 1997).

...Romania sold Jews to Israel for three thousand dollars each

When Nicolae Ceausescu came to power in Romania in 1965, his fondest wish was to gain most-favored-nation status from the United States. This would give Romania trading privileges on liberal terms. To accomplish this task, Ceausescu, believing that Jews were masters of "back-stairs diplomacy," called on the services of Romanian chief rabbi Rosen.

Rosen had experience as a goodwill ambassador from Romania to Jews in America. Indeed, the economy of Romania had profited greatly by allowing the Joint Distribution Committee, a worldwide Jewish welfare agency, to give money to Jewish institutions across their land. As a consideration for Rosen's efforts on behalf of the Romanian government, Ceausescu promised to lift the ban on Jewish emigration from Romania to Israel. Some 220,000 Jews resided in Romania, the densest concentration of Jews in Eastern Europe outside of the Soviet Union.

Rabbi Rosen's diplomatic foray into the United States was favorably received, and negotiations proceeded to bring about the trading status the Romanians wished for. Of course, it helped that Romania, although Communist, had been charting a diplomatic course independent of Moscow and had already developed extensive ties with Israel.

Unrelated to the Romanian quest for most-favored-nation status was that the government would be able to reduce the Jewish population of Romania. This would make available to "integral" Romanians badly needed housing and jobs then held by Jews. Indeed, Ceausescu's predecessor had begun the process by allowing thirty-three thousand Jews to leave for Israel before halting the emigration.

As the United States granted most-favored-nation trading status to Romania, Ceausescu was brokering a secret deal with Rabbi Rosen, whereby the Jewish Agency would pay up to three thousand dollars per person to leave for Israel. The total amount paid was an astounding one hundred million dollars!

The Israelis felt that the price was well worth it in the 160,000 Jews who came to Israel and the goodwill generated in Romania's diplomatic friendship.[1]

---

1. Howard M. Sachar, *Israel and Europe: An Appraisal in History* (New York: Random House, 1998), 255–56.

...Israeli intelligence helped win the Six-Day War

June 6, 1967, marked the beginning of Israel's stunning victory over an Arab coalition of armies vastly superior in numbers and firepower. The Israeli army's success was due in large part to superior intelligence about Arab planning and deployment of resources.

Israeli intelligence determined that the Egyptian radar and anti-aircraft installations were faced east. Acting on this knowledge, the initial Israeli attack planes came from the north and the west.[1]

The Egyptian Air Force expected the Israelis to attack between four and seven in the morning. The Egyptian reconnaissance flights took place during those hours; then they would be back on the ground. Knowing all this, the Israelis attacked shortly after seven o'clock, precisely hitting all their previously pinpointed targets.[2]

During the battle, the Israelis intercepted President Nasser's order to the Egyptian army to fall back to the Suez Canal. This knowledge enabled the Israeli army to shift some forces to counterattack the Syrians on the Golan Heights.

The Israelis had also broken the Egyptian army code and used it to confuse the Egyptian military by issuing false orders. On one occasion, they ordered a MIG pilot to jettison his bombs into the Mediterranean Sea. The pilot was suspicious and asked for further proof that the order was genuine. The Israelis then supplied the pilot with details about his wife and children. Convinced, he dropped his bombs into the sea and parachuted to safety while ditching the plane.[3]

In another feat, the Israelis deployed a dummy force to mislead the Egyptians into thinking that their attack into the Sinai Desert would take a more southerly route than actually planned. The Egyptians diverted forces of elite units to counter the Israeli token force, while the main Israeli thrust went elsewhere, meeting only light resistance.[4]

One would have to search far and wide to find a war in which intelligence played a greater role than that played by the Israeli secret services in 1967.

---

1. Ian Black and Benny Morris, *Israel's Secret Wars: A History of Israel's Intelligence Services* (New York: Grove Weidenfeld, 1991), 224.
2. Ibid.
3. Ibid., 232.
4. Ibid., 232–33.

...Yasser Arafat was a KGB creation

According to Ion Mihai Pacepa, the highest-ranking Soviet bloc intelligence officer ever to defect to the West, Yasser Arafat was almost entirely an invention of KGB resourcefulness.[1]

Yasser Arafat was born in Cairo, Egypt, in 1929. Gravitating toward communism, he received training in the Soviet Union at the Balashikha special operations school near Moscow. It was then that the KGB decided to promote Arafat as the leading spokesman of the Palestinian cause.

Their first task was to destroy his birth records and replace them with documents stating he had been born in Jerusalem.[2] The KGB's next step was to beef up Arafat's four-page tract called "Falastinuna" (Our Palestine) into a forty-eight-page monthly magazine. After that, they created an anti-Zionist persona for him and engineered his election to the post of chairman of the Palestine Liberation Organization. They also set Arafat up with the line that Israel was a tool of Zionist imperialism. Labeling others as imperialists is a favorite Soviet euphemism for anybody who disagrees with them.

As Arafat evolved into a full-time terrorist, the Romanian intelligence services began to serve as a cover for Arafat's terrorism, while at the same time building him up as a statesman. The trick, as stated by Pacepa, was to keep on promising to break with terrorism while never getting around to actually doing so.

All this time, the Romanian intelligence services were serving as a conduit for some two hundred thousand dollars a month to the PLO. Presumably, other monies were coming from a variety of other sources to fund their terrorist operations.

How well all this chicanery worked was summed up in 1998 when President Clinton, speaking to Arafat, concluded his remarks by thanking Arafat for "decades and decades of tireless representation of the longing of the Palestinian people to be free, self-sufficient, and at home."[3]

Toward the end of Clinton's presidency he was able to convince the Israelis to agree to the Palestinian demands and give up a large portion of Jerusalem in exchange for "a lasting peace." This however was not enough for Arafat and he walked away from the negotiations, never to return.

President Clinton would later change his tune into a denunciation of Arafat's duplicity.

1. Ion Mihai Pacepa, "The KGB's Man," *Wall Street Journal* (September 22, 2003), http://online.wsj.com/article/SB106419296113226300-search.html.
2. French biographers Christophe Boltanski and Jihan El Tairi wrote in their 1977 biography that Arafat was born in Cairo, Egypt. According to the Jewish Virtual Library, the Palestinian Authority's Ministry of Information lists Arafat as having been born in the Gaza Strip, which has been a part of Egypt.
3. Pacepa, "The KGB's Man."

...Jewish immigration to Palestine was good for Arabs

When journalist Joan Peters went to the Middle East in 1973 to cover the latest Arab-Israeli conflict, she became interested in the much-talked-about "refugee" problem. In her perusal of United Nations documents, she became familiar with the usually accepted definition of refugees as "those people who were forced to leave their 'permanent' or 'habitual' homes."[1] She also noticed what she termed "a seemingly casual alteration of the definition of what constitutes an Arab refugee from Israel."[2] The UN broadened the definition of an Arab refugee to include persons who had lived in Palestine for only *two* years before Israeli statehood.[3]

Ms. Peters questioned why it was deemed necessary to amend the definition of a refugee. The answer she found is that the Arabs' claim to having lived in Palestine "from time immemorial" is untrue, and the amended definition served the purpose of padding population numbers in order to strengthen the Arabs' position in laying claim to the land. Ms. Peters's exhaustive investigation into the "refugee" problem led to the title of her book *From Time Immemorial.*

Another Arab claim was that the Jews were displacing Arabs. Ms. Peters's data show that the Arab population in the mainly Arab section in the time period recorded increased about 121 percent, while the Arab population in the mainly Jewish area increased an astounding 401 percent.

The conclusion to be drawn from the data is that the immigration of Jews actually *attracted* Arabs rather than displacing them as has been claimed by the Arabs.[4]

---

1. Joan Peters, *From Time Immemorial: The Origins of the Arab-Israeli Conflict over Palestine* (Chicago: JKAP Publishing, 1984), 4.
2. Ibid., 4.
3. Ibid.
4. Ibid., 255.

...Alexander Haig saved Israel in 1973

When the Arabs launched their surprise attack on Israel on Yom Kippur in 1973, the Israeli armed forces found themselves on the defensive and expending ammunition at a rate faster than they had anticipated. An immediate call went out to the United States for help in replenishing their rapidly diminishing supplies.

Secretary of State Henry Kissinger was of the opinion that if the Israelis were denied a decisive and quick victory, they would be more amenable to make concessions in the peace talks to follow. His theory, as told to Secretary of Defense Schlesinger, was "to let Israel come out ahead, but bleed"[1] before shipping the necessary matériel to the Israel Defense Forces.

What Kissinger failed to recognize was that at that point, the Israelis were in danger of losing the war, and that they would have *no* bargaining power at all at the peace table. So desperate was the Israeli military situation that Prime Minister Golda Meir ordered the arming of nuclear weapons to be used in case of an enemy breakthrough.[2]

Without waiting for authorization, General Alexander Haig, at that time President Nixon's chief of staff in the White House, began rounding up TOW missiles from Germany and the eastern seaboard of the United States and started sending them to Israel. He then invited senior Israeli military officers to Fort Benning, Georgia, for an orientation session in how to use the deadly anti-tank missiles.[3] The Israeli officers were amazed to learn that the missiles had a 97-percent kill rate "and could be fired from a foxhole and destroy a moving tank three kilometers away."[4]

The Israelis returned to the battlefield in time to employ the TOW missiles and repel the attackers. They then launched a successful counterattack, which turned the war around and resulted in an Israeli victory. By acting on his own, Alexander Haig had aided in Israel's victory, saved the Arab nations from a nuclear holocaust, and helped Nixon and Kissinger avoid a major political disaster.

---

1. Seymour Hersh, *The Samson Option: Israel's Nuclear Arsenal and American Foreign Policy* (New York: Random House, 1991), 227.
2. Ibid., 226.
3. John Loftus and Mark Aarons, *The Secret War against the Jews: How Western Espionage Betrayed the Jewish People* (New York: St. Martin's Griffin, 1994), 316.
4. Ibid.

...Israel saved Anwar Sadat's life

In 1977, Egypt and Israel were close to signing a peace treaty. For Anwar Sadat, this was an especially dangerous undertaking. Hard-liners throughout the Arab world would have no part of any sort of accommodation with Israel, and death threats were issued to any Arab leader who would engage in such negotiations.

The Israelis, anxious to keep the nascent peace process alive, arranged a meeting between Egypt's director of military intelligence and the Mossad's General Hofi. The Israelis informed the Egyptians about an elaborate plot that they had uncovered to assassinate Egyptian president Anwar Sadat. The stunned Egyptians were provided with the names and addresses in Cairo of the conspirators, and the plotters were quickly arrested.[1]

With that threat ended, President Sadat was able to continue his quest for peace with Israel. A peace treaty with Israel was signed in 1978. Ultimately in 1981, Sadat was assassinated by a dissident soldier while reviewing a military parade.

ISRAEL: Building and Defending a Nation

---

1. Howard M. Sachar, *A History of Israel from the Rise of Zionism to Our Time* (New York: Knopf, 1996), 845–46.

Bibliography

Abrahams, Israel. *Jewish Life in the Middle Ages*. Philadelphia: Jewish Publication Society, 1896.

Aguirre, Adalberto. *Racial and Ethnic Diversity in America: A Reference Handbook*. Santa Barbara, CA: ABC-CLIO, 2003.

Aharoni, Zvi, and Wilhelm Dietl. *Operation Eichmann: The Truth about the Pursuit, Capture and Trial*. Hoboken, NJ: John Wiley and Sons, 1997.

Alexander, Catherine M.S., and Stanley W. Wells. *Shakespeare and Race*. Cambridge: Cambridge University Press, 2000.

Alpern, Sara. "Estee Lauder." *Jewish Virtual Library*, 2007. http://jewish virtualli-brary.org/jsource/Lauder.html.

Anderson, Herbert L. "Early Days of the Chain Reaction." *Bulletin of the Atomic Scientists* 29, no. 4 (April 1973): 8–12.

Arditi, Benjamin. *Yehudei Bulgaria bi-shnot hamishtar hanatzi, 1940–1944* [Bulgarian Jewry under the Nazi regime]. Holon, 1962.

Bard, Mitchell Geoffrey. *The Complete History of the Holocaust*. San Diego, CA: Greenhaven Press, 2001.

Bartlett, John, and Justin Kaplan. *Bartlett's Familiar Quotations*. New York: Little, Brown, 1992.

Behar, Ruth, and Humberto Mayol. *An Island Called Home: Returning to Jewish Cuba*. Piscataway, NJ: Rutgers University Press, 2007.

Benbassa, Esther. *The Jews of France: A History from Antiquity to the Present*. Princeton, NJ: Princeton University Press, 1999.

Bellis, Mary. "The History of Blue Jeans." http://inventors.about.com/od/sstartinventors/a/Levi_Strauss.htm.

Bendersky, Joseph W. *The Jewish Threat: Anti-Semitic Policies of the US Army*. New York: Basic Books, 2000.

Ben-Sasson, Haim Hillel, ed. *A History of the Jewish People*. Cambridge, MA: Harvard University Press, 1976.

Bingham, Robert Kim. *Courageous Dissent: How Harry Bingham Defied His Government to Save Lives*. Greenwich, CT: Triune Books, 2007.

Birmingham, Stephen. *The Rest of Us: The Rise of America's Eastern European Jews*. Boston: Little, Brown, 1984.

Bjarkman, Peter C. *Diamonds around the Globe: The Encyclopedia of International Baseball*. Westport, CT: Greenwood, 2005.

Black, Edwin. *IBM and the Holocaust: The Strategic Alliance between Nazi Germany and America's Most Powerful Company*. New York: Crown, 2001.

Black, Ian, and Benny Morris. *Israel's Secret Wars: A History of Israel's Intelligence Services*. New York: Grove Weidenfeld, 1991.

Blau, Joseph L., and Salo W. Baron, eds. *The Jews of the United States, 1790–1840: A Documentary History*. New York: Columbia University Press, 1963.

Bodner, Allen. *When Boxing Was a Jewish Sport*. Westport, CT: Praeger, 1997.

Boyadjieff, Christo. *Saving the Bulgarian Jews in World War II*. Ottawa: Free Bulgarian Center, 1989.

Bronner, Stephen Eric. *A Rumor about the Jews: Antisemitism, Conspiracy, and the Protocols of Zion*. London: Oxford University Press, 2000.

Buchholz, Todd G. *New Ideas from Dead CEOs: Lasting Lessons from the Corner Office*. New York: Collins, 2007.

Carroll, James. *Constantine's Sword: The Church and the Jews*. New York: Houghton Mifflin, 2001.

CBS News, "Cosmetics Mogul Estee Lauder Dies," April 12, 2004. http://www.cbsnews.com/stories/2004/04/12/national/mail/main611403.shtml.

____. *People of the Century*. New York: Simon and Schuster, 1999.

Clark, Alan. *Barbarossa: The Russian-German Conflict, 1941–1945*. London: Weidenfeld and Nicolson, 1995.

Clark, Ronald W. *Einstein: The Life and Times*. New York: Avon Books, 1984.

Chaucer, Geoffrey. *The Canterbury Tales*. Translated by Burton Raffel, with an introduction by John Miles Foley. New York: Modern Library, 2008.

Cohen, Rich. *The Avengers*. New York: Random House, 2000.

———. *Tough Jews*. New York: Simon and Schuster, 1998.

Connecticut State Register and Manual. Hartford, CT: Secretary of the State, 2001.

Crampton, R.J. *A Concise History of Bulgaria*. Cambridge, UK: Cambridge University Press, 1997.

Cropper, William H. *Great Physicists: The Life and Times of Leading Physicists from Galileo to Hawking*. New York: Oxford University Press, 2001.

Cross, Milton, and David Ewen, eds. "Felix Mendelssohn." In *Milton Cross' Encyclopedia of the Great Composers and Their Music*. Vol. 1. New York: Doubleday, 1953.

Dalin, David G., and Alfred J. Kolatch. *The Presidents of the United States and the Jews*. New York: Jonathan David, 2000.

Dawidoff, Nicholas. *The Catcher Was a Spy: The Mysterious Life of Moe Berg*. New York: Random House, 1994.

Dershowitz, Alan. *The Case for Israel*. Hoboken, NJ: John Wiley and Sons, 2003.

Douthaut, Ross, and David Hopson. *SparkNotes: The Merchant of Venice*. New York: Spark Publishing, 2002.

Dubnow, Simon M. *History of the Jews in Russia and Poland*. 3 vols. Philadelphia: Jewish Publication Society, 1916–20.

Eban, Abba. *My Country: The Story of Modern Israel*, New York: Random House, 1972.

———. *My People: The Story of the Jews*. New York: Behrman House, 1968.

Eco, Umberto. *Six Walks in the Fictional Woods*. Cambridge, MA: Harvard University Press, 1994.

Eliach, Yaffa. *There Once Was a World: A 900-Year Chronicle of the Shtetl of Eishyshok*. Boston: Little, Brown, 1998.

Encyclopedia Britannica Micropedia, 15th ed. Chicago: Encyclopedia Britannica, 1990.

Encyclopedia Judaica, CD-ROM Edition. Jerusalem: Keter, 1997.

Engerman, Stanley L., and Robert E. Gallman. *The Cambridge Economic History of the United States*. Cambridge, UK: Cambridge University Press, 2000.

Epstein, Edward Jay. *Dossier: The Secret History of Armand Hammer*. New York: Carroll and Graf, 1996.

Falsani, Kathleen F. "Wallenberg Aide Shares Tale of Rescuing 80 Jews." *Chicago Sun Times*, November 12, 2004.

Felder, Deborah G., and Diana Rosen. *Fifty Jewish Women Who Changed the World*. New York: Kensington, 2003.

Feldman, Louis H. *Jew and Gentile in the Ancient World: Attitudes and Interactions from Alexander to Justinian*. Princeton, NJ: Princeton University Press, 1993.

Fisher, Gordon. Introduction, "About *The Protocols of the Elders of Zion*." H-Net Humanities and Social Sciences Online. H-Antisemitism: Documents, Issue no. 1, March 22, 2000. http://www.h-net.org/~antis/doc/graves/graves.a.html.

Fitzpatrick, Donovan, and Saul Saphire. *Navy Maverick: Uriah Phillips Levy*. New York: Doubleday, 1963.

Friedlander, Gerald. *Shakespeare and the Jew*. New York: Dutton, 1921.

Gay, Peter. *Freud, Jews, and Other Germans: Masters and Victims in Modernist Culture*. New York: Oxford University Press, 1978.

Ganzfried, Rabbi Solomon, *Code of Jewish Law: A Compilation of Jewish Laws and Customs*. New York: Hebrew Publishing Company, 1961.

Gleick, James. *Genius: The Life and Science of Richard Feynman*. New York: Pantheon Books, 1992.

Goetze, Katharina. "Hitler's Jewish Counterfeiter." *The Forward*, February 16, 2007. http://www.forward.com/articles/10099/.

Bibliography

Goitein, S.D. *A Mediterranean Society: An Abridgement in One Volume*. Revised and edited by Jacob Lassner. Berkeley: University of California Press, 1999.

____. *Jews and Arabs*. New York: Schocken, 1984.

Golden, Harry, and Martin Rywell. *Jews in American History: Their Contribution to the United States of America*. Charlotte, NC: H.L. Martin Co., 1950.

Goodman, Matthew. "How the Radanite Traders Spiced Up Life in Dark-Ages Europe." *Forward*, May 30, 2003. http://www.forward.com/articles/8926/.

Goodwin, Doris Kearns. *No Ordinary Time: Franklin and Eleanor Roosevelt: The Home Front in World War II*. New York: Simon and Schuster, 1994.

Gordon, Cyrus H. *Before Columbus: Links between the Old World and Ancient America*. New York: Crown, 1971.

Graetz, Professor Heinrich. *History of the Jews*. Vols. 2–5. Philadelphia: Jewish Publication Society, 1893–1894.

Greenbaum, Masha. *The Jews of Lithuania: A History of a Remarkable Community, 1316–1945*. Jerusalem: Gefen Publishing House, 1995.

Greenberg, Daniel S. *The Politics of Pure Science*. Chicago: University of Chicago Press, 1999.

Gresser, Moshe. *Dual Allegiance: Freud as a Modern Jew*. Albany: SUNY Press, 1994.

Hall, Kermit L. *Shaping Justice: Landmark Cases of the US Supreme Court*. CD-ROM. Portable Professor Series. Barnes and Noble, 2004.

Hatton, T. J., and Jeffrey G. Williamson. *Global Migration and the World Economy: Two Centuries of Policy and Performance*. Cambridge, MA: MIT Press, 2005.

Hentschel, Klaus. *Physics and National Socialism: An Anthology of Primary Sources*. Basel: Birkhäuser, 1996.

Hersh, Seymour. *The Samson Option: Israel's Nuclear Arsenal and American Foreign Policy*. New York: Random House, 1991.

Hertz, Rabbi Dr. Joseph H., ed. *The Pentateuch and Haftorahs*. London: Soncino Press, 1952.

Heyer, Sandra, ed. *Even More True Stories: An Intermediate Reader*. White Plains, NY: Longman, 1992.

"Hiram Bingham IV." http://www.ct.gov/sots/cwp/view.asp?a=3188&q=392620.

Horvitz, Peter S., and Joachim Horvitz. *The Big Book of Jewish Baseball: An Illustrated Encyclopedia and Anecdotal History*. New York: SPI Books, 2001.

Hoyt, Edwin P. Jr. *The Guggenheims and the American Dream*. New York: Funk and Wagnalls, 1968.

Isaacson, Walter. "Citizen Ben's 7 Great Virtues." *Time* (July 7, 2003): 40–53.

Jacobs, Joseph. *Jewish Contributions to Civilization: An Estimate*. Philadelphia: Jewish Publication Society, 1919.

Jewish-American Hall of Fame. History of Jews in America Virtual Tour. http://www.amuseum.org.

Jewish Virtual Library. "Emanuel Celler." http://www.jewishvirtuallibrary.org/jsource/biography/Celler.html.

____. "The Nazi Olympics." http://www.jewishvirtuallibrary.org/jsource/Holocaust/olympics.html.

____. "Sugihara." *http://www.jewishvirtuallibrary.org/jsource/Holocaust/sugihara.html*.

Johnson, Paul. *A History of the Jews*. New York: Harper and Row, 1987.

Kaganoff, Benzion C. *A Dictionary of Jewish Names and their Origins*. New York: Schocken, 1977.

Katz, Steven T. *Jewish Philosophers*. New York: Bloch Publishing Company, 1975.

Kaufman, Louis, Barbara Fitzgerald, and Tom Sewell. *Moe Berg: Athlete, Scholar, Spy*. New York: Little, Brown, 1974.

Kayserling, Meyer. *Christopher Columbus and the Participation of the Jews in the Spanish and Portuguese Discoveries*. Albuquerque, NM: Hubert Allen and Associates, 2002.

Kertzer, David I. *The Popes against the Jews: The Vatican's Role in the Rise of Modern Anti-Semitism*. New York: Knopf, 2001.

Konner, Melvin. *Unsettled: An Anthropology of the Jews*. New York: Viking Penguin, 2003.

Kurzman, Dan. *The Day of the Bomb: Countdown to Hiroshima*. New York: McGraw-Hill, 1986.

———. *Genesis 1948: The First Arab-Israeli War*. New York: World, 1970.

Laird, Gordon. "The Kimhi Family: Their Writings in the Reformation." http://www.glaird.com/kim-hom.htm.

Learsi, Rufus, and Abraham J. Karp. *The Jews in America: A History*. Jerusalem: Ktav, 1972.

Lehmann, Manfred R. "The Book of Ben Sira." http://www.manfredlehmann.com/news/news_detail.cgi/141/0.

Levin, Nora. 1973. *The Holocaust: The Destruction of European Jewry, 1933–1945*. New York: Schocken, 1973.

Levine, Hillel. *In Search of Sugihara: The Elusive Japanese Diplomat Who Risked His Life to Rescue 10,000 Jews from the Holocaust*. New York: Simon and Schuster, 1996.

Levy, Carol. "The Olympic Pause: 1936 Olympic Games in Nazi Germany." *The Jewish Magazine* (autumn 2000). http://www.jewishmag.com/36mag/olympic/olympic.htm.

Liber, Maurice. *Rashi*. 1906. Reprint, Whitefish, MT: Kessinger Publishing, 2004.

Liebreich, Fritz. *Britain's Naval and Political Reaction to the Illegal Immigration of Jews to Palestine, 1945–1948*. London and New York: Routledge, 2005.

Loftus, John, and Mark Aarons. *The Secret War against the Jews: How Western Espionage Betrayed the Jewish People*. New York. St. Martin's Griffin, 1994.

Maisel, L. Sandy, and Ira N. Forman, eds. *Jews in American Politics*. Lanham, MD: Rowman and Littlefield, 2001.

"Making a Buck." *Time Machine*, History Channel, 2001.

Manchester, William. *The Last Lion: Winston Spencer Churchill*. Vol. 2, *Alone, 1932–1940*. Boston: Little, Brown, 1988.

Mandell, Richard D. *The Nazi Olympics*. Champaign, IL: University of Illinois Press, 1987.

Marcus, Jacob R. *The Jew in the Medieval World: A Source Book, 315–1791*. New York: Atheneum, 1938.

Margolis, Max L., and Alexander Marx. *A History of the Jewish People*. Philadelphia: Jewish Publication Society, 1927.

Markle, Gerald E. *Meditations of a Holocaust Traveler*. Albany, NY: SUNY Press, 1995.

Marks, M.L. *Jews among the Indians: Tales of Adventure and Conflict in the Old West*. Chicago: Bennison Books, 1992.

Marrus, Michael R., and Robert O. Paxton. *Vichy France and the Jews*. New York: Basic Books, 1981.

McIntosh, Elizabeth P. *Sisterhood of Spies: The Women of the OSS*. New York: Dell, 1998.

Medoff, Rafael. *Jewish Americans and Political Participation: A Reference Handbook*. Santa Barbara, CA: ABC-CLIO, 2002.

Menachemson, Nolan. *A Practical Guide to Jewish Cemeteries*. Bergenfield, NJ: Avotaynu, 2007.

Mendes-Flohr, Paul R., and Jehuda Reinharz. *The Jew in the Modern World: A Documentary History*. New York: Oxford University Press, 1980.

Mirabella, Grace. "Estée Lauder." *The Time 100*, December 7, 1998.

Mogulof, Milly. *Foiled: Hitler's Jewish Olympian; The Helene Mayer Story*. Oakland, CA: RDR Books, 2002.

Moore, Deborah Dash. *GI Jews: How World War II Changed a Generation*. Cambridge, MA: Harvard University Press, 2004.

Moskowitz, Milton. *Everybody's Business: An Almanac; An Irreverent Guide to Corporate America*. New York: Harper and Row, 1980.

Murphy, Sean D. *United States Practice in International Law*. Vol. 2, *2002–2004*. Cambridge: Cambridge University Press, 2006.

Nadler, Steven. *Spinoza: A Life*. Cambridge: Cambridge University Press, 1999.

Noveck, Simon, ed. *Great Jewish Personalities in Ancient and Medieval Times*. Clinton, MA: Pioneer Press, 1959.

Pacepa, Ion Mihai. "The KGB's Man." *Wall Street Journal*, September 22, 2003. http://online.wsj.com/article/SB106419296113226300-search.html.

Patai, Raphael. *The Jewish Mind*. New York: Scribner, 1977.

Peters, Joan. *From Time Immemorial: The Origins of the Arab-Jewish Conflict over Palestine*. Chicago: JKAP Publishing, 1984.

Peterson, Ivars. "The Eclipse That Saved Columbus." *Science News*. http://www.sciencenews.org/view/generic/id/7809/title/The_Eclipse_That_Saved_Columbus.

Pollack, Michael. *Mandarins, Jews, and Missionaries: The Jewish Experience in the Chinese Empire*. Philadelphia: Jewish Publication Society, 1980.

Radin, Max. *The Jews among the Greeks and Romans*. Philadelphia: Jewish Publication Society, 1916.

Rapoport, Louis. *The Lost Jews: Last of the Ethiopian Falashas*. New York: Stein and Day, 1983.

Rigg, Bryan Mark. *Hitler's Jewish Soldiers: The Untold Story of Nazi Racial Laws and Men of Jewish Descent in the German Military*. Lawrence, KS: University of Kansas Press, 2002.

____. *Rescued from the Reich: How One of Hitler's Soldiers Saved the Lubavitcher Rebbe*. New Haven: Yale University Press, 2004.

Rippon, Anton. *Hitler's Olympics: The Story of the 1936 Nazi Games*. Barnsley, South Yorkshire, UK: Pen and Sword, 2006.

Rose, Norman. *Chaim Weizmann: A Biography*. London: Weidenfeld and Nicholson, 1986.

Rosenberg, Eliot. *But Were They Good for the Jews? Over 150 Historical Figures Viewed from a Jewish Perspective*. Secaucus, NJ: Carol, 1997.

Roth, Cecil. 1970. *A History of the Jews*. New York: Schocken Books.

____. *The Jews in the Renaissance*. Philadelphia: Jewish Publication Society, 1959.

____. *The Magnificent Rothschilds*. London: Robert Hale and Company, 1939.

____. *Personalities and Events in Jewish History*. Philadelphia: Jewish Publication Society, 1953.

Royal Household. "Henry VIII (r. 1509–1547)." The Official Website of the British Monarchy. http://www.royal.gov.uk/HistoryoftheMonarchy/KingsandQueensofEngland/TheTudors/HenryVIII.aspx.

Runco, Mark A., and Steven R. Pritzker. *Encyclopedia of Creativity*. Vol. 1. San Diego, CA: Academic Press, 1999.

Runes, Dagobert D., ed. *The Hebrew Impact on Western Civilization*. New York: Philosophical Library, 1951.

Sachar, Abram Leon. *A History of the Jews*. New York: Knopf, 1964.

Sachar, Howard M. *The Course of Modern Jewish History*. New York: Vintage Books, 1990.

____. *A History of Israel from the Rise of Zionism to Our Time*. New York: Knopf, 1996.

____. *Israel and Europe: An Appraisal in History*. New York: Random House, 1998.

Schaap, Jeremy. *Triumph: The Untold Story of Jesse Owens and Hitler's Olympics*. New York: Houghton Mifflin, 2007.

Schaffer, Kay, and Sidonie Smith. *The Olympics at the Millennium: Power, Politics, and the Games*. Piscataway, NJ: Rutgers University Press, 2000.

Scharfstein, Sol. *Jewish History and You*. Jersey City, NJ: Ktav, 2003.

Scheeres, Julia. "Europeans Outlaw Net Hate Speech." *Wired* News, November 9, 2002. http://www.wired.com/techbiz/media/news/2002/11/56294.

Schlesinger, Arthur M. Jr. *The Age of Roosevelt: The Politics of Upheaval*. Boston: Houghton Mifflin, 1960.

Schwarz, Leo W., ed. 1956. *Great Ages and Ideas of the Jewish People*. New York: Random House, 1956.

Shakespeare, William. "The Merchant of Venice." In *The Riverside Shakespeare*, edited by G. Blakemore Evans. Boston: Houghton Mifflin, 1974.

Shapiro, James. *Shakespeare and the Jews.* New York: Columbia University Press, 1996.

Shapiro, Sidney. *Jews in Old China: Studies by Chinese Scholars.* New York: Hippocene, 2001.

Simonhoff, Harry. *Jewish Notables in America, 1776–1865: Links of an Endless Chain.* New York: Greenberg, 1956.

———. *Jewish Participants in the Civil War.* New York: Arco, 1963.

———. *Saga of American Jewry, 1865–1914: Links of an Endless Chain.* New York: Arco, 1959.

Slater, Elinor, and Robert Slater. *Great Jewish Women.* New York: Jonathan David, 1994.

Slater, Leonard. *The Pledge.* New York: Simon and Schuster, 1970.

Spencer, Charles. *Leon Bakst and the Ballets Russes.* London: Academy Editions, 1995.

Spiegel, Steven L. *The Other Arab-Israeli Conflict: Making America's Middle East Policy, from Truman to Reagan.* Chicago: University of Chicago Press, 1985.

St. John, Robert. *Ben-Gurion: A Biography.* New York: Doubleday, 1971.

Szulc, Tad. *The Secret Alliance: The Extraordinary Story of the Rescue of the Jews since World War II.* New York: Farrar, Straus and Giroux, 1991.

Taitz, Emily. *Holocaust Survivors: A Biographical Dictionary.* Vol. 1. Westport, CT: Greenwood Press, 2007.

Togyer, Jason. *For the Love of Murphy's: The Behind-the-Counter Story of a Great American.* University Park, PA: Penn State Press, 2008.

Tovey, D'Blossiers. *Anglia Judaica, or, A History of the Jews in England.* Edited by Elizabeth Pearl. London: Weidenfeld and Nicolson, 1990.

Trachtenberg, Joshua. *The Devil and the Jews: The Medieval Conception of the Jew and Its Relationship to Modern Anti-Semitism.* New York: Harper and Row, 1943.

———. *Jewish Magic and Superstition: A Study in Folk Religion.* New York: Behrman's Jewish Book House, 1939.

Tucker, Jonathan B. *Toxic Terror: Assessing Terrorist Use of Chemical and Biological Weapons.* Cambridge, MA: MIT Press, 2001.

Tuchman, Barbara W. *A Distant Mirror: The Calamitous Fourteenth Century.* New York: Ballantine, 1978.

US Citizenship and Immigration Services. "Immigration Act of May 26, 1924 (43 Statutes-at-Large 153)." http://www.uscis.gov/files/nativedocuments/Legislation%20from%201901-1940.pdf.

Waldman, Mark. *Goethe and the Jews: A Challenge to Hitlerism.* New York: Putnam, 1934.

Warburg Institute. http://warburg.sas.ac.uk/institute/institute_introduction.htm.

Wein, Berel. *Herald of Destiny: The Story of the Jews in the Medieval Era, 750–1650.* New York: Shaar Press, 1993.

Wigoder, Geoffrey, ed. *Illustrated Dictionary and Concordance to the Bible.* Jerusalem: Jerusalem Publishing House, 1986.

Wyman, David S. *The Abandonment of the Jews: America and the Holocaust, 1941–1945.* New York: New Press, 1984.

Will, George F. *The Morning After: American Successes and Excesses, 1981–1986.* New York: Macmillan, 1986.

Winteler-Einstein, Maja. "Albert Einstein: A Biographical Sketch." In *The Collected Papers of Albert Einstein: The Early Years, 1879–1902*, by Albert Einstein, translated by Anna Beck and Peter Havas. Princeton, NJ: Princeton University Press, 1987.

Ziolkowski, Theodore. *The Sin of Knowledge: Ancient Themes and Modern Variations.* Princeton, NJ: Princeton University Press, 2000.

Zweig, Ronald W. *The Gold Train: The Destruction of the Jews and the Looting of Hungary.* New York: Harper Collins, 2002.

Unusual Stories in Jewish History